Staging Wales

STAGING WALES
Welsh Theatre 1979–1997

Edited by

ANNA-MARIE TAYLOR

UNIVERSITY OF WALES PRESS • CARDIFF • 1997

British Library Cataloguing in Publication Data
A catalogue record for this book is available from
the British Library.

ISBN 0-7083-1419-8

Published with the financial support of the Arts Council of Wales

Typeset at the University of Wales Press
Printed in Great Britain by Dinefwr Press, Llandybïe

Contents

Preface

Theatrical art is the most ephemeral of all artistic forms, frequently unrecorded, not documented, and once the performance has passed sometimes only hazily recalled. In compiling this collection of essays, this sense of transitoriness seemed all too apparent, as I got actors out of rehearsals, spoke to directors on their way to places as diverse as Bangor, Barcelona and Harare, and distracted writers from their word processors and production deadlines.

I should like to thank all the contributors to the volume for their commitment to the project, and I know I am speaking on their behalf by emphasizing that we hope that our various preliminary examinations of Welsh dramatic practice will stimulate further discussion and analysis of theatre in contemporary Wales, a debate at present still in its cradle stage. Further thanks must be extended to Ned Thomas at University of Wales Press for his support and interest throughout, to Ceinwen Jones and Liz Powell at the Press, to the Arts Council of Wales Literature Board Committee for helpful and illuminating comment on the volume and to the many workers in Welsh theatre who have given up time in frequently over-full schedules to talk so openly and informatively to us all. Final and perhaps most grateful thanks must go to Christine Nutt in the Department of Adult Continuing Education, University of Wales Swansea, for her highly efficient and much appreciated secretarial help.

Anna-Marie Taylor
Department of Adult Continuing Education,
University of Wales Swansea

To Seona for being a rewarding fellow theatre-goer

The Contributors

Gilly Adams grew up in the Mumbles, Swansea. She studied English and arts administration before joining the Welsh Arts Council as Drama Officer. She was drama director at WAC until 1981 when she joined Made in Wales Stage Company as artistic director. She left Made in Wales in 1995, and at present is working freelance.

Ewart Alexander is a dramatist with thirty-one television, six stage and eight radio plays to his credit as well as eighty-seven episodes of television series including contributions to *Softly Softly* and *Juliet Bravo*. Born in Cwmgïedd, Ystradgynlais, Breconshire, he was educated at University College, Swansea. Formerly a teacher, he is now a full-time writer.

Simon Baker was born in Mancot, Clwyd. After a career as a professional footballer, he was educated at the University of Wales Swansea where he obtained an MA in Welsh Writing in English and a Ph.D. on the modern short story. He now lectures in English at Swansea, where he has contributed various articles and chapters in books on writers ranging from Caradoc Evans, Dylan Thomas and Rhys Davies to Anton Chekhov, Frank O'Connor and James Kelman. He is currently preparing an edition of Ron Berry's short stories.

Paul Clements trained and worked as a teacher in Birmingham before joining the staff of the Midlands Arts Centre in 1970 as Director of Community Theatre. He was one of the founder-directors of Contact Theatre Company in Manchester. He has subsequently taught drama in colleges and universities in England and Wales and was artistic director of the National Youth Theatre of Wales. His publications include *Teaching Drama* (Vancouver, 1978) and *The Improvised Play: The Work of Mike Leigh* (London, 1983). He has also contributed a chapter to George Brandt's edition of *British Television Drama in the 1980s* (Cambridge, 1993). He is now principal of Mountview Theatre School, London.

Greg Cullen has been based in mid Wales since 1983 when he was appointed as writer in residence at Theatr Powys. For Theatr Powys and the Mid Powys Youth Theatre, he has written and worked on numerous productions including *The Snow Queen, Taken Out, Mary Morgan, Tarzanne, Frida and Diego* (which has been produced throughout South and North America and Europe). He has also had a number of plays broadcast on BBC Radio, most recently *The Informer's Duty* and *Tower*. Mid Powys Youth Theatre has won several awards for its high standards of achievement. He was the first writer in residence at the Welsh College of Music and Drama.

Paul Davies is artistic director (with Fern Smith) of Volcano Theatre Company. He has appeared in all the company's major productions. He has a Ph.D. from the University of Wales Swansea on 'The Crisis of Socialism and the Exhaustion of Utopian Political Energies'. Most recently, he has written and directed *Vagina Dentata*. Under his directorship, the company has won *Time Out*, BBC, *Manchester Evening News* awards and the Grand Prix Belgrade.

Dic Edwards was born in Cardiff, and studied English and Philosophy at Lampeter. A prolific playwright, he has written over twenty plays, which have been performed throughout Britain, including the Citizens Theatre Glasgow and Leicester Haymarket.

Dafydd Arthur Jones was born in Bangor, and was educated at the Universities of Bangor and Aberystwyth. He was awarded a Ph.D. on popular Welsh-language author Thomas Levi (1826–1916) from the University of Wales Aberystwyth. He is senior lecturer in History at Trinity College, Carmarthen. He has also written plays for which he has received the first prize in several National Eisteddfodau and for radio, and has published in Welsh academic journals.

Lucy Gough grew up near Fishguard, and studied drama at the University of Wales Aberystwyth. She studied playwriting at the University of Birmingham, and has had a number of plays performed professionally, both for the stage and BBC Radio 3.

Geoff Moore studied fine art at Newcastle and Leeds before starting in theatre at Edinburgh's Traverse in 1965. He founded Moving Being in 1968, and has received choreographic and drama awards for his work. He moved to Wales in 1972 with the nucleus of his company, based at Chapter Arts. In 1982 he converted St Stephen's Church in the docks, where the company remained until 1992.

Gill Ogden has lived in Ceredigion since the late 1960s. She studied drama at the University of Wales Aberystwyth and is completing a research degree on identity and theatre in contemporary Celtic nations. She has worked as a director and writer for Welsh-language Theatre in Education companies such as Cwmni'r Frân Wen and Arad Goch, and also for Theatr Gwynedd. She has contributed articles and reviews on modern drama to journals in Wales.

Mike Pearson has been involved in experimental theatre in Wales since the early 1970s when he was a member of RAT Theatre. Educated at the University of Wales Cardiff, where he studied archaeology, he was closely associated with Cardiff Laboratory Theatre, and was a founder member of Brith Gof theatre company. He is a director of Brith Gof, and has written several articles on interdisciplinary approaches to performance for international journals.

Bob Roberts is a retired schoolmaster. He has had countless reviews published in *The Stage* and the *Western Mail*. He has acted as adjudicator at play festivals, and chaired the Drama Panel, North West Association for the Arts and the National Eisteddfod Drama Panel.

Nic Ros studied drama and English at the University of Wales Aberystwyth, and worked as an actor and director in Welsh-language theatre for over a decade. He is currently a lecturer in drama at Coleg Normal Bangor.

Charmian C. Savill grew up near Llangeitho, Dyfed, and was trained as an actress at Rose Bruford College. She taught drama at the University of Wales Aberystwyth where she also completed an M.Phil. on Brith Gof theatre company. She works as a dramatist and freelance writer, and has co-managed a community nursery.

Anna-Marie Taylor studied drama and German at the Universities of Bristol, London and Lancaster. She lectured in drama at the University of Wales Aberystwyth from 1982 to 1994, and is currently a lecturer in Continuing Education at the University of Wales Swansea. She has published widely on European drama and on contemporary world literature.

Introduction:
Staging Wales

Anna-Marie Taylor

If one of the main features of postmodernity is being severed from a
shared sense of tradition, then Welsh theatre in the last decade and a
half has certainly experienced such discontinuity. Oddly out of step
with other artistic and literary forms in Wales, for example music and
poetry, that draw inspiration from and often valorize connections
with the past, Welsh theatrical practice and dramatic writing
frequently seem to inhabit an eternal artistic present. Unlike other
cultural forms that share a sense of continuity and have been seen to
occupy an often privileged place in Wales's heritage, the drama of the
contemporary period has frequently been cut adrift from earlier work.

This break with the past is documented by Simon Baker in the
opening chapter of our volume with his account of writers such as
Gwyn Thomas, Dannie Abse and Alun Richards who established
professional Anglo-Welsh writing for the stage in the 1960s and 1970s.
Simon Baker's essay reminds us of the neglect of their work in the
present-day theatre, with their plays overlooked nowadays because
they are either (in the case of Gwyn Thomas) seen as too 'Welsh', or
(as with Dannie Abse) perceived as not 'Welsh' enough, a perennial
difficulty all too well known by today's playwrights.

Dramatic writing in the Welsh language has fewer problems with
cultural identity. However, Nic Ros in a wide survey of playwriting
from 1979 onwards locates a crisis in theatrical direction in many of
the plays he has encountered. Amongst writers such as Siôn Eirian,
Gareth Miles and Meic Povey, there is a forthright confidence in
material chosen, particularly that dealing with national, local and
sexual politics. However, Nic Ros bemoans the fact that so few
playwrights have absorbed the theatrical experimentation of the
1980s, retreating to the mainstage and not challenging received ideas
of dramatic structure and form in any radical way.

Another salient characteristic of 'postmodern' discourse is the
existence of contending histories, with different accounts of artistic

practice and historical fact jostling for authority. As Mike Pearson points out in his chapter on experimental theatre, the tracing in of a history of avant-garde practice is very much dependent on collating accounts of participants and witnesses (some highly partial and embroidered), as experimental theatre very rarely depends on a conventional literary text. Due to the lack of play publishing throughout this period, and with only limited academic and press coverage of theatrical events, this need to track down oral histories of performances extends of course beyond experimental work to Welsh theatre as a whole.

Gill Ogden and I examine the entire period, offering versions of the development of theatrical forms and company practices, and locating artistic and institutional decisions that have shaped individual groups' work. The exciting and extensive provision of Theatre in Education throughout Wales, as outlined by Gill Ogden, is clearly one of the great successes of the period, an adaptation of a foreign form (originating in the Soviet Union and Germany in the 1920s and widely developed in England in the 1960s and 1970s) 'to fulfil specific cultural requirements peculiar to the Welsh context and to express . . . a Welsh identity'. Yet, its success is rarely publicized and this now indigenous, well-rooted educational form is presently under threat because of reorganization to unitary authorities. More visible is the work of the larger companies such as Mold's Theatr Clwyd and Cardiff's Sherman Theatre. I have sketched in the development of particular companies and the theatrical establishment as a whole, contrasting the localized, community-based Welsh theatre of the early 1980s with the more metropolitan, centralized desire for a National Theatre in the 1990s.

Another achievement of the post-war period has been the establishment of professional drama training in Wales through the Welsh College of Music and Drama, and through programmes of academic study in departments of Drama and Theatre Studies in Further and Higher Education. Paul Clements examines the interesting history of the establishment of the Welsh College, and outlines the nature of the training offered to students that is based on a recognition of each actor's idiosyncratic self.

Despite his obvious care for the craft of the actor, Paul Clements is uncertain about the future of live theatre, and wonders whether it is in fact in terminal decline, as 'smaller numbers of people are attending fewer live performances mounted by fewer companies in a diminishing number of theatre buildings'. This grim prognosis is counterbalanced by Dafydd Arthur Jones's account of Theatr Fach Llangefni that, amongst various essays locating discontinuity and possible decline in professional Welsh theatre, portrays a lively amateur theatre that has a distinctive tradition of playing that stretches back to its founder's belief in an art theatre before the war.

The enduring popularity and productiveness of amateur drama are also celebrated by Ewart Alexander who relates one specific theatrical history, that of his own work in his native Ystradgynlais. Using a felicitous mix of amateur and professional actors, Ewart Alexander has mounted a trilogy of plays based on warfare this century: *Objection* (1993), set between 1916 and 1918 and dealing with protest against war; *Atrocity* (1994), located in 1943 and based on the making of Humphrey Jennings's anti-fascist film *The Silent Village* in Cwmgïedd; and *Cruise* (1995), placed aboard a cruise liner after the Falklands War. Ewart Alexander's chapter deals with the 1994 production of *Atrocity*, and offers an impassioned alternative to touring theatre, that of a sophisticated and relevant community drama based in localities all over Wales.

This plea for a theatre that recognizes specific histories and individual geographies is shared by Mike Pearson, who addresses the nature of alternative theatre in Wales, outlining its particular modes of rhetoric, spatial organization and performance. In his poetics of performance, he does not mourn the absence of a tradition of play-writing in Wales, but sees this lack of shared literary rules as liberating as it has enabled experimental practitioners to draw 'themes and subjects from the current currency of myth and religion, a rich literary tradition; a political history of bureaucratic and state intervention, of industrial and economic decay, of emigration and immigration and from a love of language, landscape and justice'.

The desire to engage with such a rich store of subjects, both theatrically and politically, has resulted in over seventy performance events by Pearson's company Brith Gof, some quite remarkable for performer and witness, that have consistently tested the bounds of stage experience. Charmian Savill provides a detailed overview of Brith Gof's diverse practices, surely one of the most significant companies in Wales over our period for the diversity, range and serious purpose of its work, as well as for its ability to forge ever new relations between the Welsh- and English-language cultures of Wales. She identifies a radical break in the form and practice of the company's work when in the mid-1980s it reshaped the way its performances were presented. The 'poor theatre' of the early 1980s that depended on dynamic and immediate interaction between performer and local community was eschewed in favour of more technologically dependent, large-scale events that were multi-voiced and much more unstable in the meanings they generated.

The shifting boundaries between 'real life' and theatrical performances that preoccupy Brith Gof are further opened up in my chapter relating events off-stage to the preoccupations and practices of formalized drama. Charmian Savill quite rightly mentions the failure of Brith Gof to establish a Theatr Ymchwil Cymru (Research Theatre Wales) during the company's stay in Aberystwyth as a lost opportunity to set up serious study of Welsh performance. Performances of an international character, though, could be studied through the efforts of the Centre for Performance Research in Cardiff (now in Aberystwyth) and the Magdalena Project in the capital that since its inception in 1986 has researched and brought together many aspects of women's performance in a committed and fruitful series of events celebrating female creativity.

The absorption of international influences along with the desire to break down boundaries between seemingly self-contained art and literary forms has been more than evident in Welsh dance theatre, and I have taken the liberty of adapting an article I originally wrote for the journal *Planet* in 1994 to acknowledge the challenging and imaginative work conducted by dance practitioners that has frequently overlapped with contemporary stage practice.

In the absence of any sustained academic study of modern Welsh theatre, the press critic has played a crucial role in informing a wider public of theatrical activity in Wales. Bob Roberts, long-time and even-handed reviewer for *The Stage* and the *Western Mail*, casts an eye over the organizational and artistic development of Wales's only large-scale repertory theatre, Theatr Clwyd, making a strong plea for its survival.

Moving away from seasoned observers of drama, *Staging Wales* ends with individual tales of what it has been like to survive as a dramatist, performer or director during the period under scrutiny. In an honest and engaging survey, Greg Cullen records the triumphs and tensions of his career as a writer transferred from London's East End to a small Powys town. Geoff Moore, director of the often exhilarating and visually daring Moving Being, whose presence in Cardiff from the

1970s helped to establish the city as a focus for experimental theatre in Britain, details the nature of the group's work within a wider context of innovative work across the arts. He bemoans the timidity of the arts establishment in not supporting challenging and ambitious work that does not fall into easy artistic and administrative categories, a lack of faith that is reiterated openly or acknowledged tacitly by other practitioners and commentators throughout this volume.

Lucy Gough and Dic Edwards discuss the purpose and nature of their work as stage authors, examining the process of writing and touching upon the differences between stage work and television writing. In the hope of broadening our range of inquiry and stressing the various histories that contribute to any understanding of Welsh theatre, I have also included Paul Davies's spirited assessment of Volcano Theatre's work. Volcano can be seen as being part of the exciting 'second wave' of Welsh experimental theatre from the mid-1980s that encompasses such groups as Man Act, Alma Theatre, Frantic Theatre, U-Man Zoo and Earthfall Dance, all of whom have developed a physically demanding, highly visual and iconoclastic approach to theatrical work.

The final contribution (reprinted from *New Welsh Review*) is from Gilly Adams, until recently director of Made in Wales Stage Company, which did much to foster and found professional dramatic writing in English. Adams looks back over twelve years of playwriting, and offers invaluable and experienced comment on the range and style of contemporary Welsh drama in English.

For this volume, I have adopted a deliberately eclectic approach, mixing first-hand testimonies of theatrical practice with more general overviews of the theatre in Wales from 1979 to 1997. For those who know that theatre well, I am conscious that a book that at first aimed to be a complete survey of the period has ended up as a partial account, with some theatrical histories uncovered more definitely than others. Above all, I hope that further investigations might arise from this volume (at present the only full-length study of modern Welsh theatre), and would wish that any obvious areas left dark in our coverage (for example, the place of design, women's stage practice, television and radio drama and popular forms such as pantos, pageants and stand-up comedy, in the overall picture) might be illuminated in subsequent assessments.

For those who are not familiar with Wales and its theatrical communities, the demarcation of the period (1979 to 1997) may seem arbitrary. Certainly, the use of the term 'contemporary' to describe well over a decade and a half of theatrical endeavour may seem over-generous, particularly to younger people than myself. However, the experiences of 1979 in Wales – the overwhelming vote against devolution in the St David's Day referendum (243,048 in favour of an assembly, 956,330 against) and the coming to power of Margaret Thatcher in May of that year – were political events that had a bearing on our lives well on into the 1990s. We were all for a long time and in many ways contemporaries of our 1979 selves.

The implications of those electoral decisions were felt by those working in Welsh theatre throughout the period, not only in the underfunding and philistine undervaluing of artistic work in market-led Britain, but also in the ambiguous and contradictory perception of Wales's national identity that permeated the practice of the period. Was Wales a colony? Could (and should) Wales be free of London? Was it possible to create theatre that bypassed the English mainstream? What was the place of the highly successful Welsh theatrical diaspora who established careers 'away' over the border – and of productive, talented 'incomers' such as Greg Cullen, Geoff Moore and Mike Pearson who stayed to enrich Welsh theatre?

Returning to my earlier contention that drama and theatre in Wales have not been able to develop a shared sense of continuity with other artistic and literary forms, it may be that Welsh theatre has not been quite so cut off from cultural experience in Wales this century. The search of stage writers and theatre practitioners for modes of organization and expression that would act as alternatives to those promoted by a free-market Conservatism were shared by many throughout Wales.

Collective practices, commitment to specific communities, challenge to orthodoxy, and an awareness of the underrepresented and disinherited in Britain are salient features of the work of many of the companies and writers discussed here. These convictions also underpin oppositional social, educational and employment practices, and constituted the central beliefs of labour movements and self-help organizations throughout Wales this century. So, it is likely that Welsh theatre-making is not such an isolated activity after all, as it is these challenges to orthodoxy that link modern Welsh dramatic practice to wider cultural histories this century. Were a more 'literary', more mainstream theatre established, the social and political commitment expressed, directly and indirectly, by many of those working in theatre in the period under discussion might recede in favour of less communitarian artistic aims.

1 • The Wounds of Possibility:
Welsh Drama in English in the 1960s and 1970s

Simon Baker

Writing a survey essay which sketches in the vestiges of a tradition can be a thankless task. It is the section at the beginning of most contemporary arts books which readers either skim or miss out altogether. After all, many would dispute the very terms of such an argument. What is the value of an artistic phenomenon? A series of patronizing stereotypes for the more sophisticated and enlightened to react against? Or, if an amalgam of this were not problematic enough, two further complications to surveying Welsh drama in English suggest themselves. The first centres on whether drama consists of the performance as text, or the text as literature. The reason that stage plays come to be taught as literature is because they are imaginative texts which lead a double life. On the one hand, they are blueprints for the alchemy of live performance, and on the other hand, they survive as a branch of literary study precisely because they have value as fictional texts consisting almost entirely of dialogue. The problem is exacerbated in Wales because very few new plays are ever performed, and the few which are, together with the best from the recent past, are largely unavailable in printed form.

The second complication is well-known to all Welsh readers. Those whom the gods wish to destroy they first afflict with a language problem. It is already a convention to say that Wales has no continuity of cultural experience comparable to that of nation states like England or France. It is equally conventional to make a virtue of discontinuity, and to argue fragmentation itself constitutes the only continuous experience we have. Conversely, it is also claimed that there is a continuous and subterranean Welsh tradition, repressed by foreign domination and internal treachery. These are all popular versions of more specific and sophisticated attitudes which underlie much historical and literary discourse, in both the languages of Wales.[1] It is impossible not to raise the spectre of a single, unified geographical and political entity when using the word 'Wales'. Yet this is only ever an imagined community, and in artistic endeavour no writer can legitimately claim to be disinterested, or to speak authoritatively on behalf of everyone involved.

Having noted the formal, dramatic and cultural limitations of writing on the Welsh dramatic tradition, you might be wondering where the argument can possibly go from here? In the spirit of Beckett's *Endgame*, my contention is that this should not mean the end of discussion. The tradition, such as it is, can be dispensed with fairly quickly. The literature or performance debate is elided by the fact that there is virtually no performance, so the only recourse is to discuss the plays as literature. And a journey into the cultural quagmire is thankfully beyond the scope of this brief survey, whose remit is to focus principally on Welsh drama in English.

In Roland Mathias's informative *Anglo-Welsh Literature: An Illustrated History*, the section entitled 'The dramatic tradition' is the shortest in the book.[2] This is undeniably a fair reflection of the paucity of the subject. As Carl Tighe succinctly put it: 'Since Wales is marginal to England, and theatre is marginal to Wales, and the playwright is marginal to Welsh theatre . . . the business of being a playwright in Wales can be a very unrewarding experience.'[3] In the latest edition of *Theatre Guide*, there are over 3,000 separate entries.[4] Apart from hundreds of dramatists and plays, the range of reference covers such diverse groups as Field Day in Ireland, Glasgow Citizens in Scotland, Asian, black, gay, lesbian, Yiddish, Graeae (disabilities) and various women's companies. There are two Welsh entries: yes, two.

That Emlyn Williams's *The Corn is Green* (1938) and Dylan Thomas's *Under Milk Wood* (1954), better known as a film and a radio drama respectively, should still represent Welsh dramatic achievement nearly half a century after they were written is bad enough. What is more disconcerting is the image of sentimental melodrama and irreverent fantasy, which they doubtless inculcate in the minds of the non-Welsh reader/viewer/listener. Lest you doubt the power of images, I refer you to the *Daily Mail*'s 'No-Good Boyo' headline the day after Kinnock's Labour Party lost the 1992 general election. The collective efforts of J. O. Francis (*Change*, 1913; *The Poacher*, 1914; *Cross Currents*, 1923), Caradoc Evans (*Taffy*, 1923) and Richard Hughes (*The Sisters' Tragedy*, 1922; *A Comedy of Good and Evil*, 1924) might have established a platform for further writing, but this never materialized. Of the five writers mentioned, only Francis and Hughes displayed any real dramatic talent, but even they tend to reproduce characteristics rather than interpret characters, and both quit the stage early.[5]

It is the misfortune of Welsh drama in English that so little cross-pollination has been achieved with its Welsh-language counterpart, because either side of the Second World War the latter's achievement was undoubtedly the more impressive. The plays of J. Kitchener Davies (*Cwm Glo* (*Coal Valley*), 1935; *Meini Gwagedd* (*Stones of Emptiness*), 1945), Huw Lloyd Edwards (*Y Gŵr O Wlad Us* (*The Man from the Land of Uz*), 1960; *Pros Kairon*, 1967) and Gwenlyn Parry (*Y Ffin* (*The Border*), 1973; *Y Tŵr* (*The Tower*), 1978) were all lively, entertaining and well-received. Yet none of these achieved the lasting influence of Saunders Lewis, perhaps the foremost Welsh dramatist of the twentieth century in either language. Throughout his remarkable career Lewis channelled his energies into a kind of literary *Kulturkampf*, arguing that there should be no division between culture and politics. In plays such as *Blodeuwedd* (1948), *Siwan* (1956), *Gymerwch Chi Sigaret?* (*Will you Have a Cigarette?*) (1956), *Brad* (*Treason*) (1958), *Cymru Fydd* (*The Wales of the Future*) (1967) and *Branwen* (1975), his range extended from mythic folklore to tragic realism, and beyond to incorporate the influences of Corneille, Sartre and Beckett.[6] At his best, his writing managed to convey aspects of the human predicament whilst still being culturally specific. The tensions between love and lust, free choice and duty, or faith and doubt made for searing drama, but his artistic vision became increasingly embittered. To adapt Seamus Deane's description of W. B. Yeats, Lewis began his career by inventing a Wales amenable to his imagination, but ended by finding a Wales recalcitrant to it. If Welsh dramatists in English have been little influenced by their Welsh-language compatriots, then they have suffered an enormous anxiety about influence from their English cousins. Whilst poetry thrived in the 1960s and 1970s (one thinks of R. S. Thomas, John Tripp, Gillian Clarke, Harri Webb, Leslie Norris), and fiction held its own (Raymond Williams, Emyr Humphreys, Ron Berry, Alun Richards), drama all but disappeared. Only the efforts of Gwyn Thomas and Dannie Abse on the stage, and to a lesser extent Alun Richards, Ewart Alexander and Elaine Morgan on screen, kept the genre alive. The reasons for this are not easy to fathom, but Carl Tighe has pointed to three overlapping 'effects' which have dictated this relative silence, namely the margin effect (extremity of), audience effect (apathy of) and experience effect (lack of).[7]

With no dramatic models on which to rely except rewritings of the post-Dylan, sub-Emlyn Great Welsh Play, Gwyn Thomas and Dannie Abse looked to the English and European theatre for guidance. That versatile Welshman Raymond Williams has identified two distinct movements in British theatre from the late 1950s onwards.[8] The first is socialist, working-class or alienated lower middle-class in its focus, anchored on plays like Osborne's *Look Back in Anger* (1956), Arden's *Live Like Pigs* (1958) and Delaney's *A Taste of Honey* (1958). The second is European and experimental in style and orientation, usually eschewing an overt political standpoint. Beckett's *Endgame* (1957) and Ionesco's *Rhinoceros* (1960) are obvious and influential examples. Gwyn Thomas wrote a series of distinctively Valleys plays from the late 1950s onwards, which are nevertheless rooted firmly in the British socialist drama of that period. Abse, in contrast, produced a number of outstanding but underrated plays, influenced by the experimental European theatrical modes of the early post-war era. As befits all enduring and distinctive drama, neither writer entirely conformed to the rather neat pattern laid out above.

In his book *Political Theatre* (1929), Erwin Piscator lamented that the working class had been excluded from theatre, by price, by tradition, and in terms of subject-matter.[9] Yet all this was to change in the late 1950s when a movement that was social in character and political in consequence transformed the face of British drama. If writers like Beckett, Pinter and Orton suggested that language was exhausted, that words had been drained of meaning, detached from any world of verifiable reality, then the socialist playwright had to respond otherwise – and respond they did. A number of writers whose careers began in the 1960s were to become the driving force of British theatre, especially after the removal of censorship, a huge psychological barrier, in 1968. Arden, Bond, Hare, Brenton, Edgar, McGrath, Griffiths and Churchill represented a loose collective whose justification was eloquently expressed in David Hare's 1978 lecture delivered at King's College, Cambridge: 'I would suggest to you crudely that one of the reasons for the theatre's possible authority, for its recent general drift towards politics, is its unique ability to display an age in which men's ideals and men's practice bear no relation to each other.' In the vanguard of this movement (although he has rarely been seen there, especially by English critics) was Gwyn Thomas.

Throughout a career of 'nicotine poisoning and explosive disbelief', Thomas wrote eight plays, the first six of which made it into performance. *The Keep* (1960), *Loud Organs* (1962), *Jackie the Jumper* (1963), *Sap* (1974), *The Breakers* (1976) and *Testimonials* (1979) all had runs in London or Cardiff, whilst two plays on Aneurin Bevan, *Return and End* and *A Tongue for a Stammering Time*, remain unproduced.[10] Most of the plays centre on a reimagining of the sprawling, throbbing, deindustrializing Rhondda of Thomas's youth, irrespective of time or place. He captures the lives of his 'voters' in an uproarious comic prose, which is rarely interested in grasping people precisely, only in exaggerating them precisely. Yet his exaggerations have a visible boundary, avoiding the pessimistic grotesqueries of Caradoc Evans and the sentimentalized clichés of Dylan Thomas. The multiple forms of irony, bitter satire, bawdy comic farce and verbal wit which pervade the idiolect of his plays work best when they are controlled within a tight narrative and dramatic structure. In short, when the humour knows its place. Dreams of fulfilment and perfectibility are held in the steady gaze of his central characters, Miriam Morton, Jackie Rees and Jim Bumford, who see institutional oppression inculcate itself into the minds of the passive and the powerless. Moral outrage transforms itself into comic art, invariably made more poignant by his defeated characters' capacity to respond but not to act, and their vague awareness that doubt deludes itself as much as faith.

In a stagnant provincial society blanketed by disillusionment, cushioned by self-deception, and populated by small imaginations and large grievances, Con Morton in *The Keep* articulates a life surviving on undernourished hopes:

Ben: No need to be bitter, Con. You'll bring on that rash on your neck again. We all have our crosses to bear.

Con: I'm with you there, Dad. I've been a pack pony in the cross-bearing business. In all the chambers of that Town Hall to which I've given my life there is no more over-worked nerve of social awareness than I.

Ben: You've been active Con, and no mistake.

Con: That's a fact. On nineteen committees, Secretary of three, treasurer to two and ideas man to the lot. My life's been a meeting, dad, one long meeting. Even on the few committees I don't yet belong to, the agenda winks to me when I pass.[11]

The Keep is probably Thomas's best-known play, which in itself is a mixed blessing. The fact that it reproduces most of the strengths of his prose (sense of place, communal bonds, adversarial wit) is counterbalanced by its weaknesses (undifferentiated characters, static action). Although he continued to produce the same basic elements in his plays – a closed community, a hidden story, a traumatic revelation, politicized wit – his *œuvre* is not nearly so narrow as many people imagine. He was a Spanish scholar and Lorca may have had an influence on his dramatic development, for his work became less claustrophobic and naturalistic as it proceeded, employing farce, folklore, song, dance and the kind of magical realism favoured by the Andalusian writer.

Jackie the Jumper experimented with historical drama, and *Loud Organs* used a Cardiff docklands club as a metaphor for post-industrial decay in south Wales (a self-fulfilling prophecy if ever there was one). His next two plays, both long out of print and no longer performed, are even more radical reworkings of the expected Welsh socialist play. He never lost his belief that whilst his characters made their world, the world also made them, but *Sap* is surely as imaginative a play as has been seen on the post-war Welsh stage. Commissioned by the Welsh Arts Council and produced by the Welsh Drama Company, *Sap* philosophizes, poeticizes and sings its way from the south Wales pits to the First World War, through the medium of a central character who changes roles quite a few times. *The Breakers* moves spatially from Pennsylvania in 1776 and 1876 to south Wales in 1976, using successive generations of the same family. Neither play ever gained the recognition it deserved, most English critics coming not to review but to bury Thomas, whose television appearances had by then defined him as a caricature comic Welshman. Nor, sadly, have his plays received their due recognition in Wales, where his reputation as a political humorist seems to preclude discussion of him as a serious dramatist. For once, I will not allow him the last word, but turn instead to Howard Brenton to put Thomas in context: 'the only thing that bonds us together today is a profound unease, and laughter is the language of that unease'.[12]

Just as Gwyn Thomas particularized socialist drama of the period to suit his own particular vision, so Dannie Abse, the other major Welsh dramatist in English of the 1960s and 1970s, adapted the formal innovations of the post-Beckettian play to his own ends. Abse's six published plays *House of Cowards* (1960), *The Joker* (1962), *Gone*

(1962), *In the Cage* (1964), *The Dogs of Pavlov* (1969) and *Pythagoras (Smith)* (1976), all focus on, to varying degrees, the loss of unique, creative, individual identity in the face of dehumanizing, oppressive, external forces.[13] Abse himself has written the most perceptive introduction to his drama:

> My experience of human irrationality, the discovery of it in my own behaviour and in other people, as I encounter it in my personal life and in my medical practice, as I am affected by it in the absurdity of public political action, as indeed I am threatened by jt in the clash of public powers, makes me feel sometimes that the earth is no ordinary hospital but a lunatic asylum whose inmates live out suffering lives in black comedy.[14]

Abse has received little critical acclaim for his drama within Wales, principally one feels because there is very little Welshness (and I do not propose to define that term) on display. His Jewish background and his career in medicine are much stronger elements, especially his by now familiar white coat/purple coat dichotomy. In *House of Cowards*, the Godot-like speaker fails to arrive and transform the expectant Hicks family ennui of daily existence, whilst the capacity of ordinary people to obey evil instructions lies at the heart of *The Dogs of Pavlov*. The play's subtext, with allusions to Auschwitz, Hiroshima and Vietnam, makes the frequent laughter induced as the drama unfolds all the more disturbing. Both plays are arguments, and arguments are dynamic: they move from point to point and from scene to scene. This means not only that the play's events progress, but also that their intellectual life is on the move. A dialogue is implied between the audience/reader and the dramatic events, particularly in Abse's finest work, *Pythagoras (Smith)*. In the following scene Dr Aquillus, rather than trying to understand Mr X's condition, attempts to use it to amuse his students, whilst Pythagoras articulates a completely contrasting view of the world.

X: My bowels are made of glass.
Aquillus: Yes, yes.
X: I feel dead inside.
Aquillus: We'll talk about it later. As a matter of fact I want you to
                 volunteer for a demonstration.
X: No! Definitely not.

Aquillus:	Why not?
X:	Definitely, definitely, definitely not. [*Mr X begins to exit*]
Aquillus:	Don't be alarmed, there's nothing to it. [*Exit Mr X*]
X:	[*Off-stage*] You're not going to exploit me.
Aquillus:	[*Shaking head*] Like you, he lives in the suburbs of punishment. But you – you feel inspired.
Pythagoras:	I do see the correspondence of disparate things. That is inspiration. I know too, the secret of irrationality, and I have the gift of approximate prophetic insight.
Aquillus:	Approximate?
Pythagoras:	It's like a smell. I can't always be sure. If I told you of my other powers you'd poke fun at me.[15]

This play investigates the relationship between, and ultimately the incompatibility of, science and art, reason and imagination, medicine and magic. The play's final image of Christmas cards and choirs suggests how the miraculous is repackaged into the ordinary and mundane, just as the central character is 'cured' of his Pythagorean imagination into being plain Tony Smith. Yet despite the dismal endings to all his plays, Abse's drama is not wholly negative. His work suggests that it is no longer enough to know that we are all at the mercy of external pressures; it is necessary to understand that such a sealed fate should not, indeed cannot, be accepted. His fascination with the visual aspects of theatre and the ambivalence and ambiguity of his language place him firmly in the experimental, postmodern dramatic movement. However, Abse, like Pinter and Stoppard, is too immersed in the experience of the apparently commonplace and ordinary to divorce himself from an identifiable concern with the social and political realities of Britain, and indeed Wales, in the 1960s and 1970s.

The 1970s saw changes in the theatrical landscape, which were themselves a part of a wider social and cultural transformation. A number of legislative reforms affecting abortion, homosexuality, divorce and equal pay came into being, and whilst many of these themes found voice in an increasingly disparate English theatre, the response in Wales was largely one of silence. Only Alun Richards and Ewart Alexander could be considered to have had any success on the stage. Richards's dramatic output is far more varied than his fiction, both in range and, unfortunately, in quality. *The Big Breaker* (1965), *The Victualler's Ball* (1969) and *The Snowdropper* (1973) all reflect contemporary Welsh concerns, whilst *The Horizontal Life* (1973) is an ambitious dramatization of desire and betrayal based on the life of Gabriel D'Annunzio.[16] Alexander's best stage plays remain unpublished, notably *Buzz Buzz Critch Critch* (1969), *The Rose-Tinted Pelicans* (1972) and *White Plains* (1976).

Increasingly throughout the 1970s and into the 1980s these two dramatists, together with Alun Owen, Elaine Morgan and Siôn Eirian, have turned to television as their primary outlet. The advent of S4C has removed almost the entire (semi-) professional Welsh-language drama community from the stage and put them on screen. The doyen of bilingual Welsh fiction and drama, Emyr Humphreys, stated recently that he has earned more money from Welsh-language adaptations on screen and radio in the last ten years than he did from the entire sum of his writing output over the previous five decades. Faced with its rivals offering greater accessibility, more security and higher financial rewards, it is hardly surprising that so few Welsh writers were attracted to the stage in the 1970s and early 1980s, especially given the disdain with which successive Thatcher governments treated the performing arts.

And yet, to adopt Antonio Gramsci's famous dictum, before the old world can die and the new one can be born, a plethora of dire symptoms manifest themselves in the interregnum. Perhaps that is an apt description of the Welsh dramatic scene in the 1960s and 1970s. John McGrath, writing a Marxist-based analysis of contemporary theatre, identifies three main elements of literary production: the residual, the dominant and the emergent.[17] The residual myths of kith and kin are dead and buried in Wales, the deindustrializing, consumerist 1980s saw to that. The dominant was and is the English theatre powerhouse of the post-war period, although perhaps its finest proponents have gravitated toward the small and the large screens, which leaves the emergent. Let us be recklessly optimistic, and hope that the emergence of Made in Wales, Brith Gof, Volcano, Theatr Clwyd, the Sherman, Greg Cullen and Ed Thomas, to name but a few, augurs well for the future. My title, which may have perplexed you, is taken from Søren Kierkegaard: 'The wounds of possibility remain open.'[18] It is a powerful phrase with many applications, holding together as it does elements of bitterness, despair and pain, with a vague suggestion of potential and hope. I can think of no better epigraph for the plight of Welsh drama in English.

Notes

1   See, for instance, the opening chapters of M. Wynn Thomas's seminal study, *Internal Difference* (Cardiff, University of Wales Press, 1992). This book also includes a fascinating chapter on the drama of J. O. Francis.

2   Roland Mathias, *Anglo-Welsh Literature: An Illustrated History* (Bridgend, Poetry Wales Press, 1987).

3   Carl Tighe, 'Theatre (or not) in Wales', in Tony Curtis (ed.), *Wales: The Imagined Nation* (Bridgend, Poetry Wales Press, 1986), pp. 239–60.

4   *Theatre Guide*, ed. Trevor R. Griffiths and Carole Woddis (London, Bloomsbury, 1994).

5   For a brief but useful survey of Welsh drama in both languages see *The Oxford Companion to the Literature of Wales*, ed. Meic Stephens (Oxford, OUP, 1986).

6   The best introduction to Lewis's work is still *Presenting Saunders Lewis*, ed. Alun R. Jones and Gwyn Thomas (Cardiff, University of Wales Press, 1973).

7   Tighe, 'Theatre (or not) in Wales', p. 248.

8   Raymond Williams, 'New English drama', in John Russell Brown (ed.), *Modern British Dramatists* (Englewood Cliffs, New Jersey, Prentice-Hall, 1968), pp. 26–37.

9   Erwin Piscator, *The Political Theatre: A History*, tr. Hugh Rorrison (New York, Harcourt-Brace, 1978).

10 The most accessible introduction to Thomas's drama is *Three Plays* ed. Michael Parnell (Bridgend, Seren, 1990).

11 Ibid., p. 26.

12 Howard Brenton, 'Petrol bombs through the proscenium arch', *Theatre Quarterly*, 5/17 (March–May 1975), 10.

13 The best introduction to Abse's plays is *The View From Row G: Three Plays*, ed. James A. Davies (Bridgend, Seren, 1990). The opening section makes particularly perceptive comments on Abse's drama, as does Tony Curtis's *Dannie Abse* (Cardiff, University of Wales Press, 1985), pp. 41–60.

14 Dannie Abse, *Pythagoras* (London, Hutchinson, 1979), p. 11. Abse's short introduction explains the genesis of the play in his poem 'Funland'.

15 *The View From Row G*, pp. 160–1.

16 All these plays are collected in Alun Richards, *Plays for Players* (Llandysul, Gomer Press, 1975).

17 This reference is taken from C. W. E. Bigsby, 'The language of crisis in British theatre', in Malcolm Bradbury and David Palmer (eds.) *Contemporary English Drama* (London, Edward Arnold, 1983), p. 33.

18 Søren Kierkegaard, *The Present Age*, tr. Alexander Dru (London, Fontana, 1978), p. 19.

2 • Leaving the Twentieth Century:
New Writing on the Welsh-Language Mainstage 1979–1995

Nic Ros

> Wales in the sixties was a much more interesting place to live and be young in . . . It remained that way until the end of the seventies. It was then that things turned sour. The seventy-nine Referendum.
>
> (*Fel Paent yn Sychu (Like Paint Drying)*, Angharad Tomos, 1988)

The year of the first devolution Referendum, 1979, also saw the election of the Conservative government that was to rule Wales for so many years. These momentous events cast their shadow over much Welsh theatre and certainly influenced the more political playwrights.

Also in 1979, a development specific to Welsh theatre was signified by the production of *Bargen (Bargain)* by Theatr Bara Caws in the Caernarfon National Eisteddfod. The massive success of this collectively written show prefigures the belated rise, in the 1980s, of the ensemble and the group-written performance which had massive implications for writers: it was at a performance of *Gernika!* (Cwmni Theatr Cymru/ Brith Gof, 1983) that the only member of the audience remaining seated at the end was a prominent Welsh playwright. This performance, utilizing song and poetry rather than dialogue, was a watershed because of its high profile as a collaboration between the National Theatre of Wales and one of the country's most radical companies. The institutionalization of group work was signalled by a parallel development in educational theatre. Welsh-language Theatre in Education is the only area of definite growth in provision over the period, but at the time of writing of this study even the future of TIE in Wales is in jeopardy.

In studying the history of writing for the Welsh-language mainstage in the period 1979 to 1995, the most obvious feature is the glaringly low number of writers who have produced more than one or two plays. While a great number have dabbled with stage writing, it appears that there are only three serious writers who have written three or more plays.

A convenient starting-point for analysis is Gareth Miles's *Diwedd y Saithdegau (End of the Seventies)* (Hwyl a Fflag, 1982), convenient for the title but also because Miles is the most prolific dramatist of the period, with seven full-length plays and six adaptations or rewrites ranging from Euripides and Webster to Bond and Bulgakov. This most political of writers utilizes Thatcherism as the spark for the play, which also touches on the referendum. Miles concentrates on a former rebel who has become respectable, signified by her marriage to a police officer. This very cynical play has the common fault of being too verbose, but is prefigurative in its display of soured revolutionary rhetoric, precluding one of the constant themes of Siôn Eirian who will be discussed later. The play fails because of its lack of theatricality: it reads like a radio play.

In *Unwaith Eto, Nghymru Annwyl (Once More, Dear Wales)* (Hwyl a Fflag, 1984) a Welsh rebel hero returns from working for the ANC to confront his political future in the light of his recent experience. Miles questions the changes brought about by S4C, this just two years after the formation of the channel, as the television journalist's integrity is under fire from one of the old rebel guard. Our Madog figure stands between the opposing factions, unsure of his position. The allegorical element is not fully incorporated into the play, and is therefore unsuccessful. The play is more interesting, however, for its reversal of expectations, as the dutiful wife who has been left to guard family and home decides that they must live apart in order for her, too, to discover herself. Here is the first obvious indication in Miles's work of his interest in women's issues. The play is naïve in its attempt to pontificate on a number of issues, which it does unsubtly, through general political statements tacked on to the end of scenes. This contextualizing betrays the influence of Brecht, whose legacy we see even more clearly in his next play.

If *Ffatri Serch (Love Factory)* (Hwyl a Fflag, 1984) is, as Miles called it, a 'comedy', then it is a comedy in the sense that Brecht's best work is comedy. This distant cousin of *The Good Person of Szechuan* revolves around the evils of capitalism and the forfeiting of principles that it encourages. Characters are sketched rather than painted, yet the play works through the pace of the episodic structure and the satire which raises smiles if not belly-laughs. Only occasionally teetering over into farce, the play is carried by the sparkling dialogue.

Like all of Miles's most stirring work, *Ffatri Serch* benefits from a clear purpose that is sorely lacking in his next play *Y Lleidr Da (The*

Virtuous Thief) (Hwyl a Fflag, 1986). There are touches of typically unflinching analysis, but it is foremost a mystery thriller based on murder and corruption in a small north Walian town. The social satire evident in the title – the thief being the most honest character depicted – is unconvincing because of the incredibility of the situation, the superficiality of the characterization and the playwright's uncertainty of style.

Sibling rivalry would seem to be the theme of *Chwiorydd (Sisters)* (Cwr y Llen, 1988), a play more suited to television than the stage, because of its time scale. An intriguing if minor work in his canon, this play shows two embittered lonely sisters battling for supremacy. The first part is particularly interesting, a virtual monologue as the famous opera singer sister has doctor's orders not to talk at all for a month. The conclusion, that the two are in essence more alike than either would otherwise admit, is facile, but at least the playwright avoids the seemingly inevitable melodramatic climax.

Miles's best play is probably *Hunllef yng Nghymru Fydd (Nightmare in Future Wales)* (Dalier Sylw, 1990): it is also undoubtedly his most exciting. His cool disdain for political platitudes is at its most obvious here, portraying a future independent Republic, and he is acerbic towards the expedients necessary to the upkeep of that 'independence' – political loyalty to England is exchanged for that of the USA – and to the past crimes committed to establish such a republic. Comparisons with South America abound as we hear of Wales being embroiled in a 'Dirty War' where the perpetrators were never brought to justice. Concentrating on the political leaders on all sides, the rhetoric is for once justified, yet the play graphically demonstrates as well as discusses the economic basis of class difference. The play nevertheless works as a thriller, and was dynamically staged as a site-specific work at the Jacobean mansion Llancaiach Fawr.

In Miles's desire to weld the political and the personal he turned to the Second Branch of the Mabinogion for *Dyrnod Branwen (Branwen's Blow)* (Hwyl a Fflag, 1993). Cleverly inverting Branwen's passive role in the original tale – here she is a pro-IRA convert who contrasts with her moderate Irish husband – Miles forges a multi-faceted commentary on Welsh–Irish relations, meshing his political allegory with the social and the domestic.

An interest in society rather than politics typifies the work of Siôn Eirian, and in particular an interest in areas unfamiliar to a Welsh audience: 'My plays have examined and tried to understand the workings of the lives of people outside my own experience, and what is their meaning.' This summation by the author of his œuvre hints at the controversy likely to follow his work for the stage as well as the page and the screen. It is certainly true of his *Wastad ar y Tu Fas (Always on the Outside)* (Hwyl a Fflag, 1986), one of the greatest plays discussed here. This truly revelatory work, for a Welsh-language audience at least, succeeds on its own terms despite an obvious debt to Martin Sherman's *Bent*. The play has at its difficult core a comparison between the explicit oppression of homosexuality in the Nazi death camps and the surreptitious censorship of today. The play succeeds through its evocation of a specific modern-day context: Martin wants to keep secret his sexual identity, believing it will harm his budding DJ career, and refuses to join in his partner's campaigning. The play ultimately deals with the sacrificing of love on the altar of ambition, a constant in Siôn Eirian's work. The relationship of the two protagonists is credibly evoked, and the stage production was emboldened by memorable performances from both Mei Jones and Tom Richmond as the troubled lovers.

Eirian's *Elfis, Y Blew a Fi (Elvis, The Hair and Me)* (Hwyl a Fflag, 1988) is a difficult piece, ultimately defeated by its own structure, concentrating as it does on two friends in 1968, 1978 and 1988, and the development of their relationship from college students to professional media people. A collage of impressions lacking a satisfactory dramatic backbone, and not aided by a convoluted time structure, the play again deals with compromise abetted by ambition. The author himself admitted later that the failure of this play (in his eyes) led him away from the theatre for seven years.

It may be that Eirian's most enduring works will turn out to be his most issue-based plays. Turning away from the obvious biographical influences which forged *Elfis*, *Epa yn y Parlwr Cefn (An Ape in the Back Room)* (Dalier Sylw, 1994) confronts head on issues surrounding prostitution, and was inevitably savaged by reactionaries. It was the gutter realism of the language that upset most people, but it is not the presence of four-letter words that is most shocking but the matter-of-fact attitude to sex that characterizes the working girls. The first half is almost documentary drama, maintaining interest as an exposé of a seedy underworld unseen in the Welsh media. The second half is unsatisfactory because of the predictability of the plot, and because of the author's decision to forego the presence of the more interesting of the two main prostitutes for most of the act. Although as issue-based as Miles, Eirian never attempts a state-of-the-nation address. Miles on the other hand has Wales in two of his titles, and looks in different works to Ireland, South Africa and South America to locate Wales in the global political picture.

Turning from the work of Miles and Eirian to other writers with an interest in politics, it is Wales and in particular its relationship with England rather than the world that interests writers, the Conservative government offering an at times too easily recognizable foe: 'Every other show in Wales recently claims to be an allegory for Thatcherism and what is happening to our society.' So claimed Siôn Eirian as late as 1994, yet the theme is obvious in much earlier work, and in some unexpected places.

A modern melodrama may seem a contradiction in terms, but Gruffydd Jones's play *Bedlam* (Hwyl a Fflag, 1985) does succeed in inverting the conservative tendency of the form to produce a thinly veiled critique of the dog-eat-dog mentality. The play is based in London in 1883, but the contemporary allegory is clear, as we see business prioritized instead of people, and the hypocrisy of the public espousers of family values. The characterization is of course reliant upon stock, yet the author creates tension around exactly who is fit for the institution of the title. The young hero Sam Byn is an effective source of comedy, and the play is only let down by a weak ending, incredible even by melodrama's loose standards. The final scene is unintentionally hilarious, an absurd farce which attempts a cynical twist on the typical happy ending, uniting young hero and villain in business in an attempt to emphasize further the insidiousness of market values.

In a more realistic vein, and yet located in an alternative present, Gwion Lynch's *Dim Ond Heno (Only Tonight)* (Cwmni Theatr Gwynedd, 1991), has as its central device the unlikely scenario of English settlers in north Wales striking back against the arsonist campaigns of Meibion Glyndŵr, the paramilitary terrorists so successful in burning down summer homes. Yet again a play is centred on an embittered former revolutionary, the owner of a tuppence ha'penny Welsh press wanting to publicize the English attempts at arson, but compromised by his own private life – a one-night stand with his friend's wife: an interesting concept which is let down by simplistic pontificating at the expense of rounded characters.

Gareth Ioan's *Tŷ Ni (Our House)* (Araḍ Goch, 1993) also looks at English immigration into rural Welsh Wales, but thankfully without overt sloganeering. This he manages by analysing racism and bigotry on both sides of the political fence. Emphasizing the human dimension, he looks at the relationship between an English grocer's daughter raised in Wales and a young migrant from north Wales. Ioan is an interesting example of a writer who has graduated to the professional stage by a curiously old-fashioned method: by honing his craft on the amateur stage. This development, which is quite rare today, is only made possible by this writer's location in a particularly active community in west Wales. After a very promising first professional production, *Sgrech (Scream)* (Arad Goch, 1995) was a huge disappointment, a patronizing study of the problems of youth set in an alternative present or near-future. Stereotypical characterization and uncertainty of style are the worst of its many faults.

William R. Lewis's *Golff (Golf)* (Cwmni Theatr Gwynedd, 1993) is another play which seems unable to decide if it is a serious drama or a satirical comedy. The play has in its favour obvious contemporary relevance, discussing as it does corruption and bribery in north Welsh council circles, an idea so familiar that the comedy is often one of recognition rather than revelation. The play's strength and weakness ultimately have the same root in the familiarity of the milieu, the specificity of any political points it has to make. Within the same field of what might loosely be called political writing, the next two plays are, literally, a world apart.

Pam Palmer's *Yn Ein Dwylo (In Our Hands)* (Arad Goch, 1992) is notable for being the last winning play in the National Eisteddfod drama medal competition. This hamfisted play about Lithuanian independence is not notable for any other reason. The characters talk in Constructivist conceits, unbelievable in an otherwise non-epic style, and in an attempt to evoke the massive political forces crushing the small nation, the writer resorts to reportage for the whole of the static third act, which a sympathetic staging could not save.

Plant Kalev (Children of Kalev) (Hwyl a Fflag, 1991) is on a more human scale, and is accordingly rather more successful. The declaration of Estonian independence is shown realistically as a starting-point only for the growth of the small nation, and the play partly succeeds because of its deliberate underlining of comparisons and contrasts with the political situation in Wales. Excepting his one man study of Lewis Valentine, *Val* (Hwyl a Fflag, 1990), this was the first full-length play by the multi-talented Dyfan Roberts.

Dyfan Roberts is not the only performing and directing talent within the Welsh theatre world who felt a need to increase his œuvre.

Cefin Roberts's *Janine* (Hwyl a Fflag, 1989) unfortunately begins with
an unexpected reunion of college friends in a village in the south of
France. Despite this unbelievable plot device the second half is
interesting, depicting the emancipation of two middle-aged, middle-
class wives under the bewitching spell of the seventeen-year-old wild
child of the title. The fantastical and allegorical elements of the
second half are, however, stylistically inconsistent with the pre-
valently realistic first half.

Examples abound of writers of novels and poetry turning their
hand to the stage, almost as if through a misguided sense of duty to
attempt every literary form at their disposal. Unfortunately this tends
to exacerbate the already word-bound tendency of much Welsh
writing. Iwan Llwyd's *Hud ar Ddyfed (Dyfed Under a Spell)* (Hwyl a
Fflag, 1993) had particular potential, creating at times a ghostly filmic
atmosphere, aided by a marvellous score. While the poet's
imagination is clearly inspired by using themes from the difficult
Third Branch of the Mabinogion, Manawydan, the playwright is
seriously misguided in his attempt at naturalistic dialogue which
comes over as soap opera.

That poetry can be converted more easily into effective theatre as
'shows' rather than conventional plays is also illustrated by *Y Forwyn
Goch (The Red Virgin)* (Dalier Sylw, 1992), a study of Simone Weil by
Menna Elfyn which makes no attempt at a biographical explication of
her contradictory life. Using the figures of Plato, de Gaulle, Trotsky
and St Francis of Assissi to define Weil's position, the play is also
evocatively written, if terribly edited, and even has a dramatic
backbone: the underused device of Weil's interrogation after landing
at Liverpool docks. The piece is structurally untidy, and of course
wordy, but the stage adaptation alienated by introducing comedy into
the proceedings, almost as if apologizing for the poetic content.
Although only one of the plays by Menna Elfyn can be analysed here
(she has written at least two amateur or semi-professional pieces), she
is one of the few writers in other media who does have an ongoing
relationship with the theatre, and who will continue to write for the
stage.

The vastly experienced actress Sharon Morgan set herself one of
the most difficult tasks for a writer and actress: that of a monologue.
Her adaptation of a Simone de Beauvoir short story *Gobeithion
Gorffwyll (Mad Hopes)* (Theatr y Byd, 1994) was a searing piece of
theatre, an at times almost too intense study of a woman on the cusp

of madness. The monologue form is here reclaimed by the theatre, similar work too often plumps for televisuality under the ubiquitous influence of Alan Bennett. One such example is the three monologues by Richard T. Jones, *Chwith Meddwl (It's A Sad Thought)* (Cwmni Theatr Gwynedd, 1993), a deeply disappointing evening with little connection between the three pieces, only one of which was saved by a *tour de force* performance by Valmai Jones as an isolated old woman.

Cyn Daw'r Gaeaf (Before Winter) by Meg Elis (Hwyl a Fflag, 1987) portrays in a sensitive way the politicization of a pastor's wife who decamps to Greenham Common, and subsequently struggles to reintegrate into middle-class society. The play's origin as a novel is betrayed in the episodic nature of the first act, yet the play works because of the credible characterization and lack of sentiment. Despite occasional clichés, the writer never succumbs to preaching nor to offering simple solutions.

Like *Cyn Daw'r Gaeaf*, *Mysgu Cymylau (Blending Clouds)* by Branwen Cennard (Dalier Sylw, 1991) unapologetically centres on women's experience, but is more notable for its unpatronizing treatment of Welsh-language working classes in south Wales. The play uses an intriguing concept, a concert by the Welsh folk/pop singer Heather Jones (playing herself) which is both background and point of departure for a series of monologues and memories of three women's lives.

Reading *Tanddaearol (Underground)* (Hwyl a Fflag, 1992), it would seem that the novelist Angharad Tomos had created a bewitching fable on the memory of a nation, with hints of Sartre's *Huis Clos* in her display of the afterworld (the underground of the title). Yet this ambitious piece seemed rambling and incoherent on stage, because despite the rigour and heartfelt intelligence of the words there is no theatricality, and the very promising conceit falls apart when the dead return to the earth. This is a major disappointment after the success of Tomos's first stage play *Fel Paent yn Sychu (Like Paint Drying)* (Theatr Crwban, 1988), a credible attempt at linking teenage ennui to the stoicism of the elderly. Around an unhappy couple the son and grandmother establish an unlikely rapport. The central relationship is skilfully and coolly evoked, and works despite the essential verbosity of the piece which underlines the overstated dramatic climax.

It is no coincidence that much of the best new writing derives from individuals with a background or training in theatre rather than literature, for the simple reason that these have a theatrical eye as well as an ear. Much promise was shown by actress/director Siân Summers in her semi-comic *Un Funud Fach (One Little Minute)* (Hwyl a Fflag, 1993), an enchanting mesh of absurdity and romance set against the realistic background of a taxi rank on New Year's Eve and contrasted throughout the play with a simultaneous showing of *Brief Encounter*. Despite an occasional uncertainty of tone, as might be expected from a play which can count Ionesco and *The Wizard of Oz* among its myriad influences, the play shows some maverick touches.

The contributions of many to female writing for the stage are polymorphous. A female playwright of undoubted commitment to the stage is Sêra Moore Williams, the actress/director/writer who also formed the company Y Gymraes (The Welsh Woman) to create theatre from a female perspective. Her *Byth Rhy Hwyr (Never Too Late)* (Y Gymraes, 1992) was their first production. *Byth Rhy Hwyr* is a diverting state of the world address. Utilizing a unique twist on a Pirandellian idea, the play has three actresses' 'real' lives interrupting their presentation. The twist here is that all three are aliens on a fact-finding mission to our troubled planet. The flow of this absorbing bitter comedy is only occasionally marred by the constant diversions.

Her second play for the company, *Trais Tyner (Tender Violence)* (Y Gymraes, 1994), takes an idiosyncratic look at the varying perspectives of three generations of women. Mother and grand-mother are ghosts who advise, cajole and castigate the daughter as she attempts to make sense of her relationship with her man. Not always certain of direction, the result is nevertheless an engaging and chal-lenging mix of bitter comedy and realistic romanticism.

A feature of these last two writers is their confidence in mixing levity and seriousness, of charging their ambitious and difficult conceits with humour which is often black and incongruous. Despite occasional vagaries of tone, their plays work when the humour arises naturally from character and situation. Conversely, much of the more obviously comic writing of the period would seem to be composed as a series of punchlines which never make a composite whole, an example of which is *Plas Dafydd (David's House)* (Cwmni Theatr Gwynedd, 1988). Following *Hywel A* and *Pontrobat*, the first of which was particularly engaging, this was Huw Roberts's third farce. His occasional success with familiar elements is too dependent on stereotypes such as the stupid policeman, while the plotting is weak in what is essentially comedy of situation, and the dialogue disappointing.

A young author of great potential is Emlyn Gomer, whose first stage comedy *Dim Byd Ynni* (Hwyl a Fflag 1990) has an untranslatable title due to a pun on the Welsh word for energy. This very humorous script simultaneously celebrates and satirizes the farce, combining stereotypes with alienated asides. The throwaway plot, concerning murder and corruption in the energy industry, is not important, but the original production, which unfortunately did not develop into a tour, was a hilarious, scathing romp which delighted its audience.

His next play was the modern interlude *Brawd Herod (Herod's Brother)* (Rhiniog, 1992), again combining familiar elements with a modern, cynical world-view. Written in verse, the play was nevertheless accessible and proved popular with seasonal audiences, assisted by a competent young cast who utilized elements of *commedia* and strong physical characterization. The play climaxes with a very effective darkening of tone, with the birth of the Antichrist contrasting with that of the Messiah.

By the end of the 1980s themes pursued in serious drama had become familiar enough for comic use. In *Barbaciw (Barbecue)*(Hwyl a Fflag, 1990) the character of Martell, the conscience of the piece, is the most pathetic and meandering of a group of successful media professionals. Ultimately he is shown to be as dishonest a hypocrite as his peers. William O. Roberts's play fails because of its uncertainty of style – he wants to write a farce and a satirical drama, yet the play's funniest moments are provided by incursions of the absurd. Here is a writer of undoubted yet heretofore unrealized talent. His first full-length play was *Bermo yn y Nos (Barmouth by Night)* (Dalier Sylw, 1989). This naturalistic and almost Ibsenite play sees the familiar return of the past to haunt a segregated family. The time scale is confusing for an audience and the characterization bland.

Two plays, connected by setting and production company, which straddle the serious/entertaining divide with aplomb are worth consideration. Gareth F. Williams's success in *Siôn a Siân (Siôn and Siân)* (Cwmni Theatr Gwynedd, 1989) is in formulating an old-fashioned, almost Hollywoodian romance, founded on the Christmastime liaison of two lonely people. Its greatest asset is a lack of sentimentality throughout, and despite the melodramatic conclusion, the play works, primarily because of its strong characterization, deftly balancing sympathy with an understanding of the reasons for these people's loneliness. The play's main fault is typical, a tendency towards teleplay rather than theatricality, but the three-day development of the relationship is credibly rendered.

Christmas is also the setting for Dewi Wyn Williams's *Leni* (Cwmni Theatr Gwynedd, 1990), a play formulated on the commonplace idea of the tragic clown. The title character is a bitter stand-up comedian whose misogyny extends beyond his act, until the double threat of his wife's infidelity and his own cancer bring him humanity and a bruised dignity. The first half is the funnier, the second heavily pregnant with irony, and the whole work is skilfully crafted without resorting to mawkishness, aided by the unsentimental characterization.

The work of the much-vaunted Edward Thomas is difficult to pigeonhole for a different reason: as a writer he works as much on image as on words to create pieces of theatre which need to be seen rather than read. Following the explosive impact of *House of America* (1988), expectations were very high for his first Welsh-language play *Adar Heb Adenydd (Birds without Wings)* (Dalier Sylw, 1988), an adaptation of his own *The Myth of Michael Roderick*. Although the play is not as wholly successful as his first, it is far more ambitious stylistically and thematically. Its surreal comedy is obviously indebted to Beckett and particularly Ionesco, as the play discusses loudly if sometimes incoherently the need for new mythologies and heroes. Tending towards farce at the close, there remains a feeling of intense desperation behind the clowning and visual humour. This original and idiosyncratic writer has not written in Welsh for the stage since. This loss is made all the greater by the lack of theatricality of much of the writing discussed here. Thomas, despite his rather obvious need for an editor at times, is a poet of the stage.

It is unarguable that Welsh Wales produces greater writers of words than it does stage poets. Only one playwright of any prolificity unequivocally deserves to be placed in this category. At the end of the 1970s Gwenlyn Parry produced his masterpiece *Y Tŵr* (*The Tower*) (Cwmni Theatr Cymru, 1979), the zenith of his linear development outlining the crisis of faith in modern Wales. His training in science and his interest in religion ensured a fascinating grapple between faith and reason, and he concentrated on the gradual erosion of spiritual values, culminating in the urban godlessness of *Y Tŵr*.

Gwenlyn Parry's work in the 1980s was an anticlimax. *Sal* (Cwmni Theatr Cymru, 1980) sidesteps into history, taking the case of the so-called miraculous Starving Girl of the nineteenth century. His preoccupation with the nature of faith is again evident, but the play is inconclusive and, even worse for the one dramatist considered a literary giant with a very imagistic imagination, static. He forgoes his Beckettian use of the evocative stage picture, for a historical curio staged rather unimaginatively as part inquest. Conversely, the notion that the use of inquest or trial as dramatic backbone can succeed is demonstrated by Maldwyn Parry's *Euog Di-euog (Guilty, Not Guilty)* (Hwyl a Fflag, 1990). A somewhat controversial piece, the play was believed to be based on a real-life murder scandal in Dolgellau in the 1950s, despite protests to the contrary by the author. What might have been yet another courtroom drama is rendered more interesting by the use of the tabloid reporter as a structural backbone, allowing a more theatrical treatment of events and saving the inevitable courtroom until the end. The play ultimately deals with the rights and responsibilities of the press, with the question of guilt left to the audience to decide. This courageous ambiguity works for the play, while Gwenlyn Parry's *Sal* is rendered even more frustrating by its inconclusive ending.

Gwenlyn Parry's last play *Panto* (Cwmni Whare Teg, 1986) is a farcical farrago unworthy of his name. In theatre as in other art forms the desperate artist struggling to serve his muse finally turns his glance to art itself. A play within a play, a stage split between stage and dressing room, and much clever but ultimately empty play on the correlation between life and art, are its constituent components. The play is no more than an occasionally humorous diversion, and is an unworthy epitaph. He left four great stage plays which ensure his future on stage as well as in print. His last two should be forgotten.

The contrast between Parry and Meic Povey, the last of the three dramatists previously mentioned, could not be greater. Povey did not write for the stage until Parry's last play had been produced, and his work obviously betrays the influence of television. His writing is not as political as that of either Siôn Eirian or Gareth Miles: Meic Povey's greatest asset is that he remains within the confines of an easily recognizable Welsh domestic context.

By the end of the 1980s the idea that S4C had monopolized most of Wales's writing as well as acting talent was something of a cliché: dramatists such as Gareth Miles may well earn their crusts by writing scripts for television, but their theatrical work is often diametrically opposed in style and theme. It was in fact the fourth channel that gave Povey the chance to mature his craft by the time he returned to writing for the stage in 1987: he had, after all, begun as a writer of one-acters. One of his strengths is his ability to edit his own work, to pare down to the bone. His disciplined attitude means that his plays are usually no longer than ninety minutes, and better for it.

The comparative brevity of his work is a positive advantage in dealing with the grim theme of incest in his greatest play *Perthyn (Related)* (Cwmni Whare Teg, 1987), a brilliant exposition of family tensions which miraculously persuades us that even if the relationship between father and daughter is an illicit one, it is nevertheless the most loving in the triangle of father, mother, daughter. It is the debunking of the monster myth, implying that both women are almost as guilty as the ineffectual patriarch, that makes this play truly disconcerting.

In his next play *Gwaed Oer (Cold Blood)* (Cwmni Whare Teg, 1990) Povey revisits some of the themes of *Perthyn*. Again we have an adolescent girl of burgeoning manipulative sexuality, although this does not excuse the unhealthy attentions of father and grandfather. Once again the characterization is skilfully balanced, and the dialogue subtle. But Povey overloads the plot with infidelity, blackmail, unemployment, and suicide, and as implied by the title the play is in reality a thriller as we await the climactic ending. The retrospective device of the psychologist's interrogations in *Perthyn* is sorely missed, and the play asks too much of an audience's expectations that all these cathartic events happen within five days.

Povey's disappointing, but enthusiastically received *Wyneb yn Wyneb (Face to Face)* (Dalier Sylw, 1994) shows yet another family crisis, and the social pressures brought to bear on an essentially private crisis. The play deals even hands to the three characters: mother, gay son, lover, and is refreshingly low-key in dealing with HIV, perhaps too much so, as Povey nobly foregoes hysteria for a Pinteresque use of telling pauses and silences, but gives us little of dramatic or visual power to replace it. Ultimately this is yet another radio play. With a broadly similar topic to that of Siôn Eirian's *Wastad ar y Tu Fas (Always on the Outside)*, the contrasts between the two come to the fore. Povey is not really interested in issues, and all his work for the stage, like his screen-writing, concentrates on family situations and personal politics, and offers us no obvious political slant, unlike Miles's Marxism or Eirian's socialism.

'Dramatic presentation is in essence unreal. Writing for the stage can be a very exciting experience (and it is possible to "say" more on stage).' This quote from Povey in 1987 would imply a chasm between his stage and screen work, but in fact both fields weld in terms of style and themes. His theatre work is ostensibly televisual, but his success in both fields can be primarily ascribed to his rugged use of realistic dialogue. It is also worth noting that Povey is the one writer in this study who is writing more and more for the theatre: he has also written three plays for Theatr Bara Caws, whose community theatre based largely on devised work is outside the concerns of this study.

A great deal of the new writing discussed here was produced by Hwyl a Fflag, and the loss of their grant in 1994 brings sharply into focus the desperate need for a company totally committed to developmental work. Gareth Miles's debt to the company is obvious, and they also fostered a number of younger writers of whom more will hopefully be heard in the future. Equally the loss of the same company's Codi'r Hwyl Festival is crucial, not only as an outlet for new writing but also as the closest approximation in Wales to a national festival of theatre outside the boundaries of the Eisteddfod. Although the August jamboree remains an important event in the Welsh theatre calendar, the axing of the drama medal, partly precipitated by the failure of the experiment which saw professional productions of winning plays until 1992, is another negative step for new writing.

There is now once again talk of a national Theatre of Wales, a full decade after the débâcle of the closure of Cwmni Theatr Cymru just two years after the ground-breaking *Gernika!* It is ironic that the other company involved in the collaboration continues to flourish. The recent history of Welsh theatre shows us unequivocally that there is a paucity of writers of stature, while it is difficult to see how in the present climate they might be nurtured.

The period 1979 to 1995 will no doubt be little more than a footnote in dramatic history, primarily because the work of worth that has been produced remains unpublished. The death of Gwenlyn Parry in 1991 signified the end of a period, Gwenlyn being the last dramatist accorded the honour of having all his work published, ensuring his immortality on page as well as stage. The bitter irony of Gareth Miles's position is that he has had more success in publishing his adaptations than his own work.

The contribution of ensemble or co-operative processes was recently acknowledged by the publication of *Bargen* as the first in a new play-publishing initiative. The artistic process of ensemble groups, and their radical stagings, offered in the 1980s a challenge which seems for the most part unanswered by dramatists and production companies. Few companies have reacted to the *Zeitgeist*: Dalier Sylw with their site-specific *Hunllef yng Nghymru Fydd* being an exception. This is surprising, given that the easy definitions of mainstage work on the one hand and experimental on the other seemed for an exciting period in the 1980s to have been broken down. Unfortunately the 1990s have seen a reversal of this possibility, with each company solidly defending its own corner.

3 • Surviving on the Edge:
Patterns of Contemporary Theatre-Making

Anna-Marie Taylor

In August 1980 a Danish theatre company toured Wales, working within local communities and with professional actors. The company Odin Teatret, based in the provincial town of Holstebro, was almost unknown in Britain. This event may seem of little consequence, a friendly exchange between practitioners from small countries on the edge of Western Europe that was perhaps only remembered by its participants. However, the visit from Odin Teatret that summer had an impact on Welsh theatre that persists until the present in the work of companies as diverse as Arad Goch, Brith Gof and Alma Theatre, and in a decisive way pointed those involved in drama towards a way of working and forms of dramatic expression that seemed to be particularly appropriate for Wales.

Founded in 1964 by Eugenio Barba who had settled in Denmark from Italy, and who had worked as an assistant to Polish visionary director Jerzy Grotowski in the 1960s, Odin Teatret is characterized by the intensity and rigorousness of its performance work.[1] Barba's main focus is on the performer, and over the years this experimental project has developed a challenging, often collective, programme of physical training that integrates both oriental and occidental dance, gymnastic movement and acting techniques. Barba's setting up of an International School of Theatre Anthropology in 1979 further advanced such interculturalism, forging and investigating links between performance in both East and West.[2] The result of Odin's training is a dynamic theatre that experiments relentlessly with dramatic enactment; a reinvigoration of the conventions of Western theatrical performance.

Apart from the obvious life and commitment of the actors' performances, Odin's work was attractive to those involved in Welsh dramatic experiment for two main reasons. First, in a linguistically divided culture, it offered a working practice that was not based on a word-bound, literary theatre. Furthermore the roots of the group's practice lay in the dramatic expression of folk and non-Western cultures. Odin stood outside the European mainstream associated with the political and cultural hegemony of metropolitan centres such as Paris, Berlin and London.

Even more significantly, the members of the group brought vibrant, often processional, examples of performances that could be toured to communities with little history of regular theatre-going. In the same way that Peter Brook had tested his experimental theatre work in Africa in 1976, the company had taken its performance research outside the confines of Holstebro: to Peru, to Barba's native Italy, and in 1980 to Wales.[3]

This 'Third Theatre' idea (not necessarily of the Third World but a utopian search for a theatre outside the mainstream) informed the foundation of Brith Gof in Aberystwyth in 1981 and the group's exploratory work in the village halls, chapels and streets of north Dyfed. Such immediacy, interculturalism and vitality were also apparent, alongside the absorption of American and European experimental influences, in the carnivalesque quality of productions by Paupers Carnival, Cardiff Laboratory Theatre and Moving Being, whose inventive *Mabinogion* staged in Cardiff Castle in 1981 and at sites throughout Wales was one of the high points of the early 1980s.

In this exciting period (which had much of the 1968 spirit in its belief in the power of the imagination in transforming the everyday), forms of theatre were created that would, as with Grotowski's and Barba's theatres, go beyond words, privileging the visual and the physical in their expression. The artistic (and also political) desire to create a specifically Welsh theatrical language, that would bypass the English mainstream and establish kinship with other culturally overshadowed countries such as Catalonia, Poland and Denmark, dominated the practice of the early 1980s, giving rise to models of performance and vital dramatic forms for a theatrically under-represented country.

A decade and a half later, as I write this chapter, the theatrical ground in Wales has shifted considerably. The debate over national appropriateness now focuses on the question of establishing a National Theatre (very much under discussion before the referendum debate, but, particularly after the demise of Cwmni Theatr Cymru, only whispered about in private in the fifteen years afterwards). As we have seen, the most compelling model for Welsh theatre in the early 1980s was a small-scale one, localized yet part of a network of similar groups on the edge of the theatrical (and political) establishment throughout Europe. The proposal for a 'Welsh' theatre in the 1990s looks towards a much more conventional and formalized 'First Theatre'. In the various plans put forward to set up a National Theatre for Wales,[4] the emphasis is on a federal system of housed theatres that would be responsible for a repertoire of Welsh or Welsh-inflected plays. Such a venture it is hoped would give Welsh theatre a place among those of other European countries, but this time firmly in the centre, not offering an alternative model from the margins of the literary and theatrical establishment.

Thus, the period from 1980 to the present offers us two visions of a theatre for Wales; it opens with a localized avant-garde and closes with the dream of a well-subsidized state system that would link training, touring and theatrical venues. In this chapter I shall trace the main characteristics of theatrical organization and practice that have occupied the terrain between these two visions of a theatre for Wales, outlining some examples of individual organizations and aims, to give an indication of the way in which companies have survived and progressed.

The Repertory System

It may be helpful to begin with the most familiar of British theatrical institutions, the 'First Theatre' of housed playhouses. Wales is unusual in Britain for not having an established system of repertory theatres. Whilst before the Second World War Welsh towns and cities boasted theatre buildings galore (frequently later converted into cinemas) to accommodate tours, short runs and variety performances, with theatrical families controlling touring circuits and buildings, Wales as a whole lay outside the inter-war regional repertory movement that made an influential mark on the cultural life of many British towns and cities.

The setting up of the Gaiety Theatre in Manchester by wealthy theatre enthusiast Annie Horniman in 1907 established in its philosophy and practice modes of operation that would be adopted by future repertory companies, for, as Anthony Jackson observes:[5]

[it] became the benchmark of repertory for at least the next 80 years. Thus the company was committed to presenting a wide range of high

quality drama, classical, foreign and recent; it consisted of a permanent company of director, stage management and actors; it fostered the development of new, home-grown writing, it aimed to appeal to a specifically Manchester audience; and it set a high standard of production and performance. It was against staging plays simply for their box office potential, against long runs and against the star system.

Such a template for a progressive theatre imprinted itself upon the establishment and running of theatres all over Britain in the 1930s and 1940s, resulting in a network of like-minded organizations that included the Liverpool Everyman, Glasgow Citizens, Sheffield Playhouse and Birmingham Repertory Theatre. All of these alternatives to a commercialized variety theatre were supported by private subscriptions and by prosperous individuals like Horniman committed to the arts. Methods of production and a repertoire were founded that were serious, ambitious and often drew strength from the theatre's locality.

Post-war expansion of state patronage through the Arts Council and local government consolidated a system of repertory companies, mainly in the ambitious building of new theatres in most British cities and large towns. The construction of Coventry's Belgrade Theatre in 1958 began this cycle of expansion. Leeds's West Yorkshire Playhouse in 1990, as Jackson speculates,[6] may be the last: although, if the National Theatre for Wales campaign gains momentum, an additional theatre in Cardiff may be more of a millennial possibility than the much maligned opera house project.

In many ways, this sudden confidence in theatre-building mimics the civic pride of emerging cities last century who outbuilt each other with ever more grandiose city halls and council chambers. Instead of the bold Neo-Gothic châteaux, mansions and secular cathedrals so beloved of Victorian city elders, inward investment was made in bold concrete façades and ever more ingenious thrust stages and auditoria.

There was Welsh investment in such modern-day palaces of culture, although at times in the unlikeliest of places. In 1976 the small town of Mold (1990 population 8,180) saw the opening of the large-scale complex of Theatr Clwyd, whilst the following year Milford Haven (population 13,960), gained the Torch Theatre, partly through public subscription. The University of Wales's expansion in the 1970s also established half-way houses for toured 'work. Attempts were made to set up repertory companies in some of these centres, failing in

Aberystwyth but succeeding in Bangor with Theatr Gwynedd launched in 1986, occupying the space vacated by Cwmni Theatr Cymru. This demographically eccentric arrangement, with Theatr Clwyd the only true 'rep' of the kind Jackson describes, has left Swansea (1990 population 171,520) with a beautifully refurbished Grand Theatre but no permanent repertory company, and centres of population such as Wrexham and Bridgend with no theatrical provision.

Cardiff must be the only European capital city without any established 'art' theatre. The Sherman Theatre is often regarded as being such an institution, but it is much younger and has evolved differently from equivalently sized theatres in other British cities. Like Theatr Y Werin in Aberystwyth, the Sherman opened as part of the university campus in 1973, here as a result of a private bequest. The theatre was a receiving venue alone until 1985 when a repertory company was briefly created to serve south-east Wales. From 1985 to 1989, the Sherman team tried to establish an artistic direction, with a repertoire comprising modern classics such as Arthur Miller's *Death of a Salesman* and Anton Chekhov's *The Seagull*, musicals and, somewhat surprisingly, as its presence was decreasing in 'reps' elsewhere in Britain, new writing. For the management of the theatre, these years were also crisis times, since an unexpected financial deficit at the University of Wales Cardiff caused the college authorities to withdraw most of their subsidy to the Sherman in 1987. The theatre survived through the foundation of a limited company which gained funding from private and public bodies.

In 1989, the theatre's policy was changed from running a mainstream repertory company with a leaning towards modern drama to developing a producing house for young people's theatre. One major reason for this radical shift in identity came from *Theatre is for All*, published in 1986 by the Arts Council of Great Britain (as it was before devolution in 1994). This document, known widely as the Cork Report, extended the arguments put forward in William Rees-Mogg's highly influential policy report, *The Glory of the Garden* (1984), that made the case, in admittedly patrician tones, for devolving arts provision to the English regions. The Cork Report dealt specifically with the future of the theatre in Britain, arguing for regional 'centres of excellence' and for investment in a future audience by establishing community and young people's initiatives.

The Drama Department of the Welsh Arts Council, with its proven commitment to Theatre in Education, responded to the wider policy

statement by shaping the Sherman as a centre for youth theatre
activity and by supporting Phil Clark, with a strong background in
educational theatre, as artistic director in 1989. Clark's directorship
has given the Sherman a distinct character, with a prominent
emphasis on children's drama and contemporary writing.[7] In the
latter area, the Sherman has cultivated an especially productive
relationship with dramatist Frank Vickery whose bitter-sweet
dissections of south Wales life have proved popular with the theatre's
audience.

The Sherman has implemented the recommendations of the Cork
Report in an extensive programme of events and institutional
practices to broaden the theatre's audience and attract young people
into what is often seen as the leisure pursuit of an older generation
and another class. There are 'pay what you can' evenings and a
relaxed, youthful image has been created in the foyer. Running from
the building are a number of separate youth theatres, a summer
school, shows for children in both the main house and the studio, and
a scheme to encourage young writers through a series of lunch-time
performances. The theatre has also mounted major youth projects
such as *A Generation Arises* (1994),[8] a collaboration between
established writers (including Greg Cullen, Siôn Eirian and Charles
Way) and young dramatists articulating the contemporary hopes,
fears and experiences of young people living in Wales.

The success of the Sherman lies at present in its demotic
informality and its management's espousal of a democratic, cultural
experience targeted at young adults. Its achievements, in the view of
its present director, have, however, been hard-earned, as a large
theatre's output is constantly governed by box-office returns, with the
budget for productions in a large theatre proportionately smaller, as
well as the rehearsal period shorter (at three to four weeks), than is
often the case in a small touring company.

The Touring Companies

With almost all the large companies housed far away from the
majority of the Welsh population (a pattern of building that mirrors
the placement of other cultural institutions in Wales),[9] the period
1980 to the mid–1990s saw an expansion in touring to serve
communities, both urban and rural, that did not have easy access to

theatre-going. In its annual report for 1980,[10] Welsh Arts Council-supported companies were limited in number (to fourteen) with Cwmni Theatr Cymru as the only major touring company receiving a royal share of available funding (£253,000). In the financial wings of the balance sheet were, however, a number of small groups such as Cwmni Theatr Crwban and Gwent Theatre in Education that reflected the Welsh Arts Council's enlightened support of companies serving schools and the communities in all the counties. From the annual report of 1992/93, it is clear that investment and development have taken place; most notably in the repertory companies, in experimental work and in touring groups (twenty-two companies with recurrent funding).[11]

Many of the touring companies in the period under discussion had a distinct remit to provide education as well as entertainment. Some remained small-scale and rooted within a particular locality, others such as Arad Goch, Bara Caws and Theatr Powys worked in their immediate community but also toured well beyond their particular counties (although only rarely out of Wales) to develop an identity that was decidedly localized but that also became increasingly national.

Very few touring companies had the resources, nor perhaps for Welsh-language groups the need or political will, to work both in Welsh and English; notable exceptions being Brith Gof, Theatr Powys and Theatr Gorllewin Morgannwg (Theatre West Glamorgan). It may be worth focusing on the creation and evolution of the last company to sketch in some of the effects of funding and cultural policies on a group's work. Theatre West Glamorgan, now one of the largest and most ambitious of the erstwhile schools' companies, came into being as a result of the aforementioned policy from the Drama Department of the Welsh Arts Council (backed up by Local Education Authorities) to establish Theatre in Education (TIE) throughout Wales. Replacing Open Cast Theatre, which had seen its grant-funding withdrawn in 1980, ostensibly for artistic reasons, Theatre West Glamorgan was originally attached to Sandfields Comprehensive School in Port Talbot, later moving to its own headquarters in Neath. Its present director Tim Baker joined the company in 1984 when he came from north Wales's Bara Caws to work on a musical drama *After You've Gone* that dealt with Valleys people's involvement in the Spanish Civil War. A major decision by Baker on taking over the running of the company was to work bilingually and thus serve both language communities. This policy has remained in place, and Theatre West Glamorgan is still the only company working in both languages as a core activity.

The evolution of the company has been twofold. It serves a specific (majority English-speaking) area and an educational purpose, yet, particularly after the Newport Eisteddfod in 1986 when *Jeremiah Jones*, an agitational piece about the rise in house prices and the inability of many Welsh people to buy a home, was performed, Theatre West Glamorgan has also been steadily seen as a national company by Welsh speakers, representing a certain kind of Welsh-language theatre. Theatre West Glamorgan probably tours more extensively than any other company, taking its Welsh-language productions on the road for up to nine weeks at a time, and serving venues from well-equipped Theatr Clwyd to fairly spartan village halls. Its schools' performances, however, take place in the company's base centre in Neath and are not toured at present. Although the company may not necessarily desire it, the more nationally directed work may become more prominent, as the reason for Theatre West Glamorgan being set up, and for which it receives local authority funding, may be severely threatened by a combination of schools having devolved budgets and the reorganiza-tion of local government to unitary authorities.

Evolving from the direct confrontation of actor with audience in schools and community playing, the group's style is visual, fast-moving and highly theatrical with frequent use of music. The work is popular yet politicized. Public identification with the company's work and an expectation of a distinct theatrical experience have, ironically, caused problems in Theatre West Glamorgan's development. It has proved difficult to change direction. In recent years, the company has broken with its policy of devising shows entirely between actors and director, and has begun to commission writers and to perform existing plays, an unexpected choice being Willie Russell's dream of female escape *Shirley Valentine* (performed 1992). In the absence of Hwyl a Fflag (the Welsh writing development company), Theatre West Glamorgan has developed a summer writing school for prospective Welsh-language playwrights. It has also further tested its autonomous identity by linking up with other companies on productions, such as with Theatr Gwynedd on the annual Welsh-language pantomime.

Theatre West Glamorgan, which has developed a distinct and recognizable style of playing in such joint ventures across Wales, should be able to maintain its theatrical identity. In view of the financial uncertainty facing arts organizations, this movement away from artistic independence to partnerships with other groups may protect and sustain small- and middle-sized companies. However, there is always the danger, as has happened with some co-productions between English repertory companies, that the individuality of a company's playing style and underlying philosophy may be diminished.

Writers' Companies

Collective work on scripts and performances has informed much of the practice of community-based companies, as with Bara Caws and Theatr Powys from the late 1970s onwards. Several companies were founded, though, to promote individual voices for the theatre. In a pioneering and much emulated move, Gilly Adams who had been Director of Drama at the Arts Council helped to set up Made in Wales Stage Company in 1981[12] to give emerging playwrights an opportunity to develop their work through workshops and productions. Cwmni Hwyl a Fflag in north Wales was later founded to promote play-writing in Welsh in the same fashion. Other companies have been associated with a single author, namely Y Cwmni with Edward Thomas, Theatr y Byd with Ian Rowlands, and Theatr Powys with Greg Cullen.

As Simon Baker outlines,[13] professional play-writing in Wales received little critical attention and even less status in the 1960s and 1970s, despite a flourishing amateur drama tradition. It is a credit to the developmental companies that Welsh theatre now has several established playwrights whose literary strengths have been further promoted in other media, above all by BBC radio. Authors have also had considerable opportunities to write for television, a lucrative although not always an artistically successful option.[14]

Cardiff-based Dalier Sylw was founded in 1988 in response to the need for a writer-led company to work in Welsh in south Wales. The company is concerned above all with supporting writers who have already worked professionally, rather than, as with the writing schemes attached to the Sherman Theatre and with Made in Wales in its early days, in discovering fresh dramatic talent. Writers associated with Dalier Sylw include Gareth Miles, Siôn Eirian, Geraint Lewis and Meic Povey, all of whom have been able to extend the form and practice of their stage writing. Building on the success of this venture, the company has recently implemented a policy of lending artistic and administrative support to emerging writers and directors.

The company mounts three productions a year (two directed by artistic director Bethan Jones, one by a guest director such as the very experienced Ceri Sherlock). The process of moving a script to the stage is a relatively lengthy one, with the play commissioned between eighteen months and two years before the production. The playtext is worked on intensively by writer and director before the rehearsal period begins. Unlike some other companies that commission new writing, there is limited development of the script in rehearsal (usually of three and a half weeks), so that the author is 'not thrown off course'. For playwrights, Dalier Sylw's high standards of production provide an attractive and intensive opportunity for stage work where, in contrast to television and film projects, the writer is central to and has control over the process of enactment.

With a large number of Welsh-speaking actors resident in Cardiff, Dalier Sylw has been able to cast inventively and creatively, although it has chosen not to establish an ensemble or 'stock' company as with Y Cwmni and Theatr y Byd, preferring to forge its identity through the range of writing and dramatic approaches chosen. The range of work encompasses sustained naturalism (Siôn Eirian's *Epa yn y Parlwr Cefn (Ape in the Back Parlour)*, 1994) and political satire *(Calon Ci (Heart of a Dog)* by Gareth Miles, 1993), as well as radically updated versions of classics *(The Bacchae*, 1991) and outdoor promenade productions *(Hunllef yng Nghymru Fydd (Nightmare in Future Wales))*, staged at Llancaiach Fawr Manor in Mid Glamorgan in 1990.

Despite a lack of identifiable 'product' beyond the promise of contemporary writing, Dalier Sylw has been able to build up audience loyalties, with its tours to various venues across Wales, including established theatres and community halls. The company's ability to engage a wide audience (seat capacity is more than 70 per cent in many venues) is in sharp contrast to the recent fortunes of English-language companies. Here, despite critically acclaimed writing, Arts Council investment in new writing schemes, and high standards of playing, there is a real crisis, as there has been a depressingly real failure to maintain an audience for more 'difficult' modern work. However, having said that, one audience has proved responsive to often challenging and unsettling writing, and that is young people. There has been a remarkable flourishing of writing in this area, and many playwrights (including Lucy Gough, Greg Cullen, Angharad Tomos, Dic Edwards and Charles Way) have extended the range of their work to address a young audience.

In delineating these various practices, I am reminded of those oil-filled lamps popular in the 1960s and 1970s, and which enthusiastic stage managers track down for authentic period detail in productions of Mike Leigh's *Abigail's Party*. Inside these 'lava lamps' (that now possess New Age fashionability, I believe), the patterns would shift around, never still, the image inside the glass re-forming, moving from the centre to the edge, bright colours coagulating, thinning, swimming to the centre again. Such perpetual motion could appear to characterize the shape and structure of contemporary Welsh theatre, constantly shape-shifting, offering different versions of itself, incorporating prior and new theatrical forms.

On the surface, it may appear difficult to locate recurrent patterns in the diversity of dramatic work carried out in Wales. Yet, beyond what seems like heterogeneous randomness, certain common features can be discovered in the many forms and practices that have evolved. Perhaps most strikingly, this period is one of intense theatrical (as opposed to literary) exploration, with companies and individuals striving to establish stage forms and lay down (often collective) modes of production that would have a local and national resonance. Such explorations with form and its relationship to the audience, as well as ideas of Welshness, are pronounced in experimental practice, most notably in the work of Brith Gof. It also dominates the practice of community and educational groups, where, as with Theatre West Glamorgan, companies working from a local context can find their work articulating a wider 'Welsh' theatre.

Experimentation with form and its national significance also penetrated the larger companies (although to a much lesser extent) as with Theatr Clwyd's successful transpositions of European classics such as Chekhov's *Uncle Vanya* (1994) and Ibsen's *An Enemy of the People* (1991) to Welsh contexts, and reworkings of Welsh classics such as *Full Moon* (1994), staged by Polish director Helena Kaut-Howson, whose daring and visually assured style of presentation, with its roots in European *Regietheater* (director's theatre), had much in common with the confidence of Welsh experimental theatre of this period.

Helena Kaut-Howson's departure from Theatr Clwyd is to be regretted artistically, as she was probably the only director in the larger theatres who managed to assimilate European and North American experimental influences into mainstage productions. However, the history of Welsh theatre in this period is not necessarily one of departure and diaspora, and another characteristic is the stability of personnel (although not of grant funding!), seen in the large number of people who have chosen to stay in Wales and who have remained with the same company for many years.[15]

Part of this tenaciousness can be attributed to lack of career structure within the Welsh theatre infrastructure, with the pattern of advancement found in England from small touring to middle-sized company through to large repertory theatre much less available here. However, there is another more overwhelming reason for this constancy, and that is to do with commitment to founding distinctly Welsh patterns of theatre and to developing and sustaining an audience.

Whilst Michael Bogdanov's and Phil Clark's proposal for a National Theatre should be welcomed for its vision of theatrical activity across Wales underpinned by training, archival and educational initiatives,[16] the stated aim that those working outside Wales may be attracted back seems to miss an important point. The strength of Welsh theatre since 1979 (and indeed before) lies in the abilities of those who stayed, and who have tried to establish types of playing and repertoire that are culturally appropriate to a linguistically and geographically divided and often overlooked country. A new state theatre in Cardiff may suit the architectural and economic aspirations of an undersized capital desperate to look towards Europe for a future. But, unless the repertoire and practice of such a theatre take into account the diversity of theatrical work that has grown up out of many groups' localized engagement with living in modern Wales, such a venture risks becoming, to borrow Janelle Reinelt's description of the international touring circuit: 'a court theatre display[ing] the capital and cultural wealth of their sponsors and host countries to a largely privileged elite who can afford the price of the tickets.'[17] To continue with Reinelt's assessment of 'Theatre on the brink of 2000', the theatre professor sees the future of theatrical activity as not being located in prestigious and well-subsidized centres but, as Odin Teatret demonstrated in 1980:

it is to local performances that we must turn if we are to recognize the vitality and power of theatre as a cultural and artistic resource, and if we are not to allow the string quartet [of a court theatre] to occupy the centre, pushing other forms of theatrical representation to the margins. For it is in locations formerly at the margins, newly asserting and obtaining a place nearer the centre, that contours of the new century will appear.[18]

It is this understanding of entering into a worldwide theatrical community that Wales should celebrate and not bemoan its inability to create successful large-scale models of theatre apart from reasonably resilient Theatr Clwyd. The possibility of Welsh theatre contributing to a mainstream of European cultural activity seems to lie in not emulating the centre but dramatizing and articulating the experience of surviving on the edge.

Notes

1   Ian Watson outlines the practice in 'Eastern and Western influences on performer training at Eugenio Barba's Odin Teatret', in Phillip B. Zarrilli (ed.), *Acting (Re)Considered: Theory and Practice* (London, Routledge, 1995), pp. 129–37.

2   The results of such work can be found in Eugenio Barba and N. Savarese, *The Secret Art of the Performer* (London, Routledge, 1991).

3   Documented in John Heilpern, *The Conference of the Birds* (London, Faber, 1977) and Eugenio Barba *The Floating Islands* (Holstebro, Bogtrykkeri, 1979).

4   See Mario Basini, 'Flying the flag for a theatre', *Western Mail* (22 November 1994), p. 6.

5   Anthony Jackson, 'The repertory theatre Movement in England, 1960–1990', in Klaus Peter Muller (ed.), *Englisches Theater der Gegenwart* (Tübingen, Gunter Narr, 1993), pp. 99–117.

6   Ibid.

7   The Sherman commissioned forty plays (new work, translations, adaptations) between 1990 and 1995.

8   See Phil Clark, 'Investing in a new world' for a fuller description of the project (Appendix IV).

9   Concluded by Gwyn Alf Williams to be an impediment to Welsh progress in *When Was Wales?* (Harmondsworth, Penguin, 1985).

10 Please see Appendix II: Welsh Arts Council Schedules to Accounts for 1981 and 1993, for a fuller picture.

[11] It will be interesting to look at the picture after reorganization of local government in 1995/6.

[12] Gilly Adams gives a lively account of Made in Wales's work in *New Welsh Review*, 27 (Winter 1994–5), 62–6; see Chapter 17 below.

[13] Simon Baker, 'The Wounds of Possibility' (Chapter 1, above).

[14] The standard of television drama on S4C has improved greatly in recent years, probably through the experience of over a decade of television film-making in Wales.

[15] E.g. Jeremy Turner has been artistic director with Arad Goch for over a decade, Mike Pearson has remained with Brith Gof since 1981, Gilly Adams directed Made in Wales 1981–95, and Louise Osborn and Greg Cullen were associated with Theatr Powys for well over ten years.

[16] Please refer to Michael Bogdanov and Phil Clark, *Consultative Paper on a National Theatre for Wales* (Cardiff, July 1995).

[17] Janelle Reinelt, 'Theatre on the brink of 2000: shifting paradigms', *Theatre Research International*, 20/2, (Summer 1995), 123–31.

[18] Ibid.

I should like to thank Tim Baker, Bethan Jones, Patric Gilchrist, Margaret Jones and Phil Clark for giving up so much time to discuss their companies with me.

4 • A History of Theatre in Education in Wales

Gill Ogden

Very little has been written about the history and practice of Theatre in Education[1] in Wales (TIE), and a lack of consistent archives other than the knowledge of the administrators of existing companies and the oral memories of early practitioners makes reliable documentation difficult. Exceptions are Charmian C. Savill's useful survey published in 1988[2] and an HMI report of 1989[3] which praises the achievement of the TIE companies, but raises doubts as to the ability of the schools to take full advantage of the programmes of work provided. More recent articles in the Welsh press have mainly taken the form of uncritical eulogies of the work, in a campaign to save TIE from extinction. Many TIE companies have now begun to take video recordings of their work which provide a useful documentation of later practice, but the early work is largely undocumented and very few reviews have ever been published.

In this chapter I intend to provide an introductory discussion of the form and theory of TIE, attempting a definition and clarification of the features and functions that distinguish it from other types of contemporary theatre. I shall then examine its development in Wales in some detail and attempt a survey of the present position, looking at selected examples of practice. In the process I shall propose that TIE is a form which originally was established in Wales from England by a process of cultural colonization but which then evolved and adapted to fulfil specific cultural requirements peculiar to the Welsh context and to express, in varying degrees, a Welsh identity.

Theatre in Education began in the mid-1960s as part of the post-war movement in Britain to widen the base and appeal of theatre, to rid it of its élitist overtones and create art forms that were accessible and relevant to people from different social backgrounds. The same movement that gave rise to community, alternative and Agit-prop theatre, like the earlier workers' theatre movement, embracing the idea that theatre can and should be performed anywhere, at any time, led to the desire to take theatre into schools and to make it relevant to that audience's needs and interests. At the same time, changes in the philosophy and theory of education meant a gradual introduction of more child-centred, heuristic techniques and the use of drama as a learning tool. Drama also began to be taught and examined as a subject in its own right in secondary schools and university departments, leading to an increase in numbers of young people trained and educated in theatre and eager to experiment with new forms. When the first TIE team was set up at the Belgrade Theatre in Coventry in 1965 it was jointly funded by the theatre and the local authority and its priorities were to provide well-researched, specially devised theatre pieces which, together with accompanying workshops and class visits, would comprise an educational programme aimed at the curriculum agenda and the social, even political agenda of schoolchildren. The plays produced in this way, often devised by the company, differed from the Young People's Theatre which visited schools in Britain in the post-war years in that they always included an educational aim, though not necessarily a didactic one, and were planned in consultation with teachers and other educational specialists. The personnel of the TIE team were referred to as 'actor-teachers' in recognition of the fact that the majority of them held teaching qualifications as well as being experienced theatre practitioners.

The work of the TIE team at Coventry was adopted as a paradigm by many of the new companies which sprang up all over England and Wales during the 1970s, many of them to be staffed by practitioners who had served at Coventry Belgrade and spread through England and Wales like missionaries. In Wales, as in England, before the designation of TIE as such, a number of theatre practitioners had been working in schools mainly to present performances of plays by Shakespeare or children's theatre. In addition there was a parallel development in the form of the work of enlightened county drama advisers such as Derek Hollins in Flintshire. Flint TIE was formed by him and a team of drama teachers who worked as a team in schools for two days a week in the early 1970s. Amongst their shows was *Syrcas Sulwen (Sulwen's Circus)*, which John O'Toole refers to in his definitive study of British TIE[4] as a pioneering attempt to use theatre in second-language teaching. Similarly, John Greatorex formed the Breconshire TIE company in 1971, later to become Theatr Powys.

Whilst these initiatives reflected a general awareness of the potential of theatre and drama work in schools, none of them yet incorporated the hybrid features that defined TIE as it had developed in England, such as intrinsic participation or the challenging of actors in role by the audience. It was a combination of the arrival in Wales of TIE professionals such as the 'missionaries' from Coventry and others, many of them Welsh by birth, and the initiative of an enlightened Welsh Arts Council committee that inspired the growth of TIE proper in Wales. In 1976 the drama officer at the Welsh Arts Council, Gilly Adams, in consultation with professionals such as John Prior who had worked in Coventry and Exeter TIE, proposed that there should be a TIE company in each county in Wales. This national strategy upheld the belief that this was the best way to ensure the delivery of theatre to all young people in Wales, however scattered the population, and was a breakthrough that led to over ten years of artistic and administrative growth.

The first professional TIE companies in Wales were thus formed as a result of collaborations between a proactive Welsh Arts Council, experienced practitioners and local authorities. In 1976 Action Pie was formed at Llanover Hall Arts Centre in Cardiff to serve South Glamorgan under the leadership of John Prior. In the same year the leaders of Gwent Youth Theatre, Gary Meredith and Julia Davies formed Gwent TIE. A team of ex-Swansea University graduates including Eirwen Hopkins formed a community theatre company in Swansea called Open Cast, partially funded by the Welsh Arts Council, which subsequently took on a brief from the local authority to provide TIE work in West Glamorgan. These three companies each provided practitioners, including Tim Baker, Jamie Garven, Ros Hutt and Robin Hall, all artists based in Wales who had trained in England, to create a company for Mid Glamorgan, later called Spectacle Theatre Company. When Gilly Adams became drama director in 1979, Michael Baker was appointed as drama officer to push through this policy into the rest of Wales and to ensure its adequate funding and survival.

The next important development in Welsh TIE came with the recognition that the companies based in Welsh-speaking areas should operate chiefly through the medium of Welsh. The first Welsh-medium TIE company was formed in Aberystwyth, in 1979 with the encouragement of the Arts Centre Director, Roger Tomlinson, who had experienced TIE in his time at Leeds Playhouse. Cwmni Theatr Y Werin, under the directorship of the relatively inexperienced Glyn Wheldon, was under-resourced from the outset, and was closed down by the Welsh Arts Council in 1981 and replaced by Theatr Crwban under the directorship of Emyr Morgan Evans. For the first time in Wales there existed a consistent provision, albeit variable in artistic and educational quality, of Welsh-language theatre in schools for children of all ages in Dyfed. In addition, an independent company, Jeremy Turner's Cwmni Cyfri Tri, specialized in young people's and experimental theatre in Welsh. The Welsh Arts Council, in consultation with Dyfed Education Authority, later decided that there should also exist an English-medium TIE company in south Dyfed to serve its widely differing cultural and linguistic communities, and South Dyfed TIE, later Coracle Theatre, was set up for this purpose in Milford Haven. Companies established by administrators rather than artists, such as Coracle and Cwmni Theatr Y Werin, did not often achieve the highest artistic or educational standards, and it was not until Coracle was joined by the director Ros Hutt that their work blossomed. In the mid–1980s the Welsh Arts Council supported the amalgamation of Cwmni Cyfri Tri and Theatr Crwban, combining their artistic, creative and material resources to create a new entity called Arad Goch Theatre Company. The efficient and visionary way in which the two companies achieved this transformation led Dyfed Education Authority to award Arad Goch the Welsh and English TIE and young peoples' theatre remit for the whole of Dyfed, resulting in the demise of Coracle Theatre.

By now Gwynedd was the only Welsh county without full TIE provision, the community theatre company, Bara Caws, having decided to hand over the Gwynedd Education Authority grant to make way for a specialist TIE company. The Welsh Arts Council initiated the establishment of Cwmni'r Frân Wen in 1984, based at Coleg Harlech, following a year's work bringing theatre into the community and schools by Eirwen Hopkins as artist in residence at Theatr Ardudwy. The success of the pilot scheme, originally intended to help raise the profile of the theatre at Harlech by providing a service for schools and the community, led to the funding of the resident TIE company by the Welsh Arts Council and the LEA which has continued ever since. This commitment to the only solely Welsh-language TIE company in Wales has been a policy of the funding bodies rather than the artists themselves and may be interpreted as discriminatory at (mainly English-medium) secondary-school level if one believes that TIE should be accessible to all young people, whatever their background.

This generalized review of the early politics and administration of TIE in Wales attempts to explain why, at the end of the 1980s, there had come to exist in Wales a sustained provision of TIE in both Welsh and English that was greater in scope and vision than anything elsewhere in the UK. By the time Charmian C. Savill published her survey in 1988, she was able to report that there were eight companies in existence, all funded by a combination of local authority, Welsh Arts Council, Regional Arts Associations, the Welsh Office and other minor funding sources, a provision which 'far outweighs that of its neighbouring countries Ireland, England and Scotland and is a leading example in European terms'.[5]

Theatre in Education is a form of theatre that possesses its own body of theory and practice, as a growing body of literature in the English press indicates.[6] Unlike young people's theatre, which may set out to entertain or to educate and entertain, TIE always has an educational aim, which is carried out through the medium of theatre. It may entertain, and it may, as in drama in education, ask children to act out roles and improvisations, but always as part of a structure that is carefully planned to contain a fully integrated learning process.

Until recently, the majority of TIE plays were devised by the company, partly because of a dearth of suitable scripts, but also because this enables the project to be carefully researched and tailored to meet the needs of a specific age-group in a particular part of the world. Although it is time-consuming and problematic in some respects, for instance in the efficient preparation of the teachers' resource packs and previews that generally accompany productions, the process facilitates the integration of local references and the ethical stance of the company. Increasingly new plays are commissioned by writers who will sometimes work with the company, allowing some of the fruits of the devising process to be integrated into a polished script. Plays written in isolation are often not successful for TIE. Although in the early days members of the TIE team were expected to participate in all aspects of production, increasing specialization and a raising of artistic standards has led to the creation of a pool of designers, technicians, and stage managers who are able to meet the special needs of TIE performance, where lightweight sets are assembled in a variety of halls and classrooms, with minimal or non-existent blackout facilities and little chance of absolute silence. The role of facilitator, an important feature of participatory TIE is often undertaken by a skilled stage manager or one of the actors, acting as a bridge between characters and spectators during the performance or workshop. Many companies also include education liaison officers, often ex-teachers who prepare workpacks and resources to accompany the show and arrange consultation meetings with local teachers. However, special-ized, vocational training in Wales for the TIE profession is still non-existent.

TIE offers an experience that integrates imaginative experience into investigative learning and vice versa. A specific programme may be designed to fulfil part of the national curriculum, or to enable the personal or creative growth of the individual. At best the TIE project achieves a change of understanding on three levels; the personal, concrete and universal, provoking thought and debate and using theatre as the medium to achieve these educational objectives. The balance between theatre and education in the style of presentation is a matter about which conflicting opinions have been voiced in recent years.[7] The main way in which this difference manifests itself in the work of TIE companies is in the degree of participation with which a project is endowed. Those which follow the traditional style of the earliest TIE work use integral participation, where the audience has a decision-making role built into the script and where the actors are prepared to use a certain amount of carefully structured improvisa-tion to facilitate the taking on of this role by the pupils. A central level of participation is peripheral, where the audience may take part in activities such as learning a song or dance, adding to the theatricality of the play without affecting the course of the action. Thirdly, the project may maintain its theatricality by limiting any participation to an extrinsic position, separated from the play itself, in the form of a workshop or separate role-play session.

Theatr Powys is perhaps the most outstanding example of a TIE company in Wales that often uses structured intrinsic participation as part of its work in schools. The audience is placed in a theatrical frame before or during the play in which it may make decisions that can affect the course of the action, or lead it to project its own potential resolution to a play that, in dramatic terms, has no end. In *Soil*, a project about belonging and responsibility in a small Welsh community for nine- to eleven-year-olds the children were placed in the centre of a circular set representing a series of different interiors and a school playground. From this position they meet as equals, begin to understand and even attempt to reconcile, a family that has been in dispute for a generation. The subtle themes of personal responsibility and conflicting loyalties that the play contained were introduced beforehand in an out-of-role discussion. Dramatically, the play would perhaps be judged a failure; it had no satisfactory ending, parts were re-run after a break for greater clarity, but in terms of moral and personal education it was extremely successful. Members of the audience were involved in the action to an extent not commonly experienced by young people in live theatre, and were able to appreciate and evaluate complex moral dilemmas with a degree of maturity not normally demanded or expected of their age-group. In *The Present*, a Theatr Powys project for the same age range, the children, having been prepared through discussion about the suitability of television programmes on a previous visit, were placed in frame as parents at a school like their own. They were given the responsibility of deciding whether a play performed by the company, about a Jewish girl and her German friend during the early days of Nazism and on beyond the Holocaust, was suitable for their children. The way in which the audience were framed and allowed to ask for re-runs of particular parts of the play or to question the actors in role enabled them to investigate the delicate issues at stake with a sense of responsibility and an involvement, not with the characters or the story themselves, but with the implications on their own lives.

These examples illustrate one of the most positive features of TIE as practised by experienced and perceptive practitioners, that one should always over- rather than under-estimate the intellectual and empathic abilities of one's audience, whatever their age or supposed academic abilities. Critics who believed it to be misguided or dangerous to stage a play about Nazism in Welsh rural communities failed to understand both this and the principle of framing. TIE at its best aims to challenge and does not, without good reason, indulge in the fluffy animals and squeaky voices that characterize much children's theatre. Geoff Gillham observes:

> From the standpoint of learning it is the 'negative' aspects of the experience which most stimulate the desire to understand . . . Concentration on the so-called 'positive' aspects of life . . . fails to meet the real need to know. It breeds a deep and self-annulling cynicism.[8]

The views of Howard Barker give further support to the notion that the audience should be challenged to participate, rather than absorb solutions:

A theatre which honours its audience will not therefore make an icon of clarity. If a scene might mean two things it should not be reduced to one . . . We need a theatre of Anti-Parable, in which the moral is made by the audience and not by the actor. Naturally, this means that the parable will be interpreted differently by different individuals. A good parable should provoke an argument and not a submissive nod of the head.[9]

Theatr Powys, which also provides touring community-theatre productions in English, has produced some of the most consistently challenging TIE work in Wales. Still run internally if not formally on the co-operative basis favoured in the 1970s, the company's work is mostly devised, although new scripts are occasionally commissioned. The high educational impact of their work has sometimes led to a lack of sufficient theatricality, but never to low artistic standards.

The work of Cwmni'r Frân Wen, whilst remarkable as the only purely Welsh-medium programme, also provides an example of the purposeful and non-patronizing use of animal enactment in TIE. *Amaswn (Amazon)*, a play for infants devised under the direction of Carys Huw, told the simple story of a boy and the animals he meets in the rain forest, introducing environmental issues and concepts of communication and friendship. The play used no verbal dialogue but was underscored by percussion and the 'animals' own languages. The piece, which delighted both children and adult audiences, exemplified the quality of innocence that has typified the work of the company since its inception and derives from the realization that performing for shy rural children in a medium that only some of them fully understand demands a sensitive, low-status approach to win trust and be effective. In its early days the company implemented an in-service training policy, part of which committed the actors to a careful investigation of their relationship to their audience.

The company tours extensively the scattered but comparatively culturally cohesive county of Gwynedd, always performing in the classroom or school hall to small numbers of children, and where possible taking each project to the appropriate age-group in every school in the county, avoiding so far the economically driven situation of other companies who perform for larger audiences at central locations. The work is mainly devised and accompanied by extrinsic workshops or peripheral participation. The projects often treat a specific subject in the curriculum, rather than taking the cross-curricular approach favoured by Theatr Iolo and Gwent Theatre.

Theatr Iolo in South Glamorgan and Outreach Theatre Company (administered until 1995 by Theatr Clwyd and now replaced by an 'in house' education service) were similar to each other in that their work was chiefly curriculum-led and included such diverse educational activities as Shakespeare workshops and historic re-enactment sessions as well as conventional TIE programmes, both devised and commissioned from new Welsh writers such as Lucy Gough. Whilst unique in its attachment to a major producing theatre, Outreach possessed a clearly defined statement of artistic policy that serves as a useful summary:

To promote active learning through participatory TIE.

To present TIE which encourages pupils to think for themselves.

To help pupils develop self confidence and self esteem – particularly those who may be socially or economically disadvantaged.

To present TIE which engages the audience emotionally, sensitizing them to the feelings, preoccupations and beliefs of others.

To equip pupils with ideas, arguments and information relating to contemporary social and political issues. To encourage them to:
a) evaluate their own opinions;
b) evaluate the opinions of others;
c) challenge received or dominant ideas.

To be responsive to the needs of teachers.

To link the company's work to the aims of the national curriculum when its aims coincide with the above objectives.[10]

Theatr Iolo, Theatr Gwent and Theatr Powys are obliged to recruit Welsh-speaking directors and writers to provide a language programme for which extra funding was until recently provided by the Welsh Office and now by the Arts Council for Wales. This system, which allows the production of second-language and Welsh learners' projects in non-Welsh-speaking areas, has been worthwhile in providing a bank of freelance work and training opportunities for Welsh-language practitioners, but may be viewed by the companies themselves as a potential disruption of their style and ethos, and by the Welsh-language theatre community as indicating that Welsh-language work is valued as an external appendage, only taken on because of the money.

The work of these four companies provides a solid resource for teachers to rely on, fulfilling many of the aims outlined in the Theatr

Clwyd Outreach statement. Participatory workshops, workpacks and, in the case of Gwent Theatre, integrated educational visits, are a priority, whilst the use of guest writers and directors continually raises artistic standards. Gwent Theatre, Outreach and Theatr Iolo run youth theatre activities, providing a training ground for future practitioners and instilling a love of theatre in young people.

Each of the eight TIE companies has developed its own style, often in relation to the tastes of the artistic director, but also determined by the in-service training opportunities provided by the Welsh Arts Council and other bodies such as the Wales-based Centre for Performance Research. The work of several companies, for example Theatr Powys and Theatr Iolo, has been influenced by the work of the south American theatre practitioner Augusto Boal, whose methods of enabling the spectator to participate in forms of theatre and therapeutic drama have been widely adopted by practitioners in a number of other fields such as prison and probation work. The influence of the educationalist and drama specialist, Dorothy Heathcote is seen in the recent work of Cwmni'r Fran Wen and Outreach. The TIE work of Theatre West Glamorgan, in English and in Welsh, strongly displays the influence of the company's own highly successful formula of locally inspired community theatre that includes song, dance, and first-person monologue. TIE has traditionally valued its comparative political autonomy and the brief to challenge received ideas has led to the treatment of issues that, in Wales, mainstream theatre has often failed to address – including AIDS, Third World poverty, the environment, the situations in Northern Ireland and in Bosnia.[11]

The influence of the Third Theatre and other eclectic European traditions such as *commedia dell'arte* is strongly apparent in the work of Cwmni Theatr Arad Goch. Design and skilful presentation hold priority in their largely Welsh-language work. A strong directorial influence creates a style with its roots in the work of Grotowski, Eugenio Barba's Odin Teatret and children's theatre in Europe and Scandinavia. Whilst it would be difficult to deduce the exact curricular relevance of their 1992 production *The Sky in My Pocket (Y Nefoedd Yn Fy Mhoced)*, produced in conjunction with Paraply Teatret of Denmark, the simple and visually stunning show, based on the work of the artist Magritte, was a memorable *theatrical* experience for even the youngest child and effortlessly introduced concepts of communication, symbols and imagery.

The wide range of style and emphasis in TIE in Wales has constituted some of the most innovative and dynamic experimental theatre in the country in the last ten years. The comparative security which most of the companies enjoyed until recently allowed the form to develop, alongside an equally young mainstream native theatre, and to experiment with modes of presentation and relationship with the audience in ways which conventional theatre is only now beginning to appreciate. A degree of stylistic dialogue developed between TIE in Wales and the Welsh experimental and community theatre companies during the 1980s, often as a result of exchange of personnel. TIE incorporated aspects of the innovatory physical theatre of companies such as Brith Gof, whilst Cardiff's Hijinx employed TIE techniques with community audiences. This creative dialogue, together with special grants for Welsh-language projects, and a certain bias within Welsh theatre towards issues of identity and communication led to the incipient formation of a specific identity for Welsh TIE, one that combined a high degree of concern with complex questions of roots and belonging with a willingness to experiment with visual styles of performance. This identity arises from a specifically Welsh context, where a new tradition of theatre is being created in the absence of an older one and where communities are faced with competing allegiances of culture and language.

However, the nurturing of artistic and philosophical identity is entirely dependent on stability and adequate funding, and as the economic and administrative context changes for both education and the arts in the late 1990s the nature of Welsh TIE is likely to be affected by compromise and necessity. For some years practitioners have been encouraged by financial incentives to produce TIE projects to address health education and safety issues as well as the perennial language-support initiatives. This has resulted in some excellent programmes on topics as diverse as AIDS, alcohol and drug abuse, incest and bullying. The funding bodies and organizations concerned rightly appreciate the unique way in which theatre and drama can succeed in raising awareness about such issues, leading to creative problem-solving by the individual, rather than what might be seen as 'preaching' by specialists. New partnerships have also been formed in ways of siting and presenting TIE, performances taking place in museums, art galleries and historic properties, bringing new life to local history and the understanding of art and technology. Whilst many of these initiatives have resulted in innovatory work of a high standard, the general movement towards market-led and external economic forces may undermine the artistic and philosophical autonomy of TIE, previously only answerable to artistic and educational criteria. Of greater impact in the eyes of many practitioners, is the implementation of the national curriculum and statutory testing of pupils. The low status given to the arts, together with the pressure which schools are under to meet targets and answer to market-place criteria has led to a concern that it will not be possible to present the moral and humanitarian themes that have been so well treated in the past. However, in practice these issues are adequately woven into a well-planned piece of TIE, whatever the curricular focus of the piece. An awareness of the needs of the curriculum is vital if schools are to value TIE in an uncertain future.

Administrative changes in the mid to late 1990s will have a profound effect on TIE in Wales. The service in England and Scotland is already severely affected. Two Welsh local authorities have already withdrawn funding due to financial constraints, making it necessary for Theatr Iolo and Spectacle to charge schools for TIE. The new unitary authorities are unlikely to be able to maintain TIE, and the redrawing of boundaries implies the loss of geographical delineation of the companies' remit. Local management of schools requires governors to understand and evaluate the role of TIE if they are to allocate money from tight budgets to subsidize the service. As the systems responsible for arts funding change, with the disbanding of regional arts associations, and the administration of the National Lottery funds and the former Welsh Office support grants all in the hands of the Arts Council of Wales, there is a danger that priority will be given to larger enterprises able to take advantage of capital funding, whilst the grass-roots work which requires revenue funding will be left struggling.

The best outcome would be the formation and funding of a number of smaller local companies, working within compact geographical areas and able to visit all the schools on a regular basis. Less happy would be a free-for-all, with existing companies trespassing on each other's territory and competing for little resources, or, worse still, companies from outside Wales, with no knowledge of Welsh language and culture. In between the two lies the most likely compromise, where existing companies more or less adapt to the new situation: charging the schools for their service; operating within notional old boundaries to ever larger audiences; obliged to undertake an increasing number of drama workshops on set texts; and performing theatrical pieces with little or no participation or, with the demise of education officers, follow-up work. Such a service is also likely to become an élite, discretionary one; seen as an optional extra, the poorer schools will charge the pupils for a TIE visit, meaning that the most needy will not have access to the experience.

TIE in Wales developed with the inspiration and, initially, the expertise of the English model of form and practice. The movement in Wales was then able to establish an exceptionally stable and comprehensive provision thanks to the determination of its practitioners, an enlightened Arts Council and supportive LEA's. It was eventually to forge its own identity deriving from the specific cultural context and the parallel development of experimental theatre forms derived from the European and Scandinavian models. To this extent, the TIE movement in Wales is counter-hegemonic in spite of its Anglocentric origins. It can also claim to have brought the experience of theatre to many thousands of young people in a country where it has been observed that 'the act of going to the theatre is seen to be alien, bourgeois, and unnecessary'.[12]

Postscript

Since this article was written local government reorganization has taken place and the new unitary authorities are beginning to establish practices and priorities. Many are still in the process, encouraged by the Arts Council of Wales, of drawing up arts policies for the first time. The impact of TIE companies is ongoing and varied; some of the unitary authorities in a former county region continue to support their TIE company, others do not.

Other factors continue to effect changes in practice amongst TIE professionals: these include the reaction of school heads and governors to local management, changes in the organization of the Arts Council of Wales, and the availability of lottery funding for capital and revenue costs where work for young people is a priority. A far wider choice of arts activities is now being offered to schools from a variety of sources, changing the pattern of TIE across Wales.

The flagship TIE company, Coventry Belgrade, was closed in 1996.

Notes

1   I would like to thank Michael Baker, Eirwen Hopkins, John Prior and
    members of Arad Goch, Gwent, Iolo, Outreach and West Glamorgan
    theatre companies for their invaluable help in the preparation of this
    chapter.

2   Charmian C. Savill, 'Theatre-in-Education in Wales', *Planet* 67,
    (February/March 1988), 49–54.

3   HMI in Wales, *A Survey of Theatre in Education in Wales* (Cardiff, Welsh
    Office, 1990).

4   John O'Toole, *Theatre-in-Education: New Objectives for Theatre, New
    Techniques in Education* (London, Hodder and Stoughton, 1976).

5   Savill, 'Theatre-in-Education in Wales'.

6   See most recently: Tony Jackson, *Learning Through Theatre: New
    Perspectives on Theatre in Education* (2nd edn. London, Routledge,
    1993); John O'Toole, *The Process of Drama: Negotiating Art and
    Meaning* (London, Routledge, 1992).

7   Cf. Tony Jackson, *Learning Through Theatre*, pp. 64, 69.

8   Geoff Gillham, *SCYPT Journal*, 20 (1990).

9   Howard Barker, *Arguments for a Theatre* (London, John Calder, 1989).

10 Theatr Clwyd TIE, Artistic Policy Statement, 1994.

11 E.g. Gwent Theatre, *Who Cares Wins* (AIDS education), 1988; Coracle
    Theatre, *Thine is the Kingdom* (Northern Ireland), 1988; Theatr Iolo, *By
    a Thread* by Lucy Gough (war refugees), 1992; Theatr Iolo, *Bag Dancing*,
    by Mike Kenny (homelessness, the elderly); Theatr Powys, *Red Dressing*,
    by Louise Osborn (incest), 1993.

12 Carl Tighe, 'Theatre (or not) in Wales' in Tony Curtis (ed.), *Wales: The
    Imagined Nation* (Bridgend, Poetry Wales Press, 1986).

5 • Professional Actor Training

Paul Clements

Although I write as someone intimately involved in the training of professional actors in Wales, this is an essentially personal essay and I make no claims to speak on behalf of anyone but myself. While some of the ideas discussed here inevitably have found their way into the day-to-day practice of the drama school in which I work, this is not a policy document. There is no party line being followed here.

There are many routes to an acting career in the professional theatre and its related industries but the most common is through drama school. Many colleges and universities in Britain claim, often justifiably, to offer drama and theatre courses which prepare students for work in the theatre. Drama schools, however, have a *specific* vocational emphasis, teaching the skills, crafts and techniques required of the professional practitioner. For current purposes, therefore, a drama school is defined as an institution which is a member of the Conference of Drama Schools or which runs courses of professional training accredited by the National Council of Drama Training.[1]

NCDT, as its name suggests, is a national body. It is made up of representatives of employers, trainers and practitioners and is responsible for monitoring, maintaining and improving standards in the professional training of actors and stage managers. NCDT representatives visit drama schools on a regular basis and courses which fulfil its criteria are awarded accredited status. Accreditation is important for three reasons. First, it provides public confirmation that a course is recognized as an appropriately rigorous vocational training by members of the profession. Second, few local authorities are likely to award grants to students on non-accredited courses. Finally, graduates from accredited courses enjoy immediate Equity status and may apply for jobs, under most Equity-negotiated contracts, on equal terms with other Equity members.

Students at drama schools are normally eighteen or over. Thus, while the majority of drama schools are private institutions, the few in the public sector form part of the government's general provision of higher education and attract the lion's share of their financial support from their respective Higher Education Funding Councils. There are three public sector drama schools in England: Rose Bruford College; the Central School of Speech and Drama; and the Manchester Metropolitan University School of Theatre. In Scotland there are two: the Royal Scottish Academy of Music and Drama, Glasgow; and the School of Drama at Queen Margaret's College, Edinburgh. In Wales there is one: the School of Drama of the Welsh College of Music and Drama in Cardiff.

WCMD occupies purpose-built accommodation near the city centre and adjacent to Cardiff Castle where it was first established. After the Second World War the Bute family, the owners of Cardiff Castle, incurred two sets of death duties in a very short time. As a result of financial pressures, they handed the castle over to Cardiff City Council in 1947. The castle is a prestigious – not to say exotic – building and at first the city was at something of a loss as to how to use it. The energetic Director of Education, W. J. Williams, eventually persuaded colleagues that it should serve an educational and cultural purpose as a college of music. In 1949, Dr Harold Hind, a music adviser from London, was appointed as first Principal of the 'National College of Music' housed in the castle. Dr Hind announced that he would be entering able students for external degrees of London University. The college attracted a small number of part-time music students but outside political considerations did not augur well for its future prosperity and growth.

The use of the term 'national' in the college's title had instantly offended the University of Wales which had three music departments of its own. Dr Hind's ties to London University only added more fuel to this particular fire. Further, there was considerable rivalry between Cardiff City Council and the larger Glamorgan County Council, an immediate manifestation of which was that Glamorgan refused to assist its students to attend the college.

In 1952 the city council took the decision to add drama to the existing provision. By now, 'National' had been dropped. The first appointment to the drama staff of the 'Cardiff College of Music and Drama' was Raymond Edwards. He was employed as drama adviser to the Cardiff Education Department and was charged to spend seven-tenths of his time in the city's schools and the remaining three-tenths in building up the college's drama department. Dr Edwards applied himself to his job with vision and resourcefulness and in a short while he had exactly reversed the proportions of time he was supposed to spend on his two areas of responsibility. From the outset, he says, 'I wanted to do things for the theatre in Wales.' He had been a long-time supporter of the idea – current since the 1930s – that Wales needed a national theatre 'in order to reflect the talents of its people'. He saw a vigorous expression of those talents throughout the nation in the proud amateur traditions of music-making, choral singing and drama. If the national theatre of Wales was to become a reality, however, it was his belief that the country would have to train its own theatre personnel to a professional standard.

He viewed the training of Welsh actors in particular as a priority. He believed that the Welsh were endowed with histrionic gifts and distinctively powerful vocal dexterity, and he saw acting as a medium of expression natural to the people. 'But in the early fifties most Welsh people were poor.' They saw education as the escape route from poverty. Working people's aspirations for their children tended towards secure positions as 'teachers and preachers' rather than to the notorious insecurity of the professional stage. He established a two-year, full-time course in actor training which was taught mainly by part-time and visiting lecturers. It attracted only a handful of students, most of them women. The majority of students were from England. Among the few who came from Wales in the early 1950s were Anthony Hopkins and, a year after him, Peter Gill. Raymond Edwards attributes the poor recruitment of those days principally to Glamorgan County Council's continuing boycott of the college.

In 1958 Harold Hind retired and Dr Edwards was appointed principal – a post he was to hold for the next twenty-five years until his own retirement. Under his leadership, drama came to enjoy equal status with the music department. He was able to control appointments and brought in a number of well-qualified and nationally recognized staff on both part-time and full-time contracts to enhance the quality of the teaching. It must be remembered, though, that while the castle provided an extraordinary aesthetic environment in which to work, its facilities were actually primitive and inappropriate for a busy drama school. With no performance space of their own the (by now) increasing numbers of drama students had to present their work in a variety of venues: in church halls, schools and regularly in the University's Reardon Smith Lecture Theatre. The city council recognized that the college, in terms of student numbers and its own ambitions, was outgrowing its original home but showed little interest in providing a new building until the late 1960s when Dr Edwards persuaded the Conservative chairman of the city council to back a building programme.

A site was found close to the city centre on a long triangle of scrub land between Bute Park and Cathays Park with the Cardiff Castle Mews immediately to the south. The funding level which was eventually achieved for the new building, designed to accommodate a target figure of 350 students, proved to be disappointing. At a rate of £7 per square foot the building estimate for the Welsh College of Music and Drama (the new name had been acquired in 1968) was the same as for an infants' school. The sterling crises of the early 1970s also had an impact on the construction which was by then under way. Cuts imposed on local authorities forced further economies and the length of the partially completed building was reduced by eight feet, compelling architects and builders to shunt all facilities into the truncated space. The drama department eventually moved out of the castle in 1973, followed a year later by the music department.

In spite of the manifest inadequacies of the new building – a theatre but without a fly tower, poor soundproofing and a tiny movement studio – the move did mark an enormous step forward for the college. Courses were increased to three years and a graduate-equivalent diploma in drama, validated by the University of Wales, was introduced as well as one-year courses for postgraduates. Student numbers continued to grow. Design and stage management departments were established and there were a substantial number of new appointments to the full-time staff. Local government reorganization saw responsibility for the college pass from Cardiff City to South Glamorgan County Council. Finally, with the arrival of the newly established NCDT, in the early 1980s the drama school's acting and stage-management courses acquired accredited status.

The college today is based securely on these early foundations. Although it is now an independent higher education corporation under the Higher Education Funding Council for Wales and it houses over a hundred more students than it was originally built for, the original course structure in drama is still discernible. The graduate diploma in drama has been recently upgraded to a full degree course with discrete options in acting, design and stage management. In 1989 the college took the strategic decision to reduce the number of actors it trains and to increase commensurately the numbers of design and stage-management students in order to reflect more accurately the realities of the employment market. These changes, however, have served only to develop what was there before. The drama school continues to train for professional employment and of its current enrolment about one-third of the students come from Welsh local authorities, with the remainder coming mainly from England although there are a fair number of Scots. In recent years the college has begun to acquire an international flavour with an increasing number of students from the EU, Iceland, Scandinavia and from North America.

On paper, the content of the training programmes offered by most drama schools appears quite similar. The curriculum will offer work in voice, speech and singing, in movement and dance and, of course, in acting. All drama schools offer highly specialized training in what we might call the technical craft skills of the actor. Helping the individual student to realize the full potential of his/her speaking and singing voice and to develop vocal strength and adroitness are clearly central parts of this training since the actor's voice is perhaps his/her most vital tool. Wyn Calvin recalls that during his first professional job, in weekly rep at Lytham St Annes, an elderly theatre-goer recognized him in a shop and observed to her companion, 'He's good. He can shout!' Audibility has to be the first accomplishment of the professional actor.

The development of flexibility and definition in the body is also central. A range of work is undertaken in the physical dimension of training to build up stamina, to encourage precision in movement and to liberate the individual's personal expressiveness. Various teachers in different schools will approach technical work in different ways, but there will not be much variation in the essential aims of the technical training programmes from school to school.

Similarly, with the teaching of acting, the practice of most drama schools is to offer students a variety of training experiences which reflect the diversity of theatre itself: Greek drama for elemental power and ritual and Shakespeare for non-naturalistic heightened text and classical style; Chekhov for studies in naturalism; Restoration plays and Sheridan for comedy of manners; a range of contemporary plays to embrace current debates and styles; improvisation for spontaneity and some experience of devising without recourse to an extant conventional dramatic text; radio and television acting to teach appropriate techniques for the respective media. It is also true of almost all drama schools that the philosophical and practical underpinning of their work is to be found – whether acknowledged or not – in Stanislavsky's writings about the inner resources of the actor and his central concerns for spontaneous life, believability and truth in acting.

Since the course content of most schools is quite similar, the reader may reasonably enquire, 'Well, what are the differences between them?' What makes each drama school different is the particular emphasis given to each of these disciplines it teaches and its individual perception of the industrial and cultural context in which the actor will eventually work.

Until about twenty years ago there was a sort of career structure for actors, however ramshackle it may have been. The young actor coming out of drama school usually found a first job in a small-scale local repertory or fringe company. These first jobs were widely perceived as a period of apprenticeship following basic training, with the drama school graduate developing confidence and learning further skills from the more experienced professionals with whom s/he worked. Additionally, many companies in those days were committed to keeping an ensemble of actors together instead of casting from production to production. The effect of this policy was to provide young actors with the opportunity to play a variety of roles across a broad range in a single season. Bernard Hill, for example, graduated from Manchester Polytechnic School of Theatre in 1972. After periods with the Library Theatre and with Liverpool Everyman, he joined Contact Theatre Company for the 1973/4 season. Between September and March he played Azdak in Brecht's *The Caucasian Chalk Circle*, a disturbed teenager in *A Downright Hooligan* by C. G. Bond, Feste in *Twelfth Night*, the Devil in a devised show for secondary schools about the advertising industry called *You Are What You Buy* and John Lennon in John Batty's *What Did You Expect . . . The Beatles?* – a role he later repeated with great success back at the Liverpool Everyman in *John, Paul, George, Ringo . . . and Bert* by Willy Russell and which eventually took him into the West End. From that foundation he has gone on to construct a substantial and distinguished career as an actor in theatre, television and film. While Bernard Hill became a nationally recognized figure relatively quickly after he left drama school, the early experience of many other actors whose professional lives developed at a gentler pace was broadly similar.

Today, with fewer repertory theatres and with hardly any companies able to afford to maintain an ensemble, the old (albeit precarious) career structure has all but disappeared and the young actor graduating now faces an employment future of huge uncertainty. This prevailing uncertainty affects profoundly those of us attempting to run actor training courses which manage to maintain both educational and artistic integrity and relevance to the theatre industry. The crucial question is what skills for what jobs?

The greatest of the perilous temptations attendant on trying to answer this question is that of prophecy. It seduces its victims into attempting to predict the condition of the professional theatre and the film and broadcasting industries five, ten or twenty years ahead. Those who see the future of live theatre as a landscape of twinkling marquees advertising the names of endlessly running musicals, hurl their eggs into the basket of musical theatre and gear up their training courses in that direction. One can almost hear the cry of 'Eureka! *That's* where the jobs are going to be!' Similar cries, accompanied by the sound of courses being ratcheted into other, different gears, are emitted by the prophets whose visions of the future are of television production companies as the omnivorous employers of the twenty-first century; or of non text/language-based physical theatre, with its antecedents in Poland, as the predominant middle-class art form; or even of a theatre aspiring to emulate Lazarus, with set plays and adaptations of set literary texts exhumed annually for consumption by National Curriculum audiences.

We may indeed be in a phase where theatre is in decline. There is evidence to support the view that smaller numbers of people are attending fewer live performances mounted by fewer companies in a diminishing number of theatre buildings. If it is like that now, however, none of us can be sure that it will inevitably continue to be so or that the decline is terminal. Like society itself, theatre is in a condition of constant change and none of us can predict that some act of renewal will or will not occur in the next few years.

Further, if there *is* a decline in public interest in theatre, there is no evidence at all to suggest that the public appetite for drama is similarly attenuating. Trevor Griffiths was arguing twenty years ago that the National Theatre of Great Britain exists not on the South Bank in London but throughout the nation on television where a one-off play can reach a larger and more socially diverse audience on a single evening than a play running in the West End for years. The vast audiences for soap operas, situation comedies, drama series and even, still, for one-off plays on television attest to the continuing demand, one might almost say the continuing need, for people to witness human experience represented to them in fictional form in various ways and to varying degrees of accuracy, truthfulness and complexity.

The representation of human experience is, of course, the business of all creative participants in the dramatic event in whatever medium, but it achieves its most complete expression through the work of the actor. It is the development of the individual actor's capacity to assume the joyous responsibility of this task which, I would argue, must be at the centre of actor training. The individuality of the actor is paramount. For acting is not an 'out there' commodity or external discipline to be reached out for and mastered. Its sources lie within the actor's original, particular and idiosyncratic self. I try to explain this to young actors in the following way:

Imagine yourself acting in any scene from any play with one other actor. Then, while the interpretation, tempo and blocking of the scene stay the same, another actor of equal talent takes the place of your original partner. Although the externals don't change, the acting of scene will be qualitatively different because of what the new partner brings to every moment. This won't simply be because s/he looks different from the original partner, it's because s/he *is* different. The same lines, the same words will have different resonance for the new partner and will find changed expression. There will be a different look in the eyes reflecting a different sensibility and a distinct imagination. If you're a sensitive, open actor, in subtle ways your performance will change, too, as you respond to the particular qualities the new partner brings to the scene.

The process of teaching and refining the craft skills which the actor requires to communicate to an audience with definition and exactness must not be allowed to obscure his or her quintessential personal creativity. For therein lies the spontaneity and potential excitement which gives genuine life to the dramatic event.

In practice, and particularly if students arrive in drama school with a received idea of what acting is, training should encourage them to develop confidence in their uniqueness. This does not mean simply playing to strengths, because actor training must also encourage students to extend their emotional playing range in order to open out and reveal a broad spectrum of experience.

For all of this, the education and training of the actor does not and cannot take place within an ivory tower. There is a real and pretty ruthless world of work (and probably long periods without it) waiting at the end of the process. My contention is, however, that a programme of training which places the individuality of the actor at the centre equips him/her more thoroughly for employment than any other method.

Notes

1   The eighteen member schools of CDS are listed below. All offer NCDT accredited courses with the exception of those marked *. Arts Educational London Schools, Birmingham School of Speech and Drama, Bristol Old Vic Theatre School, Central School of Speech and Drama, Cygnet Training Theatre*, Drama Centre London, East 15 Acting School*, Guildford School of Acting, LAMDA, Manchester Metropolitan University School of Theatre, Mountview Theatre School, Queen Margaret College School of Drama, RADA, Rose Bruford College of Speech and Drama, Royal Scottish Academy of Music and Drama, Webber Douglas Academy of Dramatic Art and Welsh College of Music and Drama.

6 • A Vision Undimmed:
Theatr Fach, Llangefni

Dafydd Arthur Jones

Given the general unease with the state of contemporary Welsh drama and the frequently cited conflict between the demands of the mass media and stage, it is a matter of some speculation whether the amateur theatre has any impact on contemporary arts. A common plea for community involvement is often hailed as good practice by critics and actors alike. No less heartening is the number of Welsh repertory companies which have become well established in many areas. Popular 'single-issue' plays attract generous notices and there is the feeling, confirmed by some practitioners, that the idea of a truly 'national' theatre for Wales might well emerge from the confines of the locality. But the question regarding the role of amateur theatre more often than not remains unanswered. Cultural historians are reminded of the demise of erstwhile well-established and popular companies and uninterested communities are frequently cited as further proof of the weakening of the traditional belief in the intrinsic merit of amateur productions.

A company which flies in the face of such adverse criticisms is Theatre Fach, Llangefni. Dedication to the cause of theatre on the island of Anglesey has been fairly well documented. It is a reputation firmly based upon the belief in the primacy of serving the community. A study of the various aspects of its pioneering work reveals the durability of the vision of its founding father George Fisher.

Unlike many companies, Theatr Fach boasts a long and illustrious past. Fisher, a native of Glamorganshire, whose family originally hailed from Somerset, first came to the island in 1931. He was appointed to teach mathematics at the local grammar school but he soon acquired an active interest in Welsh culture. A diligent student of literature, his passion for drama and English verse remained undimmed for many years. Much of his literary output was published in such journals as *The Adelphi* and *The Twentieth Century*. He also cultivated an enthusiasm for playwriting. November 1939 saw a production of his play *The Disinherited* produced at Swansea with a masque written by Vernon Watkins. Called up to the navy, Fisher made great use of his time by learning Welsh. His well-thumbed copy of *Welsh Made Easy* was invaluable. Such was his interest that he regularly corresponded with the author Caradar. In time his mastery of Welsh enabled him to feel sufficiently confident to write in his newly acquired language. Indeed his proficiency was severely tested when his play *Y Lleoedd Pell (Far Places)* was performed at a drama festival held at Llangefni in 1943 and *Blaidd Ddyn (Wolfman)* was sent to a one-act play competition at Eisteddfod Môn during the same year. His appreciation of literature also embraced poetry. He was attracted to *cynghanedd* and even sent an *englyn* to the National Eisteddfod at Bangor – drawing words of encouragement from G. J. Williams, one of the adjudicators. His play of the same year in the Eisteddfod was less favourably received and the criticism seemed to suggest a failure fully to apprehend Welsh idiom.

Fisher's importance as a pioneering enthusiast lies in his undertaking of ambitious plays at the school. A notable production was *Amlyn ac Amig (Amlyn and Amig – A Folk Tale)*, in 1947. Saunders Lewis had initially conceived the work as a radio play and Fisher's talents involved a radical adaptation. Such efforts were duly rewarded and the play afforded the opportunity to experiment with scene changes and movements. Critics noted the performance of a young schoolboy named J. O. Roberts as Amig. Fisher's talents at the school were widely appreciated and soon his reputation grew. Two years after his school production a drama society was formed in the town. Fisher's enthusiasm more than compensated for the lack of resources. Play after play flowed from his pen and in 1949 he won the first prize at the National Eisteddfod at Dolgellau for a one-act play *Catrin*. His interest in Welsh history was noted and his research into the Age of the Princes amply rewarded. The Drama Society undoubtedly was a catalyst for artistic endeavours on the island. Amateur theatre had been encouraged by the Annual Drama Festival already established under the auspices of the Rural Community Council. The newly formed Society staged more plays on a regular basis at Llangefni. Many of Fisher's own plays, notably a sea fantasy, *Morwyn y Môr (The Sea Maiden)*, were warmly received. Another play, *Y Ferch a'r Dewin (The Girl and the Magician)*, had its première at the Llangefni Drama Festival in 1954 under the directorship of Edwin Williams, and it was subsequently published. The period witnessed a growing interest in amateur drama as a means of providing entertainment, but Fisher's ultimate dream was yet to be realized.

In 1953 Society members availed themselves of the facilities in the old grammar school. A new comprehensive school had been built and Fisher was anxious that a workshop should be established in the vacated physics laboratory. Sets and large flats were stored in the defunct swimming pool destined for demolition by the education authority. With his usual presence of mind Fisher grasped the nettle and saw it as an excellent opportunity to establish a permanent home in the outbuildings of the Pencraig Estate. Land and property had recently been bought by Llangefni Urban District Council and Fisher was soon able to embark on his lifetime ambition and established a fully fledged theatre on the site. The buildings were initially rented from the council for a nominal sum until the Society could muster enough funds. Local enterprise and hard work combined to convert an unprepossessing barn into a theatre, which eventually led to a grand opening night on 3 May 1955. Here was a praiseworthy enterprise hitherto unique in the history of drama in Wales; a truly communal effort, which had established its own theatre, had now been officially declared open.

Two one-act plays crowned the realization of Fisher's ambition. *Rwsalca*, a stage adaptation by Cynan of a short story by Pushkin, and *It's Autumn Now* by Philip Johnson were both warmly received in the tiny auditorium seating sixty-five people. Local interest and well-wishers throughout Wales were attracted to the enterprise. The gamble had paid off and a small and lively theatre had finally become a reality. Fisher's policy of staging plays in both languages was accepted. Technicians and actors were reminded of the importance of commitment to Fisher's ideals and this became the hallmark of the early years. Given the nature of Welsh drama in the post-war period his attempt to stage new work was innovative. Longer and more ambitious productions were staged and the company boldly attempted the world's classics.

The Llangefni National Eisteddfod of 1957 provided the theatre with national recognition. The building, which had been extended to seat 110, became the focus for artistic endeavour during the week. Fisher's *Merch yw Medwsa (Medusa is a Girl)*, was a fitting testimony to his directorship. Of considerable interest was the staging out of doors of an elaborate pageant *Ednyfed Fychan (Little Ednyfed)* by Ifan Gruffydd. Fisher's endeavours were rewarded with an MBE in 1958, followed by financial assistance from the Gulbenkian Trust in 1960. In view of the relative paucity of professional productions on the Welsh stage during the 1950s, Theatr Fach gave invaluable service. The growing sophistication of actors and technical staff was well demonstrated in a production of *All My Sons* in 1961, *Mother Courage* (1963), *Blodeuwedd* (1964), *The Good Person of Szechuan* (1964) and *Siwan* (1966). Recognition of the company's growing reputation came about in the following year when membership of the Little Theatre Guild of Great Britain was confirmed. The bilingual policy was approved and recognized as an asset and the theatre was firmly established as one of the leading amateur companies in Wales. Apart from the growing range of plays and its commitment to technical expertise, Theatr Fach provided useful training for a growing number of promising actors and performers. The talents of Charles Williams, Elen Roger Jones, Glyn Williams ('Glyn Pensarn'), Elwyn Williams, J. O. Roberts, Hywel Gwynfryn, Maldwyn John, Gwenno Hodgkins, Ioland Williams among many others have been widely appreciated. Actors like Llion Williams have also featured in past productions. The role of an amateur theatre in providing such opportunities has been of lasting value and a notable number of non-professional actors have formed close associations with the company.

Fisher's death in 1970 did not affect the well-established policy of maintaining exacting standards. Continuity of artistic direction was ensured by Hazel Slade and J. O. Roberts and the chairmanship of Llewelyn Jones was a happy augury during the difficult transitional years. Fisher's labours were commemorated with the opening of a much valued rehearsal room by Sir Ben Bowen Thomas in 1972. Theatre members contributed nearly £2,000 towards the £5,000 cost, with the remainder coming from the North Wales Association for the Arts, Anglesey Rural Community Council, Llangefni Urban District Council and the County Council. The following year the theatre provided a focus for a literary conference and representatives from other small theatres came to Llangefni. Emyr Humphreys's staging of *Siwan* was highly acclaimed not only as a notable contribution but because it was the means of drawing the world's attention to the undoubted talents of Saunders Lewis.

The company's lively interest in the community has been reflected in its involvement with young people. A Saturday club provided them with films and fun and the establishment of a Youth Theatre has been one of its most successful ventures. Such an enterprise, coupled with the resources of the costume hiring department, has earned the theatre a reputation beyond the island. The staging of good and popular plays is, however, the principal aim of the company and the appointment of an artistic director and production manager has ensured a continuity of popular works. New lighting facilities were installed in the 1960s and the assistance of Frank Taylor proved to be invaluable in technical matters.

Of considerable interest was the company's willingness to export Welsh drama. In 1974 an invitation was accepted to stage *Un Briodas (One Wedding)* at the Carrolls Theatre, Dundalk, Ireland. *Pros Kairon* was staged the following year. An even greater honour came in 1975 when it was invited to be the sole Welsh and British representative to stage two plays at the International Theatre Olympiad in Detroit, USA. This indeed heralded the coming of age of a company which had firmly established its reputation in Wales and had at last gained a foothold abroad.

In 1980 the theatre celebrated its Silver Jubilee. A special fund was started as demands for greater financial recognition had been a constant source of anxiety for all theatre administrators. The idea of attracting more sponsors has been considered and the National Lottery could be a potential source of additional funds in the future. Building and further refurbishment work have assumed a greater importance and local enthusiasm has remained undimmed. A policy of commissioning plays with mass appeal has also been recognized. Notable successes include *Cariad Creulon (Cruel Love)*, directed by Tony Jones (1984), *Witness for the Prosecution* (1987), *The Crucible,* directed by J. Fuldson (1989), *The Secret Diary of Adrian Mole,* directed by Tony Jones (1989). Popular demand has also been well served with a number of pantomimes. Edgar Jones, Llanfachreth, for example, has been encouraged to write a number of popular plays, which include *Neidr Fawr Penhesgyn (The Big Snake of Penhesgyn)* and *Arch Noa (Noah's Ark)*. Since 1959 the theatre has been registered as a charity. In spite of some guarantees the threat of insolvency has always remained. More profound questions regarding artistic direction have been less daunting but channelling the ebb and flow of amateur enthusiasm may be difficult to realize.

The theatre's lasting contribution has been its willingness to provide the public with a popular and established repertoire of drama. Inevitably there must be a broadness in the number and quality of plays. Authors like Barry Williams, a native of Wales now residing in Liverpool, have earned a reputation for writing popular plays in an accessible and popular style. Plays of this kind are a fitting testimony to the memory of Fisher and his aspirants. They also confirm the reputation of an amateur company such as Theatr Fach for providing entertainment which encapsulates the true meaning and function of community spirit.

Note

I am particularly indebted to Mrs Audrey Jones, Rhostrehwfa, Anglesey, for her guidance and time. Bibliography: Llewelyn Jones, *Francis George Fisher: Bardd a Dramodwr* (Caernarfon, Argraffwyr Gwynedd, 1983); Enid R. Morgan, 'Theatr Fach Llangefni yn dyfod i oed', Y *Llwyfan* (Summer 1969), 8–9; Dilys W. Shaw, *Theatr Fach Llangefni 1955–83* (bilingual volume, 1983). I am informed that another volume about Theatr Fach Llangefni, *Deugain Mlynedd o Droedio'r Byrddau*, by J. R. Williams is about to appear.

7 • A Community Drama

Ewart Alexander

Community drama is too often associated with a thousand amateur spears pointing through bad make-up at some misty triumph in the history of Wales. Not only does this confirm the worst clichés firmly lodged in the minds of distant observers (usually across the border), but it encourages the sterile rhapsodies and the painful misinterpretations which seem to inform much of the thinking and hopes associated with that quite puny thing – drama in Wales. However, in order to make some sense of what follows, a brief outline of my own journey as a writer seems necessary. For the last twenty-six years I have, in the main, concentrated on writing for television and films. In that period, five stage plays have emerged, three of which were written specifically for a community.

This place is Ystradgynlais, sometime mining village at the head of the Swansea Valley among those seams which produced high-grade anthracite and that white betrayer, silicosis. In its days of spurious glory as a producer of fossil fuel, Ystradgynlais offered its fair share of dramatic product. Largely spilling from the once-upon-a-time vibrancy of Nonconformity and in equal measure from St Cynog (the Church of England), there were 'dramas' and the yearly offers from the two operatic societies – the Grand and the Light versions. Performances from the mid-1930s onwards took place in the Miners' Welfare Hall.

It is irrelevant in this context to rehearse the well-documented social and economic history of such communities – their decline, their semi-revival by other means – except to indicate the almost crippling tendency to oversentimentalize the things identified as the struggles and the deprivations. Indeed, it is this factor which, alongside another underestimated feature of the Welsh scene, has caused so many problems and errors of critical judgement in the drama sphere.

This other feature is the very size of Wales which, when applied to creative output, leaves far too many writers (who, anyway, too conveniently assume that title) struggling to ape and follow what is happening in other places where far more people speak English. The truth of the matter is that Wales just is not big enough to sustain a constant number of worthwhile plays; and being a fractious little place, endlessly trailing after that most unrewarding definition of identity, it all tends to end in a constant need for approval and, more dangerously and more sadly, an overvaluation of ourselves.

Ystradgynlais has, for me, been a place where I have lived and worked as a writer. For perhaps too many of those years it has been a place to be taken for granted. Familiarity breeds assumptions. Assumptions tend to become beliefs. After all it was the perfect place to work; the place that made me; the place which offered long and constant friendships; a place which provided its stillness and, in many a morning light, the sudden surprises of carboniferous limestone. Writing was for elsewhere with is successes and pleasures. Of course, in its mild insistence, the place has caught up with me. Yet, if it were not for the refurbishment of that very Miners' Welfare Hall and the need to mark its reopening during the Valleys Live Festival in the early 1990s, I would still be turning a lazy eye towards other pastures, other more beguiling outcrops.

So there it was, the challenge of putting on a play in and for the community without the comfort and safety of sitting at home watching one's own plays on television. This was for real people in a real place. Initially, I had to learn the art of stumbling towards a coherence, disguising it as clear purpose. The stumbling, I suppose, was mainly associated with defining the word community while being nagged by an unease about achieving the highest standard of production. Both considerations did not seem, in the Welsh context, to lie easily one with the other.

The solution attempted, and one which was to succeed, meant involving a strong professional component in the production. At the same time it was essential to use the relevant talent which was manifest or lay dormant in the village. Balancing both facets in order to avoid overload in one sense and underutilization in the other became a matter of fine judgement. The easier way out (money willing) would be to settle for the kind of security on offer throughout my professional life – good casts, good directors, highly professional technicians and designers – and then hope for the best.

Soon, the implications of the mix-and-match tactic became very clear. By superimposing a number of professionals as performers and technical back-up, there was a risk of alienating that very element which was most closely associated with the word community. The village might see the whole process as an indulgence by a writer who had earned his pennies elsewhere – a dormitory playwright making a gesture towards a Welsh Office initiative while at the same time falling into that trap of sentimentality which was inevitably coupled with the rebirth of a hall; a hall, do not forget, which had been built initially as a result of those miners' pennies. Furthermore, there might well be sharp resentments among the village actors who might see themselves as ignored or, at best, just making up the members in a production which, therefore, had very little connection with the venue or the place. This is where the living in and knowing of the village saved the day. The idea attracted immediate and intense interest. We were off.

It soon became evident that the community deserved a more refined definition. As it happened, the first play of a trilogy about warfare this century needed a chorus (in the Greek sense) and achieved one by means of Côr Meibion Gyrlais (in a Welsh sense). In terms of numbers this meant another forty villagers were involved in the production. The task set was not easy. During the play, the choir was asked to respond to twenty-seven cues with music of various lengths and keys. This was something outside its normal repertoire and mode of operation. In the play's run the choir performed impeccably.

The brass band was also asked to contribute relevant music in the foyer as an introduction to the production. The community was increasingly being involved. This also meant that two well-established if somewhat clichéd forms were finding new uses, and at the same time providing a clear link between the old and the new. Familiarity created far more excitement than contempt.

These two additions only went part way towards a satisfactory definition of community. It is clear that professional drama in Wales is faced with a severe problem of falling attendance. However, with the necessary effort, it was felt that selling tickets would not be too acute a problem. The real problem was that tentative progress towards fulfilling the idea of community and play as one. Who else, therefore, should be involved? Flexibility became the key strategy in opening up the notion of a play in a place to those many people for whom drama is a mystery and irrelevance and something which only 'they', the enigmatic 'they', see as worthwhile. For instance, by accident, some young people on Community Service became involved because they happened to be around while rehearsals were taking place. A kind of amused and very peripheral interest was seized upon over slow days so that by the week of production, law-breakers had become very significant contributors to the process. Happily this involvement has been maintained.

The other obvious area of potential help was and is the young unemployed. It was no use to make a goody-goody approach to get people off the street. Yet it had to be tried – somehow. The sensible and, as it turned out, the effective method was to select significant and vastly underachieving members of the non-working population and convince them that they were needed to do practical things as far removed from the text as made things non-threatening. Eventually they became leaders of the also-rans. Thus a really useful number of young people who had never seen a stage play, let alone become involved in one, became eager, sometimes overeager, helpers. A surprising number became regular attenders at rehearsals. This was the significant crossover. They got to know the professional actors, who, by this time had become temporary but very real members of the community. Gradually a sense of general involvement was building up.

Because of the costly professional element, the need for adequate funding had to be addressed while the general awareness and commitment was building up in parallel. As things developed, monies from various sources became available. It was necessary to set up an adequate administrative base. Letters and paperwork provided that irritating confetti which seem such an irrelevance when everyone is beguiled by the excitement of making something happen. An interesting result of those more mundane aspects of setting up the play was the emergence of what almost became a motto: 'But I Know A Man Who Does.' Lifted from a television commercial, this was the response to requests for various bits and pieces, for equipment, for painting and construction space and for a myriad other things necessary to achieve our aim. There was always someone, even at twice-removed, who could be, and inevitably was, of help.

It was this begging and borrowing which became an exercise in identifying the significant doers in the community, the ones who could deliver the goods. In its way it could have formed the base for some academic study. It involved far more people than had ever been envisaged. In fact, the rehearsals became a far less significant part of the production than the hurrying and scurrying surrounding them. This was a conclusion which only emerged in retrospect and has very clear lessons for whenever community drama is considered. It is also interesting to note that the search for a dozen six-inch nails (for free) led to publicity messages percolating down most unlikely avenues. Donors naturally wanted to know why the quest for six-inch nails seemed so urgent. If they didn't ask, they were told.

And related to this matter of publicity and general servicing of the production, the need to utilize the institutions already existing in the village needed to be balanced against the essential arbitrary nature of the six-inch-nail syndrome. What groups or bodies, already in the business of distributing information and organizing events, were prepared to become attached to the play? If you go for one, go for the lot. There's nothing more potentially destructive or more calculated to release the prancing little devils of Welshness than not being asked. Try approaching the Conservative Club for help and ignore the Labour Party. Try your wiles on the Church Fellowship and ignore Merched Y Wawr. Should you be so foolish, your forever gift will be as acute a definition of resentment as was ever offered to mankind; resentment tends to encourage bloody-mindedness; and bloody-mindedness will eventually lead to the quick slide of daggers when all the world seems sunny and good.

If there is, among all the institutions, a strong amateur drama company then this, above all, is the best source of support and encouragement. If potential resentments are overcome, then professional involvement has an entirely positive effect. It leads to the raising of standards in all facets of that amateur company's subsequent work. Apart from the initial need to ensure the highest possible standard of production in the community play, the cross-fertilization of the paid and unpaid has a far more profound implication for the way I see drama developing in Wales; but a little more of this later.

This kind of co-operation also allows a community-based play to buck the trend of tight budgets in the professional sphere which allow only meagre sets, and which elevate the word shoestring into an art form. All this myriad support which a properly set-up community play should engender means that the designer can be ambitious and not all that wary about costs. It is a relief and a challenge.

Thus it was in the second community play that I wrote for Ystradgynlais in 1994, which was *Atrocity*, set in 1943 and based upon the making of the film *The Silent Village* by Humphrey Jennings in the upper Swansea Valley. The designer was asked to concentrate on the set without allowing any financial constraints to force early modifications to the detriment of the final product. The philosophy which, by this time, had emerged in the process was a total concentration on the highest standards. The financial and logistical problems which might arise were left to the future. After all if a village could not cope with the challenge, then the sense of community was in no way being questioned or developed. What finally emerged was the kind of set design which did pose its very real challenges and which strained all kinds of resources to the fullest.

Another important confirmatory lesson emerged in the building of our benign monster. The ramifications of funding the vast construction place, the acquiring of immense amounts of distressed timber, the extra cost involved in taking on two highly skilled carpenters for three weeks, the cost of other raw materials which, in the end, amounted to a thousand pounds, were a test and a play in itself. While the normal rehearsals were progressing, the demands of the set became a larger thing. It became, in its way, a little legend in a little place or a big thing in a big space. The set became the topic of general conversation, and for the time being, the question as to how the set was progressing tended to push concerns about the play into the background. Again, in retrospect, this has a significance for the whole idea of drama in the community.

What also emerged was a more acute questioning about the relevant financial base for the production. Maybe, over the last twenty-five years, there has been too much dependence on Arts Council funding at all levels of drama production in Wales to the detriment of quality. Although funding policies have been established for the best of reasons, maybe the substance of what has emerged as a result does not justify the often embarrassingly large grants afforded to some companies and projects. This view can be seen as part justification for a complete reorientation of public support in the Welsh context, i.e. too much has been chasing too little. It was this thought that led to the next stage of community involvement. Why not ask the village to make substantial financial contribution to the plays?

The obvious local sources had already been approached, i.e. the banks and certain industries. (It is interesting to note that British Coal felt unable to help because of previous strident village objections to open-cast mining.) However, the proposed additions to funding were seen on a much smaller scale; and it was important not to exclude anyone. The first level of requests was based entirely on religious groups. Eventually, and upliftingly, all the Nonconformist Chapels,

the Catholic Church, the Church of England and the more
charismatic groups in the village gave generous financial support.

The more secular bodies, from the Rugby Club to the two choirs, to
the main political parties, to the pubs and clubs, played their
significant part. The smaller businesses joined the trend. But it was
the level and consistency of individual contributions which rounded
off a very gratifying picture. In the end, a large amount of subsidy
was raised from the very people who would be asked to buy a ticket
for the performances. In the context of such general support, it would
have been invidious to offer complementary seats. Even everyone
closely involved in the production was expected to visit the box office
with money in hand and any resentments firmly repressed. The village
had become a little Arts Council and was none the worse for the
experience.

As the first production approached public performances, and to an
increasing extent in subsequent community plays, a feeling of general
involvement emerged. For better or worse this was our play.
Contributing to it in whatever myriad ways was an investment which
needed to be evaluated by those who came along in such gratifying
numbers. Had it been worth their effort, worth their money? To say
that there existed tensions well above the normal anxieties associated
with producing and performing a play would be an understatement. It
was not enough to expect the kind of concession to local product
which audiences willingly give. Everything had to be right. If you ask
people to forego *Coronation Street* for something on at the Welfare,
then you had better be sure of your product; and sure of it in the only
sense that matters – a story so well told and so technically adroit that
attention is firmly held from beginning to end and that time flies. Too
much of the inadequacy of contemporary Welsh drama is disguised
under incomprehensible ranting. That alibi for lack of talent and lack
of knowledge is offered under the banner emblazoned as the
innovative. Too often the so-called innovative is at best only novel and
only too often masturbatory. Tiny coteries, out of ignorance or a
spurious fashionableness, think they are seeing profundity. You can
definitely fool some coteries some, if not all, of the time. People who
come to be entertained and to be moved and maybe, in the end, to be
made more thoughtful, make common sense and their experience of
life and heart the basis for judgement. What tends to be ignored far
too often is that drama is for audiences – especially if they have paid
for it twice over.

So what has come out of the process as manifest in Ystradgynlais in the 1990s? The first important lesson is that if community drama is to succeed and move forward, the whole effort must be informed by a relevant fusion of the professional and non-professional. The play and the varying circumstances attached to it will dictate the specific balance. Too much of a bias towards the professional might cause resentment; too little bias will prevent achievement of desired standards. These standards need not relate only to what is seen on stage. Equally important are the other daily contacts, especially on the technical side. Once a proper, non-threatening base is established between in-comers and locals, there is an eagerness to learn and a willingness to give. The results of this two-way process have been gratifying in ways which go far beyond the areas closely associated with production. Many of the disadvantaged and the uninterested young have latched on to activities and ideas through which they have, maybe for the first time in their lives, achieved a sense of competence and worth. This may or may not reflect itself in other facets of their life; but their interest in the hitherto mysterious event called a play has certainly been enhanced.

This has led to a reassessment of the whole nature of producing plays in any given community. If a comprehensive involvement is achieved then what becomes the more important, the product or the process? It can be argued that the actual event – the play – lasts only for the length of its given run. It arrives and it is over. However, perhaps it is the nature of the particular play with which we have been involved which alerts us to the question of process versus product. Considerable challenges have been entailed, especially in set-build. First, and especially where the carpenters were involved, the mystery of properly conceived drawings set in motion animated puzzlement and a parallel activity which had more to do with the very things closest to the lives of those building and eventually humping and erecting the set than it had to do with the play. Yet, as it began to shape itself, became real and made increasing demands on manpower and ingenuity, that particular effort moved closer to its basic purpose. Things began to make sense.

And it was not only the set which suggested that process is at least equally if not more important than product. As things turned out, a way through and a more relevant direction and more efficient use of public monies seemed to suggest itself. If, for instance what has happened in Ystradgynlais could occur as an experiment, say, in

twenty to thirty other Welsh communities, then drama and the nature
of Wales could, at last, rest easier one with the other. Actors,
designers, directors, writers, administrators, if assigned, cajoled or
even directed to contribute over relevantly long periods to drama in a
specific community would sharpen priorities as to the balance and
relevance between the providing and the provided-for. Gone would be
the touring companies and the scant audiences. Overambition,
overestimation as to worth, overindulgence and all other kinds of
extravagances would be things of the past – and not too soon. Smaller
can be better. Place can be more relevant than concept. Responsibility
can improve product. The people are there. They understand stories.
They tend to laugh and cry in response to the same things; and drama
can, when rid of all the frowns and the oh so patent and pathetic
imitations of worth, be such fun.

8 • Special Worlds, Secret Maps:
A Poetics of Performance

Mike Pearson

This could be some sort of chronology or a gazetteer of the manifestations of that alternative theatre practice which had its genesis in Wales in the early 1970s.[1] But that would mean remembering times, dates, places . . . For these performances, variously described as 'experimental', 'devised', 'physical', 'site-specific', rarely became part of a published record. They have their document in the endlessly elaborated (and increasingly fictionalized!) reminiscences and anecdotes of its practitioners, in a discourse akin to an oral culture. Unfortunately, memory fades. Instead of attempting an aesthetics of a unique tradition which has flourished in, and is not separate from, a particular set of social and cultural circumstances, I shall examine its specific nature.

At the Congres Internacional de Teatre a Catalunya in Barcelona in 1985, I suggested that the forms, techniques, preoccupations and placement of a Welsh theatre might bear little relation to those of its English neighbour. With no mainstream tradition defining what theatre ought to look like, with no national theatre prescribing an orthodoxy of theatrical convention, with no great wealth of play-writing, then theatre in Wales still has options. It has the chance to address different subject-matters, using different means, in spaces other than the silent and darkened halls of theatre auditoria. It need not be what Eugenio Barba called 'the noble face of show-business' or a sophisticated entertainment. It can follow other agendas, agendas of cultural intervention and stimulation, as opposed to reflection and representation. And with no one setting the rules, an experimental theatre need not be marginalized or 'on the fringe'. Indeed, as an inventive and imaginative project in and of itself, it might provide a valuable forum for the creating, challenging and changing of identities – artistic, personal, communal and national. At the very least, it has the opportunity to set in context such normative theatre practices as characterization, setting and dialogue, which are so often presented uncritically as common sense, as a universal language, as the only way 'to go on' in performance. Thus, a theatre of distinct identity might speak of, and for, a distinct identity.

Experiment begins with the questioning and affirming of the fabric of theatre, the very tenets of the form. For this, it requires clear definitions. We can define performance as something other than a set of operational devices and techniques for the staging and presentation of plays, the illustrative function of dramatic literature. It is a mode of communication and action, distinct from the 'normal' or everyday', marked out by special types of behaviour and 'registers of artfulness'. It is most often, though by no means exclusively, manifest in scheduled events bound in time and place (Chapter Theatre, Cardiff, 15 June, 8 p.m.). These may be structured, ordered, programmed. They are recognized by a co-ordinated gathering, of spectators and performers, as a heightened occasion, formally set apart from everyday life, with modifications of behaviour for all present. And they engender a sense of expectation and occasion.

The particular nature of performance is that it must be watched or witnessed for it to make sense. It resides in a complex set of contracts between two orders of participant – watchers (spectators) and watched (performers) – and in three sets of relationship: performer to performer, performer to spectator (and vice versa), spectator to spectator. This does not mean that performance need make an appeal to the outside, an overt acknowledgement of the presence of the watchers. But it does rely upon the shared competence of all the participants to identify and to mark off a strip of behaviour, framed by a series of transactional conventions. The spectator needs cultural competence to interpret this partial assemblage of activities and objects, which is characterized by omission and extra-daily juxtapositions, as a representation of a social whole. Significantly, each and all of these contracts is available for renegotiation.[2]

In performance, we can distinguish between 'the dramatic text', that produced for the theatre (the play), and 'the performance text', that produced in the theatre, everything we see and hear before us. But the latter is not subservient to the former. It is possible to 'write' in the performance text, to devise with techniques of staging, with the art of the performer. For beyond the written text, performance is manifest in four axes – space, time, pattern and detail – and theatrical material and meaning can be generated in each and all of these.

Rich and complex forms of performance can be created by the

manipulation of these principles even without a script. This is not to dismiss words and texts: they simply become features in a matrix of other modes (music, action and scenography) all jostling to create meaning. Of course, this holds true in any cultural context. What is the specific grain of Welsh experimental theatre?

The absence of a tradition of playwriting in Wales is often mourned and frequently the subject of new schemes of subsidy. But it may be that it is the very nature of dialogue itself as a means of dramatizing relationships which fails. In Wales, people continue to talk to each other, they have no choice if the language is to survive. Theatre may be better employed in developing a different repertoire with different performance structures, different ways of telling in different tones of voice, the better to address the experience, aspirations and principal concerns of a small nation: to embrace different topics or perhaps endlessly the same topics but in different ways; to constitute a reawakened interest in the experience of others as a political project; to assign fictional characters to their final fate. Naturalism is not necessarily its automatic choice of presentational style and the withdrawal to the proscenium arch and the creation of stage illusion have no primacy.[3]

Welsh experimental theatre has always drawn its themes and subjects from the common currency of myth and religion, a rich literary tradition, a political history of bureaucratic and state intervention, of industrial and economic decay, of emigration and immigration and from a love of language, landscape and justice. Whilst applying the most recent of technologies, it addresses the oldest of anxieties. It returns recurrently not only to the Bible, to ancient lyrics and to the stories of the *Mabinogion*, but also to specific instances of injustice, repression and resistance. In a traditional society, history may be experienced, or characterized, as a series of crucial, inciting incidents around which opinion accumulates and which resonate in the present. History conflates: thus the flooding of Tryweryn to make a reservoir for the city of Liverpool is still a potent metaphor for English colonialism. Performance can assume a certain level of knowledge and approbation in its audience: they are finite and already 'in on something'. With the existence of such a collective consciousness, knowledge or memory, theatrical interpretation can be audacious, detailed and diverse. And it can anticipate more acute levels of criticism! This does not mean that the tacit affirmation, by a Welsh audience, of entrenched stances such as passive resistance to bureaucracy, civil disobedience and anti-Englishness, or of such familiar notions as *hiraeth*, should go unchallenged.

This is not to suggest that Welsh experimental theatre is parochial. It is the very way in which it has dealt with the particulars of a national experience which has enabled the work to exist abroad. Its specific address may serve to illuminate that sense of loss and dislocation, deeply felt but difficult to identify, which is currently experienced in majority cultures. Nor does it imply that Welsh theatre is immune to broader issues upon which it might have a particular perspective or that it cannot use the experiences of others in the world to illuminate affairs in Wales. And whilst it naturally utilizes indigenous forms of cultural expression – annexed, modified and mutated – it has been audacious in its appropriation of other theatrical traditions, unafraid to borrow techniques and technologies to inform its work, seeking other models from sources as diverse as the classical theatre of Japan and the dissident groups of Poland.

Even the rural experience can inform the most sophisticated of theatrical experiments: it may be that the premodern and the postmodern are not so far apart. Here, we see the creation of sophisticated world pictures which draw together family history, empirical observation and make-believe into 'deep maps' in which history, landscape and genealogy are woven into a 'sense of place', a sense of belonging, in an improvised response to environment, constantly cross-referenced and updated. The medium of these constructs is 'talking'. The Welsh are used to talking, and gossip itself is a complex intertextual device which can include dizzying order of different material and sudden jumps in technique. It can encompass the fragmentary, the digressive, the ambiguous, the appropriated, in juxtaposition and in contradiction. Given all this, Welsh theatre might make different judgements about the suitability of material for dramatic purposes and might order it according to principles other than the dramatic interplay of 'I speak, now you speak'. It can include travellers' tales, poetry, forensic data, quotation, lies, jokes, a cluster of narratives – expert, witness, tangential such as gather around an event or crime, with sudden shifts, endless repetitions and interminable *longueurs*.

There are places in every society where all the other places in the culture are simultaneously represented, contested, inverted. Theatre is in and of itself such a place. In Wales, others might include the hearth, the chapel, the National Eisteddfod, Cardiff Arms Park . . . It is here that different and specific discourses – the ways in which society talks to and about itself – are generated. These are sites of anecdote and memory, of opinion and secret, of eulogy and elegy, of epic and myth and of fervour, aspiration, shouting, singing. They and their discourses are found recurrently in a Welsh theatre as points of orientation, as familiar handholds, as the intimately familiar in a sea of other material which may then be infinitely alien.

Wales has a sophisticated repertoire of musical, poetic and oratorical forms and techniques, enshrined in the competitions of the Eisteddfod, in the choral singing and preaching practices of the chapel and in the bombast of a fiery political culture. And these are highly instructive for new approaches to performance, not only in informing the expressive techniques of performers, but also in suggesting alternative types of material – poetry, song, speech – and their ordering. Welsh theatre can include performers who sing as often as they speak, particularly in moments of deep emotion, without the work ever becoming a musical or opera, and who speak with the voice of the preacher, the politician and the auctioneer. It can employ the verbal and vocal specifics of particular recitation and verse forms such as *adrodd, cyd-adrodd* and *penillion*, or *hwyl* and four-part harmony. It can substitute rhetoric and soliloquy for dialogue, declamation for discursive reason.

Performance can resemble the political meeting or the *noson lawen*, the traditional evening of song and entertainment. It can employ the conventions of chapel service and barn dance as its performance structures. It need not even be signified as distinct mode of expression: it can be as much memorial service as fictional story. Informed by the ordering principles of these models, it can exist as the dynamic juxtaposition of different varieties of material and forms of expression: music and text, the sung and spoken voice, physical image and action . . . It can order poetry, song, oratory, physical action (dance, procession, mass movement) and a myriad of technologies – video, sound recording, lighting – into complex performance structures and scenarios. It may include a libretto to carry narrative information and a musical composition to establish the dynamic pattern of emotion. It can exist as a sequence of images, as a strategy for action, as the fusion of dynamic physical action with a pattern of text in the form of verse, lyric or diatribe rather than dialogue. Or as a discontinuous and interrupted practice of different modes of expression, of varying types and intensities, in which different orders of narrative can run simultaneously, in which dramatic concept may spring from site not story and which may include rapid changes in mode and material. These performance 'hybrids', which might defy conventional labels, are not a mirror of some social issue or a simplification but a complication, which defies instant scrutiny. Yet such complex techniques of mixing and editing are not unfamiliar to an audience with a high degree of television literacy. It is not insignificant that the fullest development of experimental performance in Wales has mirrored the growth of S4C.

The pattern of performance may be more than just the evolution of a story. It may exist as an explicit scenario in which different narratives, historical and contemporary, unfold simultaneously or sequentially. It may be constituted as a strategy, in the form of rules, instructions and restrictions, both spatial and physical; as a sequence, string or series of activities with continuity or diversity of mode, style or technique (dance, song, oration, procession – continuous, discontinuous, fragmented); as a route map of sequential frames or as a chain of stepping stones of choreographed and improvised sections; as a poetic narration against a body of physical action; as the 'and then . . . and then . . . and then' of the storyteller. We may also characterize it as an unfolding of incidents and their trajectories. These are changes of consequence, crises or innovations and may include ruptures or sudden shifts in direction, emphasis, orientation. They may be most apparent at thresholds, such as entrances and exits, which are then followed by a period of change, resolution or elaboration. There may be a sequence of irrevocable acts, such as flooding of the performance area, of decay, such as the destruction of objects and of nodes, in which similar and dissimilar activities are drawn together into dense images with complex and equivocal meaning.

Performance may also have the form of a stratigraphy of tracks or layers, each carrying modes or themes in parallel: a text or libretto; music or soundtrack; physical action and scenography, the latter to include all scenic installation – lighting, amplification – prerecorded media and technical aspects. These elements may be composed, written, conceived, developed and even performed in relative isolation, against a mutually agreed sequence and a time-base. With a general agreement about the nature, purpose and emotional tenor of each section, distinct narratives may be pursued in each of the four elements in parallel. Such a pattern can be subjected to folding, faulting, compression and erasure. But it only gains coherence through a judicious use of dynamics, a graph of speeds, intensities, rhythms, 'pushing on and pulling back', increasing tension, energy expenditure, relaxation . . .

Welsh performance can employ the Welsh and English languages in concert and in conflict, each language carrying different bodies of information without the need for translation, in a truer reflection of the linguistic composition of the nation. It can include the voices of the performers – chatting, lecturing, reciting, orating, seducing – in modulations and intensifications of speed, tone, volume, rhythm, in sequence and in chorus. Yet the words need not issue from the mouths of performers. They can be part of an amplified soundtrack, a sonic architecture within which voices can be placed, mixed and moved through and around an audience.

In the early nineteenth century, Welsh rural theatre was a victim of that stern and strict Nonconformity which frowned upon such trivial pursuits. However, performance crept into the chapel in the oratorical techniques of the preacher and the harmonized voices of the congregations. And the growth of the eisteddfod preserved and established a variety of modes of verbal and vocal expression. The Welsh are used to performing, but on platforms and in contexts other than the auditorium. These are suggestive: it does not take long for a group of Welsh students to learn a four-part harmony song, albeit in the shape-note tradition of the Southern Baptists of Arkansas!

But where else might Welsh experimental theatre, particularly a visual or physical theatre, find its means in a culture short of a record of visual imagery? Performance is particular, but it is not unique. It shares characteristics with a nexus of other activities including game, play, sport and ritual. In all of them, a 'special world' is created which is under the control of the participants. This can be a fantasy world, a metaphorical world, a world with quite different rules and modes of behaviour. Yet it can be of vital importance for the participants as a forum for examining, challenging, transgressing the everyday, with real changes in status and extra-daily experiences, a place where energy is expended for purposes other than profit and where identities are created, contested and changed. These activities are all bound by rules in the form of contracts, mutual agreements, taboos and prohibitions which mark off the activity, define the 'special world' and ensure coherence, direction and momentum as well as implying the threat of transgression. They all include the dynamic interplay of strategy and tactics, of planning and operation, of choreography and improvisation. They have special ways of ordering time – as when all the activity must be achieved in a certain period, giving the activity a particular dynamic momentum – and they assign an arbitrary value to objects (props, kit, toys) beyond their material worth. Objects may be chosen from the everyday world for their intrinsic qualities: dimensions, appearance, texture, 'fit'. They need not necessarily be specially fabricated nor need they be 'ritual objects' or 'props'. But once selected by, and isolated in, the activity, an object becomes a representative of its type, and suggestive of all others. Objects are also invested with meaning and significance by the activity. We might think of this as a kind of *bricolage*, an improvised response to an environment of limited resources, which draws dissimilar objects together into images and metaphors only possible in the 'special world'. And which generates a richness of equivocal meaning. The props of a Welsh theatre may be the implements and equipment of an agricultural and industrial past, manipulated, used and misused, as the implements of cultural rebuilding.[4]

Performance may resemble, in part or *in toto*, any or all of the other activities in the nexus, in part or *in toto*. It can be as fascinating as play, as exciting as game, as coherent as ritual. It can be singular and unrepeatable. It can employ sets of rules in place of complex narratives or choreographies. It can exist as a sequence of tasks, instruction, prohibitions, restrictions. It can be 'intertextual' in its inclusion of different styles, techniques and modes of activity: it need not just tell a story. The term scenario can be used for 'that which is to be attempted': game-plan, plot, story board, shooting script. It can employ tactics as well as strategies, for although the 'what' may be fixed, the 'how', in terms of delivery, timing, qualitative improvisation, may be decided in the moment. It need not be totally planned, rehearsed, tied down. It can use various time frames manifest in sequence or in parallel. It can be a specialized form of space/time manipulation. And its performers need not pretend. They can expend energy, complete real tasks, commit irrevocable acts, in the here-and-now.

A Welsh theatre can substitute real tasks, patterns of work – such as washing shirts – for stage illusion and gesture, tasks which utilize the processes and rhythms of work, play and worship, recontextualized, mutated, re-energized. It can concern itself with the actions of nameless characters who look as much like the Neath

Rugby Club front row as actors, who behave as much like cultural activists as fictional characters. Certainly, Welsh performers are already politicized, beyond the subject-matter of the performance, in the degree of their engagement. Welsh performance need not be 'in parenthesis'. It may be as much political meeting as social simulation. Things – identities – may actually be at stake here.

Ergonomics is the relationship of humans to their working and living environment. It may be that the constructed environment of performance is 'active', much better, or much worse, than that of everyday life in 'real Wales'. And it may change from moment to moment – from acceptable, to unacceptable, to optimal. The substance of performance may be no more than the performers dealing with the ergonomic extension or restriction of their clearance, reach, posture and ability to apply strength. The methods and organization of effort, flexibility of response through improvisation, use of tools, both designed and improvised, their symptoms may be as fascinating as the fictional fate of dramatic characters. Yet this may not necessarily be an increase in hazard. It may be a perfection. The ethereal, gliding movements of Noh Theatre are only possible on the polished stages of cypress wood.

However, we do realize that the performer is 'performing'. There is something in her demeanour which tells us. Performance is revealed in the body, in the 'pathology of the performer'. Indeed, the performer may not be searching for a fictional character as prescribed in the dramatic text as role, but for a fictional body, 'a body for art'. How is this achieved? First, the body is held in a way different from that in everyday life. This is achieved principally by putting the balance in jeopardy. The complex physiological and psychological state of 'stage fright' may constitute a form of 'unbalancing' as the performer consciously 'psyches' herself up. Secondly, the line of the body includes contradictions, one force pitted against another in an internal conflict of hard and soft, straight and curved, tense and relaxed, in 'a play of opposites'. And this requires great energy to maintain. Thus seven-tenths of the performer's energy may be used in time, as endurance, and not in space, as movement. The stillness is full of energy. The body is alive in a conflict of freedom and constraint, before overt expression begins, yet there is potential for movement. This is the 'pre-expressive state'. Thirdly, the activity is characterized by omission: the gestural language of everyday life is selected, simplified and stripped of redundancy, then concentrated, mutated and recomposed. Fourthly, and most significantly, the performer can invest any action, any gesture, with more or less energy, over more or less time, than is required in everyday life. There may be no exclusive 'stage behaviour'. Any other modes of activity, other social actions and interactions – drawn from work, play or worship – can be annexed and re-energized, given new emphasis and recontextualized as dramatic carriers.

Physical communication is composed of kinesics (body movements including symptoms, signs and signals), proxemics (the relative distances of body to body) and haptics (touch of self and others). Performance takes this vast semiotic resource and begins to transform and mutate it through processes such as compression and elongation (of size, duration and intensity) and through spatial displacement, social transgressions, repetition, fracturing, and recontextualizing. The social parameters of proximity and touch are highly codified. Each individual is surrounded by four concentric zones (at least!) determined by the characteristics of sense organs, the length of limbs and cultural conditioning: intimate, personal, social and public. Entry into each zone allows different modes of physical and verbal discourse and different orders of kinesics may only be apparent within certain proxemic zones. But these zones have no sharp divisions, and they will vary from individual to individual, culture to culture, by gender, age, status and according to context. Transgression may be sanctioned by extreme circumstance or by convention: dancing cheek to cheek, the embrace of grieving adults.

A Welsh theatre concerns itself not only with the conventional theatrical representation of such phenomena but also their actual social manifestations, and then puts both under pressure. So, performance itself may include real proxemic and haptic invasion and transgression in all three sets of relationship. Performance may exist for the performer over and above 'motivation', 'character', 'blocking' as a chain of physical orientations and mutual re-engagements within a performance continuum, as an interrupted practice of different modes of expression of varying types and intensities, as a discontinuous activity including changes in style, mode, material, as a kind of incoherent behaviour, as a sensual experience – easy bits, difficult sections, rests.

Wales has only a limited range of theatre auditoria. Experimental theatre has always sought other venues. This is not solely through expediency, but challenges the notion that the auditorium is a neutral vessel of representation, seeing it rather as the spatial machine of a dominant discourse which distances spectators from spectacle and literally 'keeps them in their place', in the dark, sitting in rows, discouraging of eye contact and interaction. It dismisses the stage as a field, ploughed to exhaustion.

Performance is not context-dependent on auditoria. It can be manifest within an existing social situation or location, at a found space, a (former) site of work, play and worship. This has enabled theatre in Wales to develop in two distinctive ways. First, it can be constituted as a modular staging unit – a combination of floor, seating, lighting and scenic effects – which can be placed in any empty room or hall. Such units ensure a continuity of performing conditions and of quality of experience for the spectators, allowing detailed choreography for unchanging dimensions, extremes of action for a known surface, the proximity and touch of three-dimensional performers and the creation of complex imagery before a fixed arrangement of seating. They can be placed in the variety of opportunities presented by the cultural infrastructure of school, chapel and eisteddfod.

Or theatre can be site-specific, created for special occasions and locations, and occurring in disused factories; in and around the pulpit of chapels; in quarry, museum, barn or house; in the arena-like configuration of cattle markets, buildings in which audiences might feel more at ease than in the serried rows of the auditorium. Here, free from the rules of prudence and decorum, new relationships of watchers and watched come into being and non-theatrical techniques become possible. Performance can thus be manifest at the scale of architecture and civil engineering, with a scenography which 'brings the outside inside' and constructed from wrecked cars, dozens of trees, hundreds of tons of sand and thousands of gallons of water.

Site-specific performance recontextualizes such sites: it is the latest occupation of a location where other occupations are still apparent and cognitively active. It is conceived for, and conditioned by, the particulars of 'found' spaces, the only contexts within which it is intelligible. Site may allow the construction of a new architecture, the 'ghost' within the 'host'. Host and ghost, of different origins, are coexistent but, crucially, are not congruent. The performance remains transparent and the specifics of site – architecture, history, function, location, micro-climate – are apparent as context, subject-matter, framing, subtext. Thus site-specific performances rely upon the complex superimposition and coexistence of a number of narratives and architectures, historical and contemporary. These fall into two groups: those that pre-exist the work – of the host – and those that are of the work – of the ghost. Of the latter, some are conceptual, some spatial, some thematic, some textual. The relationship between them, whilst designed, is not complete. No single story is being told. Instead, they are conceived in such a way as to maximize their dynamic potential to create meaning recurrently through juxtaposition, conflation and mutual illumination. And they co-mingle with the host's component orders to create a dense structural poetics. This poetics is rich in opportunity and metaphor and can generate theatrical detail, image, action and language. Interpenetrating narratives jostle to create meanings. These performances are extremely generative of signs: the multiple meanings and readings of activity and site intermingle, amending and compromising one another. They reveal, celebrate, confound, criticize and make manifest the specifics of the site which begins to resemble a kind of saturated space or scene-of-crime, where, to use forensic jargon, 'everything is potentially important'.

Site may allow the suspension and transgression of the prescribed practices and by-laws of the auditorium. The non-pristine nature of the site might allow the use of resources, techniques, materials and phenomena unseen (or even illegal!) in the auditorium – the unusual, the unacceptable, the downright dangerous: fire, smoke, excessive light, animals . . . It may be possible to construct an active environment – of wind, rain, snow, machinery – in which surface and climate may change from moment to moment and present ergonomic problems to the performers. We watch their methods of coping: extreme difficulty is always interesting! Site may be directly suggestive of performance subject-matter, theme or form. Its usage, or former usage, may directly inform dramatic structure: the 'hand-in-glove' congruence of performance about war-wounded in a hospital or constituted as a religious service in a chapel or as a political meeting in a council chamber. Conversely, site may facilitate the creation of a purposeful paradox, through the employment of orders of material seemingly unusual, inappropriate or perverse at this site: an opera in a shipyard, an early Welsh epic poem in a disused car factory. Here, site serves to recontextualize the material, relocating it and suggesting environment, equipment and working processes which might mediate and illuminate it. As site, there may be an existing institutional arrangement of watchers and watched which can be annexed: the formal organization of pulpit and congregation in a chapel, sale-ring and buyers in a cattle-market or beds and visitors in a hospital. Conversely, performance may impose another arrangement, floor plan, map or orientation which confounds everyday hierarchies of place and patterns of movement: spectators may stand on islands of sand-bags in a flooded ice-hockey stadium.

Site-specific performances which fold together place, performance and public have no natural edges or frame to hold their identity discrete, no stage backdrop against which their outlines might be thrown into crisp focus and they do not rely on containment for their identity and integrity. There is no singular or external vantage point from which to view them. They are enigmatic inasmuch as any one spectator may pay more or less attention to any one event in such a multi-focus field of material. They are inherently non-hierarchical. Any of the work's components may, at any one time, provide the 'centre' or 'datum' around which other materials are working, but the responsibility for fulfilling this role is not carried by any one prime component, such as the script in conventional drama. They may constitute a 'field' of activity which will tend to escape definition, description and representation.

Performance at non-theatrical sites may dislocate and confound the preconceptions, expectations and critical faculties of the audience, that combination of previous experiences and learned contracts which defines conventional theatre orthodoxy. A new and extended contract between audience and event is then possible. A Welsh experimental theatre seeks other places, forms and functions for performance. In such constructed situations, free from the laws and by-laws of normative theatre practice, other things, real things, can happen. Performance may be in and of itself a locale of cultural intervention and social innovation. Here, extra-daily occurrences and experiences and changes in status are possible. All three performance relationships can be problematized and renegotiated and conventions and mores reshaped. Performance need not be restricted to the public or monumental zone of the auditorium. It might favour sociopetal spaces which enhance interaction by throwing individuals together.

Performance may begin to resemble a 'special world', not entirely hermetically sealed, but a 'devised' world, all the elements of which (site, environment, technology, spatial organization, form and content, rules and behaviours) are conceived, organized and ultimately experienced by its ordering of the participant. Perhaps this is an idealized world where wrongs can be righted, injustices repealed, new agendas set; where individuals work for the best of intentions, for the common good. We may all – performers and spectators – eventually have to ask, 'Who is who?', 'Whom do I watch?', 'What's going on here?' – in a virtual Wales.

Welsh experimental theatre is created within a specific social and cultural milieu. The degree to which it accepts, embraces, questions or refutes the conventions, the proscribed and recurring practices of this context, creates the tension in and around the work. It is always for, and against, chapel, Eisteddfod and the politics of nationalism. It remains sceptical of authenticity and orthodoxy. To challenge and to create identities may be its ultimate objective.

Notes

1   The notion of 'experimental theatre' – providing alternatives to the exposition of dramatic literature in playhouses – was fostered by a number of companies including Cardiff Laboratory Theatre, Paupers Carnival and Moving Being. In the former, we were particularly influenced by the austere physicality of Jerzy Grotowski's 'poor theatre' (and the work of other Polish practitioners including Tadeusz Kantor and 'student theatres' such as Osmego Dnia); the travels of Eugenio Barba's Odin Teatret and the developing concept of a 'third theatre'; the 'group theatre' techniques of American companies such as The Living Theatre, Richard Schechner's Performance Group and Joseph Chailkin's Open Theatre, and the dynamic fusion of rock music and theatre by such young touring companies as The Pip Simmons Group.

2   It may be that the rugby crowd, the Eisteddfod platform, the miners' procession, the language-act demonstration and the chapel congregation already suggest particular patterns of cultural behaviour specific to Welsh gatherings.

3   Many of these perceptions, and those which immediately follow, result from a precise history of making theatre in traditional – and to some extent monoglot – rural Welsh societies. Yet it is this very specificity and rootedness of this experience and its developed practice which might enable Welsh performance to engage in those intercultural, and interdisciplinary, or multicultural manifestations which better reflect contemporary and urban society in Wales and the multiple identities of its inhabitants.

4   'Flowers suggest weddings but also funerals or the entry of the victor.

And such meanings interpenetrate, one always present in the other. So in the surgeon washing his hands lurks Pilate. And contained in a single piece of bread is gluttony and starvation, religion and blasphemy. Revelation may mean confronting and contesting social norms. Only then can a Bible be set on fire, nailed open, devoured, cut with an axe, smothered in molten metal . . .' (Mike Pearson: 'On Objects', unpublished.)

I am deeply indebted to the work of my colleague Cliff McLucas in the composition of this chapter. Most of the thoughts on 'site' are his and his alone. His unique architectural address to place and performance are of major importance not only in the development of Brith Gof's work but in suggesting an entirely new conceptual approach to theatre-making in Wales.

9 • Brith Gof

Charmian C. Savill

Brith Gof theatre company has produced over seventy performance events since its formation in 1981. Founded by Lis Hughes Jones and Mike Pearson, the company is respected internationally and nationally as one of the most inventive and challenging theatre-making groups in Europe. It has produced work which has ranged in scale from the most intimate of settings (a farm kitchen) to large site-specific work in disused industrial areas.

In some ways, Brith Gof has appeared to be a latter-day manifestation of the alternative theatre movement which began in the 1960s, identified by Theodore Shank as dramatizing 'the moral energy of social causes and the spirit of artistic exploration'.[1] The work in the first half of the 1980s reflected a personal and artistic commit-ment to the group ethos and a rigorous devotion to the creation of a new kind of theatre in Wales, demonstrating a desire 'to improve the quality of life for themselves and for their audience'.[2] Brith Gof's resistance to establishment values, decaying cultural mores and mainstream theatre reflexes defined the 'group' as a satisfying, dignified, personal-political model of creative interaction. Richard Schechner has identified two radical responses to problems which are generated by the 'group' ethic: 'to make permanent theatres with temporary people' or to 'form an encapsulated work group, such as the Polish Theatre Laboratory'.[3] Brith Gof has oscillated between both of these models. In its early years, it gravitated towards 'the encapsulated work group'; in later years, its mode of operation has embraced the use of temporary company members. Although it has never possessed a permanent theatre site, it has a permanent core of theatre specialists. Its initial rejection of internationalist ambitions, as represented by the experimental and alternative Cardiff Laboratory Theatre in the early 1980s, was gradually re-evaluated, as its contacts with companies abroad expanded and its sense of identity as a Welsh theatre company became more assured.

From 1986, different artistic and personal ambitions fragmented the 'group' nucleus, and the individual and his or her development became a primary concern for members of the company. Mike Pearson describes the company in the first years of its inception (1981–5) as:

a poor theatre, relying on the passion, commitment, physical and vocal resources of the actor. We are drawn naturally to a theatre of physical expression and visual imagery . . . Performers sing in our performances as often as they speak, particularly in moments of deep emotion. Rhetoric and soliloquoy take the place of dialogue . . . The movement resulting from patterns of work – washing shirts, cutting stakes – can take the place of stage gestures.[4]

The primacy of its political concerns was and still is epitomized by the style of the work, as Dafydd Elis Thomas has commented:

The most political thing about their theatre . . . is its form. By working in a very direct, material way, audiences are compelled to experience the events . . . In a Britain where government censorship and political policing is increasing, we need the subversive power of the signs of resistance made by Brith Gof.[5]

Since they are their own apprentices, constantly developing systems of mutual learning, members of Brith Gof have contacts with numerous other companies, performance artists, dancers, musicians, singers and theatre practitioners from all over the world. Eugenio Barba and members of the Danish company Odin Teatret have attended private viewings of Brith Gof's work in Wales and Denmark in order to discuss critically its performance processes. This international network has enriched and informed the style, form and subject matter of its work.

The first performance by Brith Gof, in February 1981, came about as a result of a three-month study period in Japan by Mike Pearson, funded by the Welsh Arts Council. His resulting experience of Noh Theatre affected the structure and style of many subsequent productions. By inviting international exchanges with companies such as Iben Nagel Rasmussen's Farfa (from Denmark) and Osmego Dnia (from Poland), Brith Gof extended its own performance frontiers and became a major force for change within Welsh theatre and its reference points. Its ongoing work in one of the largest British university departments of Theatre, Film and Television Studies, at Aberystwyth, has challenged and encouraged the choices and expectations of performance held by many young people throughout the 1980s and 1990s. Gwenith Owen (a.k.a. Eddie Ladd), a performer with Brith Gof and founder of her own Cardiff-based theatre company (Jesus and Tracy), recalls that her student experience of working with Brith Gof helped her to develop her own sense that 'naturalism felt wrong'.[6] Brith Gof's work has been the subject of many different definitions over the last decade and a half, ranging from 'poetic' (*Le Monde,* Paris) to 'anarchist open-air event' (Johannes Birringer, *Theatre, Theory and Post-Modernism* (Bloomington, Indiana University Press, 1991)). One of the most vital aspects of its work is a fierce enthusiasm for destabilization and dislocation from previous aesthetic frameworks, re-evaluating theatrical form in a spirit of striving and search.

Reviewing *Ymfudwyr (Emigrants)* in 1983, Polish critic Piotr Kuzinski describes the performance as expressing 'the problems of disinheritance [the] search for identity in this fast changing world'.[7] *Ymfudwyr* is about the experiences of some emigrants to Patagonia and South America which are related poignantly in the first film made about Brith Gof for S4C, *I Wlad Dda a Helaeth (To a Good and Extensive Land)* in 1986. The film traces the company's experiences of performance and meetings with the descendants of original emigrants from Wales to Patagonia in 1865. *Ymfudwyr* locates 'the hopes, fears, dreams and interactions of a group of Welsh emigrants', as Brith Gof explains in its booklet *A Welsh Theatre Company:*

> Our subject matter is often specific and historical . . . but our aim is a metaphor for our current situation . . . we concentrate on the various forms of repression, we always celebrate resistance, following the example of those who struggle in more severe situations.[8]

One such instance: the production *8961: Caneuon Galar a Gobaith (Songs of Grief and Hope)*, written, devised and performed by Lis Hughes Jones in 1985, explores the grief, anger and confusion of the relatives of 'the disappeared' in Argentina. Dafydd Elis Thomas remarked how 'through her body, her movements, song and speech, the material form of oppression [was] literally acted out'.[9]

Both *Ymfudwyr* and *8961* are entirely the company's own work. However, most of its productions have been collaborations in some respect: with students, dancers, musicians, local communities, special needs groups or theatre companies. Always a complex, difficult and often problematic experience, collaboration has nevertheless proved to be an essential ingredient in the artistic development of the company. The individuals and groups who collaborate with the company are often outside conventional artistic networks, and indicate the necessity felt by Brith Gof for co-operation and challenge from the communities who receive its work. Interaction with other groups of people is itself an important catalyst in Brith Gof's own creative process, and helps to fulfil the company objectives of being facilitators and teachers of theatre. This objective developed very early on, through its work with Aberystwyth University Drama Department (now the Department of Theatre, Film and Television Studies). This opportunity was extended to the company by the late Emily Davies, a trustee of the company, lecturer in drama at Aberystwyth, and a fervent believer in the need to expand students' horizons through the experience of working with theatre practitioners from outside the university. Indeed, Brith Gof hoped in the early 1980s to create a school of theatre, what it termed 'Theatr Ymchwil Cymru (Research Theatre Wales)', and drew up a policy for such a pedagogical venture together with preliminary architectural designs, inspired by buildings owned by Eugenio Barba's Odin Teatret in Denmark. Ultimately, the faith of funding bodies in such an enterprise, and their will to make it a reality, was not forthcoming: one of the greatest disappointments the company was to suffer in its first decade of work. Nevertheless, the need to develop pedagogical frameworks and to facilitate others in the making of theatre has never left it. These objectives and methods are manifested throughout the *Trychinebau Rhyfel (Disasters of War)* projects (1987–9); during subsequent years both Lis Hughes Jones and Mike Pearson have worked as teachers of technique and facilitators of the creative processes inherent in theatre.

Welsh language and culture have been both reinforced and challenged by Brith Gof's work. Clifford McLucas, permanent company member and scenographer since 1988, comments:

Any kind of cultural activity in Wales is inevitably political, as is the decision to speak Welsh. I don't harbour notions of Welshness which tend to hover around ideas of authenticity – 'The Welsh Voice', 'The Welsh Theatre', for example. I know many young Welsh speakers in the arts who cannot associate their belief in what they do with 'being Welsh', because of the essentially reactive and repressive notion of 'Welshness' clustered around a collection of cultural and historical customs. Ideas that come from elsewhere always have to be cut down, re-shaped and made into this 'Welshness' of a precisely Eisteddfodic kind . . . There is an increasing groundswell of criticism from within the heartland implying that somehow Brith Gof has stopped being Welsh. I think it is a tightrope that the company has to walk . . . Brith Gof is working on ideas to generate a space for Welsh work to exist in Europe. Either we end up making caricatures of ourselves, and as a result become a kind of cute, exotic corner of Europe, or we do something more intelligent. Brith Gof deals with subject matter from Welsh literary, historical, social political and mythical sources. But what we've done is to weld on to those sources a form of theatre entirely alien, and made a hybrid. The idea of hybridization is very important and is entirely opposite to ideas of purity and authenticity.[10]

The importance which members of Brith Gof attach to their role in the framing of new culture is recognized by a vast cross-section of people in Wales; and the universality of the themes they tackle – oppression of minority cultures, ecology, war and peace, displacement – attracts a much wider international following. Their audience in Wales has always contained a mixture of social classes and age groups. Their later work concerns itself primarily with a younger audience, and it is the company's ambition and intention to maintain and develop this direction. Instead of the earlier supportive attitudes to the audience, Lis Hughes Jones claims that *Trychinebau Rhyfel* created 'pressure to be harder, less ready to give a simple answer. I don't think there are any answers.'[11] Jones adds that part of the essential process of making theatre involves the construction of pertinent questions. Brith Gof began its exploration of theatre form and style by focusing on the images created by the body in relation to the acoustic quality of the voice; the company has gradually complicated perceptual expectations through its use of sophisticated scenography, music and technological modifications, which synthesize and alter what is seen and heard. The company's insistence on resisting orthodoxies, including those of its own forms of theatre, makes Brith Gof a constantly regenerative force in Welsh theatre. This is particularly notable when, at the time of its inception, very little theatre of importance was being created in the Welsh language. Central to its artistic and personal vision is the sense that it represents a microcosm of the recognition, redefinition and reassertion of a minority culture breaking down through the persistent but decaying vestiges of imperialism. Lis Hughes Jones describes the complexity of this experience, referring principally to the *Trychinebau Rhyfel* project of 1987–9:

> It wasn't productions *per se* that were significant in that period, but everything else which surrounded the 'product': the decisions concerning why, where, how and who we would work with, the research into process, form and new techniques. There was a feeling that we were attempting to redefine ourselves on a personal level, through the work and through the structure of the company. The itinerant nature of our lives was reflected by the work; conflict became a way of life. The collaborations created pressure points within this process, times when we had to pull together as a group in order to work with others, which wasn't always easy, especially when there was a lot of tension between members of Brith Gof and problems within the other groups.[12]

The company has lived and worked to find ways of theatrically transcribing and transforming the poetics of its sources of inspiration from the past and present, whilst always considering the need to affirm its existence. In the first years of Brith Gof's existence, the contributions and developments of Lis Hughes Jones and Mike Pearson as theatre-makers shaped and imprinted a very particular identity upon the company. In 1981, Jones represented the linguistic and cultural specifics of the company, and Pearson was known for his innovative ideas and his ability to discover new forms of theatre to create a 'strategy of interference'.[13] Their work was inspired by their need to reinscribe Welsh social, mythic, literary, political and historical representation, through impatience with and a sense of the impotence of traditional theatre forms. Brith Gof is insistent about developing an audience alongside the company, although its journey towards a new theatre audience was initially cautious.

Pearson, in referring to the early period, remarked that 'it was based on our assumptions about our audience's expectations; we were cautious about out subject matter'.[14] Their audience consisted mainly of Welsh-speakers from rural areas and small towns at this time; their subject-matter was well-known myth and legend or socio-political content that was analogous with or connected directly to the lives of the spectators. With reference to their work from this period on *The Mabinogion* ('*Branwen*', '*Rhiannon*', '*Manawydan*', '*Blodeuwedd*'), Jones asserts that while their use

> might seem rather obvious now, the processes which led us to that decision were complex. There were many Eastern influences, not just Mike Pearson's work in Japan; I had studied Balinese dance, and the influence of Odin Teatret was very important. Whilst at Cardiff Laboratory Theatre, we had found it difficult to connect these. In *The Mabinogion*, we found a meeting point.[15]

In the early 1980s. *Gwaed neu Fara (Blood or Bread)*, *Ann Griffiths*, *Ymfudwyr* and *Rhydcymerau* all contained histories or cultural specifics familiar to the majority of the audience, or with political connotations which reverberated with an assumed collective empathy. Beyond 1986, productions such as *Pandaemonium, Y Gadair Ddu (The Black Chair)* and *Gododdin* still carried many of these resonances. Jones and Pearson continually demonstrated in their work that culture has always 'addressed itself to the specifics of expression – to the realization of the being and evolution of its collective psycho-social reality'.[16]

The need in Brith Gof to rupture the 'stable aesthetic' of the early 1980s with its progress into a more technological and consciously postmodernist phase was initiated by the 1986 production *Du a Gwyn (Black and White)*, in which performers amended the images of a projected film, *The Silent Village*, and reconstructed events using filmic techniques such as slow motion and replay, moving the audience for them to consider the action from different viewpoints.[17] Brith Gof's move into postmodernism, with its suspicion and interrogation of metanarratives, seems particularly apposite for its representations of a culture repressed and oppressed by English imperialism and internal colonization for centuries. At this time, Pearson in particular was concerned with developing a new and young audience. He felt 'the forms we were developing were anachronistic. Our audience receives information in a much more cut-up, less controlled way . . . Videotape, electronic music and film are universally helpful. They help us to exist within a spectrum of expression congruent with the experience of our audience.'[18]

Cliff McLucas believed that the fact that the company was based in Aberystwyth up to the end of the 1980s was essential to the sense of cultural placement in their work:

The ability to lock into a Welsh authenticity and the intellectual rigour this demands were possible in the environment set up by the Barn Centre [a disused university building and community centre, originally an iron foundry] . . . When I heard about the plans for Theatre Ymchwil Cymru [the research centre], I thought the notion of this kind of institution in Aberystwyth was wonderful. Its failure to be realised, and Brith Gof's subsequent departure to Cardiff, removed them from this debate; now Brith Gof is about making pieces of work.[19]

The latter half of the 1980s and the early 1990s encompassed both a change in the company's performance techniques and a radical reinvention of the ways in which it presented its work. The employment of scenographers Trevor Turton in 1987 and McLucas in 1988 deeply affected the way in which they created action and speech in the performance space. *The Arminius Project* (Germany, 1988) stimulated and confirmed an interest for Pearson in the concept of 'task as theatre' and in what semioticians refer to as the 'iconic' level of perception (where what is presented, is what it is). Congruent with this was his 'disenchantment with the elaboration of physical narrative'[20] and his need to pursue a more open and simple form of action and gesture. The presence of John E. R. Hardy as company composer and musician (1987–92) allowed for a more sophisticated and complex soundscape to augment performance and scenographic work. The permanent recruitment of Hardy and McLucas at this juncture manifested the company's pursuit of a more equal status for these three elements in its work. Because of this and other artistic and personal reasons, the core members of the company – Jones, Hardy, McLucas and Pearson – began working apart in the developmental stages of their work on particular projects. This initial 'apartness', whereby each member developed structures and frameworks concerning their own specialization, became part of their creative and working policy. This arrangement probably derived from the early 1980s when, without a central director figure analogous to Eugenio Barba to strategize a cohesive style, individuals within the company pursued their own particular training schedules and performance techniques. This led to what Pearson terms 'mixed aesthetics'. As a method, it has its problems, particularly during the collaborative stages of the work, owing to individuals' emotional and creative investment in their own ideas. The collaborative juncture may involve the rupture of each individual's established way of thought and approach concerning the work to be created, and the synthesis of the disparate art forms that are now part of the company's production structure has become one of its most urgent and problematical concerns. It was partly responsible for the resignations of Jones and Hardy in 1992. Jones explains other reasons for her departure from Brith Gof:

> I had come to feel incarcerated by the notion of being the Welsh aspect of Brith Gof. It wasn't healthy for the company. Now, if I say something, it's me saying it, I don't have to be 'Welsh'. Brith Gof's audience is changing to reflect more honestly the make-up of the company.[21]

Jones has returned to work which requires no technical support; her most recent work *Rhiannon* explores the acoustic dynamic of the voice. Similarly, Pearson's interest shows signs of returning more directly to the exploration of the actor in space, and focus on gesture and voice: he has recently stated his sense of performance as being 'primarily in the body, in the pathology of the performer',[22] whereas technology might dictate that is operators control the audience's perception of the body in action. He also still subscribes to an emphasis on 'the oral nature of performance practice as opposed to the authority of written text'.[23] He proposes that 'Performance might . . . be reconstituted as a complex form of text which incorporated map, plan, section, projection, photograph and drawing, adjacent to, and overlapping, poem, libretto, list, technical data, music, etc.'[24] Along with Julian Thomas (a lecturer in archaeology), Pearson has proposed structures for assimilating Brith Gof's performance work using methods and practices associated with archaeology (which Pearson studied at degree level).[25] For McLucas, a trained architect, his involvement with the company has involved:

> creating meaning through creating a whole architecture for a piece, setting the agenda for all kinds of things. The word 'design' in theatre means, to me, a backdrop, a prettification of something which already exists. Architecture is a word I prefer; it's about deep structures in time and space.[26]

McLucas also cites US director Robert Wilson as an inspirational influence on his scenography for Brith Gof, which predominantly features elemental constituents: earth, water, fire and air. They are often contained by decaying or recycled industrial sites, either indoors or outdoors, which permit unusually radical use of distance in terms of height, width and length. A recent Brith Gof work for television about the drowning of Tryweryn, *Pen Bas, Pen Dwfn (Shallow End, Deep End)* (March 1995), used a swimming pool as its main scenic focus. There seems to be a fruitful point of contact between Pearson's idea of 'task as theatre' and McLucas's scenographic landscapes which need the performer to rise to the challenge of activating and animating them. Sêra Moore Williams, performer in *Gododdin*, described its demands as

> the most extreme frontier of what I was able to do physically as a performer . . . you made a serious contract with yourself in order to go through with it . . . because of the challenge in intellectual and emotional terms, things seem to happen in the moment.[27]

Brith Gof's work differs from the traditional theatre paradigm of the performer wrestling with complex literary texts; they may also wrestle with objects, environments, weather (the 1992 production *Haearn (Iron)* involved technologically produced wind, rain and snow) and other physical difficulties. Thus, Brith Gof's resistance to a merely reactionary or representative form of theatre is manifested in a contrasting revelation of experience in the moment of performance, seeking to implicate the spectators in the experience of a dynamic, of 'living through', from which they can be licensed to imagine and construct their own trajectories. Theatre becomes a ground for assessment and potential reconstruction, using original Welsh sources of inspiration but 'welded on to technical and political rationality',[28] international reference points and a will to 'sustain and absorb the shock of modern civilization'.[29]

Brith Gof's theatre 'unfurls its spiritual and cultural revindication'[30] of a complex national spirit which emanates from a determination to make art that allows for changes in understanding and redefinitions of self. It walks the tightrope of invention in the face of the insecurity produced by a climate of purposeful conservatism, which involves the marginalization of theatre art. In defiance of such pressures, 'They contribute to the possibility of imagining a future, instead of clinging to the irrelevances of the past',[31] and have proved to be the most dynamic force for change in Welsh theatre culture in the twentieth century.

Notes

1   Theodore Shank, *American Alternative Theatre* (London, Macmillan, 1982), p. 3.
2   Ibid.
3   Richard Schechner, *Environmental Theater* (New York, Hawthorn, 1973), p. 284.
4   *Brith Gof: A Welsh Theatre Company* (Pontypool, Mid Wales Litho, 1985), p. 5.
5   Ibid., p. 1.
6   Quoted in C. Savill, 'Women in Welsh theatre: saying their piece', *Planet*, 91 (February–March 1992), 69–73.
7   *Brith Gof*, p. 5.
8   Ibid., p. 3.
9   Ibid., p. 22.
10 Quoted in C. Savill, 'Dismantling the wall', *Planet*, 79 (February–March 1990), pp. 20–8.
11 Savill, 'Dismantling the wall', p. 22.
12 Letter from Lis Hughes Jones to the author, 29 February 1992 (translated from the Welsh).
13 Kenneth Frampton, 'Towards a critical regionalism: six points for an architecture of resistance', in Hal Foster (ed.), *The Anti-Aesthetic* (Washington, DC, Bay Press, 1983), p. xvi.
14 Pearson in interview with the author, 20 December 1992.
15 Jones in interview with the author, 2 October 1992.
16 Frampton, 'Towards a critical regionalism', xvi.
17 *Brith Gof*, p. 4.
18 Savill, 'Dismantling the Wall', p. 22.
19 McLucas in interview with the author, 21 August 1992.
20 Pearson in interview with the author, 20 December 1992.
21 Jones in interview with the author, 2 October 1992.
22 Mike Pearson, 'The script's not the thing', *New Welsh Review* (Spring 1995), 67–71 at p. 69.
23 Ibid., p. 71.
24 Ibid.
25 'Theatre/archaeology' by Mike Pearson comments by Julian Thomas in *Drama Review*, 38/4 (T144) (Winter 1994), 133–61.
26 McLucas in interview with the author, 21 August 1992.
27 Williams in interview with the author, 8 January 1993.
28 Frampton, 'Towards a critical regionalism', p. 16.
29 Ibid.
30 Ibid.
31 Savill, 'Dismantling the Wall', p. 28.

10 • Welsh Theatre and the World

Anna-Marie Taylor

5 March 1985. Thousands of Maerdy people and their supporters from Oxford, Birmingham and other places walked up the single road to the pit in the chilly dawn to see the miners go back to work . . . As they neared the pit, the lights with the television cameras were switched on and almost by instinct, it seemed, two dozen miners at the front of the procession, raised their fists into the air and shouted slogans like 'here we go' and 'we will win'. When the camera lights went out, they stopped immediately, and soon filed into the pithead baths to start work. On the television, later that day, it looked a heroic ending to their strike. At the time it had seemed merely a sad one.[1]

In the period under scrutiny, there have been events in Welsh public life that, in the way they were mediated to a wider audience, have displayed the characteristics of more formalized staged drama. The participants' lives have been brought to our attention, creating moments of memorable power amongst the quickly forgotten ordinariness of the everyday. One significant reason for such events lingering on in our memories, long after their occurence, and for their acquiring a wider cultural resonance and not disappearing into a chaos of ill-remembered pictures and events, may be this overlapping of everyday life and the expectations of drama. The pattern of social and political conflicts can correspond to recognized dramatic structures, as does the image of the event, framed by television cameraman or press photographer as exactly and carefully as a director would place an image within the architecture of the theatre.

Thus, the triumphant defeat (or defeated triumph?) of the mining community of Maerdy, that long march back to work after months of resistance and deprivation, stays with us long after 1985. Key meanings were conveyed in the visual image of the processional return (one of the oldest forms of dramatic enactment), both to witnesses on site and to a much wider public through television later on in the day.

The courage and solidarity of the valley community were immediately and movingly conveyed. Possibly at the time, and certainly with historical hindsight, the march back in the chilly dawn also assumed a significance that reached well beyond Maerdy itself. It signalled a historical break-point; namely, the new Tory defeat of old industrial south Wales, heralding great changes in Wales's economic and social structure.

This tangible, material sense of the forces of History being acted out, being put into motion, determines our remembrance of events in Maerdy.[2] Not all the events in Wales that linger on in our memories have the dramatic force and historical immediacy of the miners' return to work. However, they still evoke particular and shared meanings. Milk gushing from farmers' tankers in revolt at EEC quotas, a highly unpopular Minister of State for Wales grimacing and miming his way through the Welsh national anthem, second homes burning – all these images contribute towards 'a community of meaning' where the underlying intention of the action is made clear. In their visual impact, they share, with certain types of literary drama, a distillation of meaning around central visual images. Nora's stripped Christmas tree in Ibsen's *A Doll's House* (1879) signalling the destruction of her family life, Lear's monstrous wall in Edward Bond's *Lear* (1972) that marks his fanatical desire to control his territory, nearer to home Edward Thomas's crazed Lewis family cooped up in their *House of America* (1988), south Wales life gone mad in its post-industrial decline, all have correspondences with the freeze-framing of actual images of Welsh public life.

These events took place on a national stage. For most of us, the locus for the conventions of formal drama invading real life is much nearer to home. As anthropologist Victor Turner maintained,[3] the everyday can be transformed when our domestic and working lives become 'social performances' that correspond to (and occasionally mimic) the observances of 'cultural performances', that is the fictionalized behaviours found on stage, screen and in ritual.[4] Through cross-cultural studies, Turner analysed the manner in which conventional codes of daily behaviour were transformed, and the fashions in which social groups coalesced and fragmented through participation in such social performances. According to Turner, many of these public dramas echoed the action of play, artistic performance and ritual; the pattern of true life conflicts often following variations on a 'breach-crisis-redress-outcome' structure (a trajectory that corresponds to much written drama and that is well understood by canny managers and elders).

Wales, as has often been remarked, is a country of small communities, each locality marked out precisely and exactly in its inhabitants' minds, if not so clearly on a formal map or to outsiders. Within all these communities, be it hamlet or suburb, Turnerian social dramas constantly take place, with outcomes that include the realignment of local identity and the consolidation of group alliances. Taking my experience of living in a closely defined community (a village just outside Aberystwyth) for almost a decade, my time there was full of countless group actions that followed Turner's scheme of events — regroupings around proposed road and building developments, conflict around sheltered housing for mental patients, consternation at the vicar's desire to modernize the churchyard. Apart from these conflicts that involved many in the village, other events remained less public but presumably 'moved through stages of Turner's observed pattern of behaviour, the private griefs, feuds, triumphs and declines, Raymond Williams's 'modern tragedies' of personal life.

The unshaped ordinariness of real life, when invaded and transformed by the extraordinary, can correspond to the appearance and structure of more aestheticized drama, as is evident in the way some news events are mediated to us and in the fashion in which local conflicts are frequently acted out and resolved. What is the result if we reverse the relationship and look at ways in which the outside world also shadows and invades the world of the theatre? How have Welsh playwrights and practitioners dramatized the experience of living in modern Wales? What is the relationship between Welsh theatre and inchoate, boundless 'reality'?

To begin with the audience for drama in Wales, the immediate interface between theatre and the world, one of the features of this period has been the theatre's apparent lack of centrality in the lives of many in Wales. A recent study of theatre-going in south Wales[5] indicates that many people went to the theatre rarely, considering themselves 'regular theatre-goers' on the strength of going to the theatre twice a year. However, despite such infrequency of attendance it would be an unusual inhabitant of Wales who had had no contact with some form of theatrical or dramatic activity over the year – be it visiting the pantomime, variety or summer season show, attending a school play, Eisteddfod recitation or amateur drama entertainment.

The connection many in Wales have with theatrical activity is a demotic, celebratory, sometimes localized one; on occasion an expensive treat, frequently a convivial night out with family and friends.

Clearly the large proportion of the theatrical activity on offer in Wales reflects such a pattern of theatre-going. Drama that falls outside the category of pure entertainment, particularly new writing, and that is challenging and radical in its concerns and presentation, has commonly had problems attracting an audience. Furthermore, the transgression of the boundaries between the stage and everyday life (exemplified by an 'all too real' display of nudity, raw language and violent action) has been denounced and discussed in the Welsh press with much more vehemence and more frequency than in the English regions where there is a longer-established tradition of theatrical work, a population that is by and large not even vestigially religious, and possibly newspapers with fewer 'slow news' days.

The suspicion of drama felt by many, and lack of attendance at the theatre, has meant that for a number of practitioners, the starting-point for the work has been the audience itself. Several companies have drawn in a public through incorporating the histories and lives of the audience into the theatrical event. Working in this semi-documentary way has been the hallmark of groups such as Bara Caws in Caernarfon, Valley and Vale in the Garw Valley and Theatre West Glamorgan in Neath who, complementing the growth in interest in oral and local history, have used their work to uncover and enact histories that have not necessarily appeared in official accounts.

A characteristic of such drama is the direct involvement of the audience, be it in critical viewing and discussion in the case of Theatre in Education or in the engagement of local amateur actors alongside professionals in the large-scale community plays seen in Wales in recent years. Theatr Taliesin's work with poet/playwright Menna Elfyn on a modern nativity play *Trefn Teyrnas Wâr (The Great and Good Kingdom)* in 1990, for example, involved the farming village of Crymych in Dyfed, and Charles Way's *Bordertown* for Monmouth in 1990 investigated Welsh/English relations in early modern times with a large cast of local players.

If we move away from the audience to the producers of drama, the democratic exchange between locality and professional theatre, as expressed in community plays has been reshaped and extended in the work of Brith Gof that has used large-scale events (such as *Haearn*

(*Iron*) (1992) and *Tri Bywyd* (*Three Lives*) (1995) to set up complex negotiations between the participants, witnesses and chosen site.[6] Thus the performance of *Haearn* on a disused industrial site in Tredegar presented not only the immediate history of the chosen place but also contained extracts from Mary Shelley's *Frankenstein*, images of the Industrial Revolution and of Greek creation myths. Here the history of the chosen place existed alongside other narratives to create a complex layering of meanings. Similarly, *Tri Bywyd* took over a specific setting, a ruined farm in the forest near Lampeter, creating three separate loci within the abandoned farmstead Esgair Frath. The life of the last generation to farm at Esgair Frath, the history of Sarah Jacob of Llanfihangel-ar-arth who starved to death (a *cause célèbre* of the last century), and the murder on James Street in Butetown of prostitute Lynette White all inhabited the site as simultaneous geographies.

The use of multiple narratives, with historical subjects placed within and alongside fictitious stories, has been a prominent trait of Brith Gof's practice since the mid-1980s. Discrete boundaries between 'social performances' and 'cultural performances' have been tested and sometimes demolished in stagings that recognize the onslaught on 'reality' through the conflation of the real and the fictional in new media and information technology.

For contemporary dramatists, this hybridity between social and cultural performances has been both liberating and problematic. Naturalism, the accepted and (through television and film) widely disseminated dramatic code in which to convey social reality has been under strident attack in recent years for its limited and limiting form – even more than earlier in the century, when naturalistic expression was lambasted by practitioners such as Brecht, Meyerhold and Piscator, and rejected by writers including Strindberg and Pirandello. For writers in Wales, it has proved difficult to find modes of dramatic presentation that have the audacity and experimental edge of groups that have worked independently of playwrights. In many ways the single unifying authority and individual imagination of the writer have been at odds with the radical pluralism and physicalized performance style of groups such as Volcano, Brith Gof and Man Act, as well as the collective process of devising central to much of Bara Caws's and Theatre West Glamorgan's work.

Some writers such as Alan Osborne, Peter Lloyd and Sean Mathias have preferred consistent realism over more experimental forms, matching up dramatic expression to their subject matter. Their plays have often concerned themselves with closely observed case studies and social histories of those denied power in modern Wales, as is evident in Osborne's tale of Merthyr losers in *The Redemption Song*, Peter Lloyd's account of petty criminality and Thatcherite business culture in *The Scam*, and Sean Mathias's portrayal of a sad, young girl desperate for affection in *A Prayer for Wings*. Such detailed scrutiny of milieu and speech, and a concern with how economic deprivation can thwart human possibilities, perhaps also links these dramatists to the humanistic realism of other Welsh writers such as Gwyn Thomas, Emyr Humphreys and Raymond Williams.

Other writers have extended realistic form more audaciously. Edward Thomas's *House of America* (1988) appropriates the claustrophobic family drama, and, as with Gwyn Thomas's *The Keep* (1960), creates a 'state of the nation' play, this time of a country playing out an endgame and in terminal decline. *The Keep* outlines the main currents of Rhondda life in the early 1950s, offering escape from Wales as the inevitable solution to the frustrated members of the family 'kept' inside the home and the inward-looking prejudices of their locality. The later drama shows us an equally imprisoned family, the Lewises, who are deprived of the promise of escape elsewhere in Britain or America. Trapped together in a house undermined by open-cast mining and presided over by a mad murdering mam, the younger generation fill their underemployed hours watching videos, drinking, popping pills and acting out incestuous desires. In *House of America* the form and structure of *The Keep* is further exaggerated to conjure up a south Wales deprived of hope, work and moral certainty.

Thomas has extended his writing in a number of powerful plays that have expressed what he sees as the dead-end situation of modern Wales, an overlooked country clinging to the edge of Europe, cut off from any kind of heroic past and communal present. This sense of being trapped in a dying land haunts *Flowers of the Dead Red Sea* (1991), a sparse and surreal meditation on life and death carried out between two slaughterhousemen, and *East from the Gantry* (1992) that, along with the depiction of a failed marriage and a teenager's death from flying from a gantry, shows us how the 'cultural performances' of television (here in the guise of soap operas, weather forecasts and Westerns) thoroughly permeate our 'social perform-ances'. *Song from a Forgotten City* (1995) pleasurably conveys this conflation of media and reality in its appropriation of *film noir* techniques to explore the nature of Welsh masculinity through the antiheroic antics of three men together in a down-at-heel Cardiff hotel.

The idea of human behaviour being a constant negotiation between surface appearances, many aped from television and film, is prominent in Ian Rowlands's plays. *Love in Plastic* (1995) depicts a hopelessly sincere young man whose honesty is tested by the hypocrisy and superficiality of both his love object, an actress of a certain age, and her odious agent. *Glissando on an Empty Harp* (1994) features two pedantic philosophizing tramps on the Thames Embankment, who along with a grotesque talking head, meander around the meaning of life and art, and the merits of beer and angels. Rowlands, like Edward Thomas, has skilfully explored the rhythms and clichés of south Walian English in his work. Such quirky affection for native idiom is also shared by Tim Rhys whose darkly comic work deflates the pretensions and cultural icons of south Wales, as in *Dead Man's Fall* (1989) and *The Ghost of Morgan Morris* (1990) which gleefully detail the kidnapping of a deceased rugby celebrity. Similarly, Laurence Allan, in plays such as *A Blow to Butetown* (1988), dealing with disempowerment caused by urban development through the personal odyssey of an old black Cardiffian, and *The Best Years of Our Lives* (1990), set ten years after the miners' strike, dissects contemporary south Wales life with mordant black humour and a keen ear for dialogue.

Writers working outside a shared cultural position have sometimes found it difficult to ally themselves to particular versions of 'Welsh theatre'. Lucy Gough in plays such as *Joanna* (1990), *Crossing the Bar* (1994) and *Lady of the Shadows* (Radio 3, 1995) has created a particular and idiosyncratic theatrical world. Entrapment (the key location of modern Welsh theatre), as well as religion's denial of physicality, feature prominently in these plays that imaginatively re-create the life of nineteenth-century visionary Joanna Southcote, a medieval nun, a young remand prisoner and Tennyson's Lady of Shalott respectively. The most prolific playwright of the period was Dic Edwards. Edward's often disturbing work is concerned like Thomas's with offering alternatives to consistent realism in its presentation, and uses highly charged, oratorial language in its desire to chart epic journeys of interior discovery. Perhaps most perturbingly, the writer delineates the ways in which particular social and economic structures can deform and distort human identity and behaviour. Edwards's plays are hard to characterize, tackling, as they have done recently, the oppression of medieval peasants in *Regan (in the Great Society)* (1992), a seedy impotent Casanova in *Casanova Undone* (1992), a philosopher's daughter searching for her origins in *Wittgenstein's Daughter* (1993), British academics' responses to a Bosnian refugee in *Three Deaths of an Idiot* (1994) and in *Utah Blue* (1995) the unsettling inner life of American serial killer Gary Gilmore.

This discussion of the fluctuating relationships between the everyday and the theatre has been highly tentative, recognizing the overlap between aesthetic and real-life drama as problematic and unstable. We live in a highly fictionalized age. We are presented by a host of stories daily. We gossip and embellish news at home and at work. We switch on the television and radio, go to the cinema, read novels and magazines. We are constantly invited to partake in the lives of others, from the vicissitudes of American footballers to the lives and deaths of former royal daughters-in-law.

For those working in theatre in Wales, staged drama's power to contend with the glossier, highly publicized attractions of television and cinema and to offer up stories within this ocean of narratives must at times seem woefully deficient. Many companies and playwrights have entered the fray by incorporating and appropriating televisual and cinematic styles of presentation, or by reclaiming an assured and adventurous theatricality. What does seem sadly lacking in much work in the theatre, however, is an ability to create images, locations and histories that have a cultural and imaginative resonance beyond the immediate. Oddly enough, whilst there is much to celebrate about Welsh theatre's success in establishing itself in the last decade and a half and, as I have outlined, there have been instances of resonant and powerful writing, the world of Wales outside the theatre does seem to have created more lasting moments of memorable drama in the widest sense.

Notes

1   Raphael Samuel, Barbara Bloomfield, and Guy Boanas, *The Enemy Within: Pit Villages and the Miners' Strike of 1984–5* (London, Routledge, Kegan & Paul, 1986), p. 165.

2   This was also seen most vividly in the fall of the Berlin Wall in 1989: the

physical destruction of the barrier between two systems showing graphically the toppling of the East German state.

3 Victor Turner, *The Anthropology of Performance* (New York, Performing Arts Journals, 1986).

4 Richard Schechner, *Performance Theory* (London, Routledge, 1988), outlines social and cultural performances in detail.

5 As discovered through audience research conducted in the Cardiff area by the Sherman Theatre in 1994.

6 Cf. Brith Gof, *Y Llyfr Glas* (Cardiff, Brith Gof, 1995).

7 Nic Ros in Chapter 2 outlines Welsh-language writing.

11 • Land of Dance:
Recent Developments in Dance Theatre

Anna-Marie Taylor

Wales has often been constructed as a land of song, but it might seem quite odd to find it referred to as a land of dance. For some, such a term may bring back distant memories of tea dances on the pier of many a seaside resort and, beyond such pleasurable remembrance of times past, perhaps even murkier ancestral accounts of *dawnsio haf* (May-dancing) in rural villages. However, modern images of Welsh people dancing are few and far between. Contestants in freshly ironed peasant attire competing at the Eisteddfod come immediately to mind, but you would have to search long and hard for commonly recognized pictures of Welsh people dancing today, possibly thinking in the end of little girls in leotards at church-hall ballet classes, the likes of Shirley Bassey and Tom Jones slinking across the stage, and maybe even boisterous women enjoying karaoke disco night in the local pub.

Unlike Scotland and several English regions, Wales does not possess that mainstay of metropolitan bourgeois culture, a housed ballet company, and it was only in 1981 that the Arts Council of Wales established a Dance Committee. Indeed, not so long ago, dance outside its eisteddfodic forms was not viewed by many to be part of Wales's cultural agenda; dance is omitted as an art and popular form from many an account of Welsh life. Unsupported in these ways, however, Wales is rapidly establishing itself as a nation of dance, the last fifteen years witnessing a real turnabout in dance's fortunes as an art form to be taken seriously. There has been a remarkable flourishing of professional and community-based work. In 1984 Wales had two full-time community dance and two professional touring companies, by 1994 these totals had grown to nine and twenty respectively. And this very swift coming of age in the areas of dance and performance was marked in 1993 by the very successful choice of Diversions, Earthfall, Emma Carlson Dance and Paradox Shuffle to promote Welsh culture at the Stuttgart festival. Wales's identity as a dancing nation has been further promoted by the tours of individual groups abroad – in 1994 Emma Carlson Dance could be found touring Germany, the Ukraine and the Netherlands, while Diversions visited Indonesia and Earthfall performed in Slovenia.

Within Wales, there have been a number of active attempts to set up community dance projects, steered by the Dance Committee of the Arts Council and Community Dance Wales who together with individual workers have extended the form's popular and artistic base. Building on the notion that, of all the means of artistic expression, dance is probably the one that most of us have participated in (even if in an amateur and self-conscious way), community dance projects have encouraged access to all kinds of dance. Popularization, though, does not mean simplification, and the members of the community dance movement have also been at pains to provide training and educational work, demystifying aspects of dance perceived as esoteric and élitist; and shaping practical work that is challenging, technically confident and socially relevant. An exemplary instance of this manner of working can be found in Dawns Dyfed's Cyrff Ystwyth that integrates professional dancers with adults with learning difficulties and whose composition Lle (Place) (1994) stretched each participant's physical and creative capacities in a group exploration of individual lives within the Ceredigion landscape. What has been evident in both professional and community dance work is not only its participants' commitment to their practice (many work very hard for modest wages or exist on small grants), but also, as with Lle, the dance-workers' desire to question and explore the bounds of their discipline. In particular, this questioning has, appropriately enough, centred around notions of Welshness and internationalism; with the former interrogated more extensively in work from outside Cardiff.

Cardiff is undoubtedly the focal point for dance and dance-theatre (the definitions are on the whole interchangeable), with an informed and enthusiastic audience, a lively performance culture that incorporates musicians, visual artists, actors, as well as choreographers and dancers (a number of whom have also performed with physical theatre groups such as Brith Gof and Moving Being), and a well-advanced plan for a National Centre for Dance and Choreography. Most of the professional companies are resident in the capital, and their body of work has been international in its focus, both in subject-matter and in its appropriation and redefinition of both Western and non-Western dance forms, traditional and modern.

Diversions, the best-subsidized and longest-lived company, provides in its repertoire forceful examples of this kind of work. The
company creates dance pieces from within the company (above all by
its artistic director Roy Campbell-Moore) as well as collaborating on
commissioned work with outside choreographers, as was the case in
its realization of *Exhibo* (1992), a hauntingly abstract evocation of
mood from Finland's Kenneth Kvarnstrom, and in *Collecting Gravity*
(1993) by the USA's Terry Beck, a bitter-sweet meditation on human
survival based around the self-interested hoarding and sharing of
green apples. The company has built up a well-received and varied
repertoire of pieces that can risk works such as *Exhibo* that refuse
stubbornly to reveal precise meanings, alongside more jokey and
ironic compositions that have a theatrical flavour and often play with
the social rituals and cultural codes of Western living. Such an
offering was the celebrated Amercan choreographer Bill T. Jones's
pleasurably cacophonous *History of Collage Revisited* (1991) that
welded together snatches of political events, accounts of dreams and
the language of clothes amongst other fragments in an unashamedly
postmodern way. The smaller Cardiff-based companies have also
displayed such abstraction coupled with an enjoyment of the vagaries
of modern living, as in Emma Carlson's 1994 *Midnight Zone* that led
us through physically exacting images of sleep and dreaming.

One of the most ground-breaking companies at present is Earthfall
Dance whose work has consistently tested limits of dance expression.
Nomads (1989) drew on the absorption by the artistic directors,
Jessica Cohen and Jim Ennis, of non-Western dance and cultural
forms into their work – an interculturalism similar to that of Brith
Gof's earlier work and seen at present in some activities within the
women's performance network, the Magdalena Project. *Nomads*
depicted with much wit a series of encounters between a masquerade
figure and two mosquito-blighted, handbag-toting Western women,
who were seen escaping from the prisons of their cultural training,
eventually celebrating their liberated physicality as barefoot co-
revellers.

This poundingly strenuous piece came close at times to elevating
the supposedly raw worlds of primitive peoples far above those
deemed to be over-cooked by Western civilization, a valorization of
the primitive not uncommon in twentieth-century performance. By
1994, Earthfall's interest in cultural exhange had become much more
developed and refined. *i and i*, which opened in Ljubljana at the

beginning of that year, dispensed with the tight narrative structure of *Nomads* and, in a much more complex dissection of cultural identity, offered a series of individual and group responses to the now almost legendary image of two lovers (one Muslim, one Serb) found dead in each other's arms while fleeing from Sarajevo in 1993. Alongside and within these responses were woven the memories (in Welsh, English and Portuguese) and relationships of six performers from different artistic and social backgrounds. Elegiac and aggressive, this powerfully structured work was partly acted out on a specially commissioned installation, creating moments of tender separation amidst violent togetherness.

It is not only the touring professional companies that have examined cultural and social identity through dance. West Glamorgan Dance project (now Tân Dance) has a well-established link with dancers in Germany, South Africa and Lithuania; there have been exchange visits in the past, and a highly complicated four-part collaboration, based on Dylan Thomas's 'The Boys of Summer', was created by its artistic director Carol Brown with its Lithuanian counterpart for 1995's City of Literature in Swansea. Within West Glamorgan itself, the enterprising project has established Dynion, a pioneering male dance group (for despite club and rave culture, it is still largely women who participate in community dance classes). Dynion features amateur dancers of all backgrounds. Its work, *Man to Man* (1994), investigated masculinity and young men's self-identity.

Questions of selfhood also preoccupy Welsh-language dance group Camre Cain, in whose work versions of Wales and different constructions of Welshness coexist and jostle for authority. Growing out of the testing dance work of its choreographer Margaret Ames with Dawns Dyfed, the pieces performed by Camre Cain since its inception in 1990 have proved to be multi-voiced and multi-layered, drawing on both high and popular Welsh culture, and trying to create a dance vocabulary that corresponds to the rhythms of spoken Welsh.

Comisiwn (Rhif 3) (Commission (Number 3)) drew its choreographic inspiration from a cycle of poems by Iwan Llwyd about human existence and nature in the Bangor area; from Brychan Llŷr the music of rock band Jess was added to create an extra level of stage interest and to draw in a young audience. *Rhif 4 (Number 4)*, performed in 1994, took as its starting-point Wales as the postmodern nation *par excellence*, each of us carrying different ideas of Welshness within ourselves. In much of Camre Cain's work media constructions of Wales are examined, not with a Baudrillardian fascination with Western culture as the overloaded land of signs, but with a sense of anger at feeling disenfranchised in Welsh-speaking rural Wales from significant centres of power and decision-making.

In contrast to the popularizing and politicized eclecticism of Camre Cain's challenging work, Sioned Huws has created dance work which is highly discreet and delicately wrought. Trained as a dancer in London and New York, Huws marked her return to her native land in *Llanw a Thrai (Ebb and Flow)* (1992) and *Distyll y Don (Ebb of a Wave)* (1993), revivifying the north Wales landscapes of her farm childhood. For these pieces, she fused her contemporary dance training (Laban and Cunningham-based) with traditional *dawnsio gwerin* (folk dance). Sioned Huws learnt Welsh country dance anew, seeing in its patterning and in its closeness to the ground a connection with a living Welsh past tied to the seasons, planet and elements – an intimation of an older agrarian existence that can be forgotten in the formal codification of such dances for competitions. A highly precise practitioner, her method of working is slow and laborious, creating deliberate and gently repetitive movements inspired by the Llŷn countryside, and devising work that can appear like a deliberate refusal of contemporary dance's fast-moving and internationalist mainstream. Uncompromisingly grounded in a north Walian rural world, Sioned Huws's work has great authenticity and courage – qualities that made themselves evident in *Carthen (Blanket)* (1994), a duet with a male dancer, in which she investigated the texture and patterns of traditional blankets, also incorporating into her choreography the sounds and movements of mill-weaving processes.

Such small-scale intimacy and quiet observation seem a long way from the outward-looking and often hard-edged dance practices prominent in Cardiff. Susan Sontag wrote in a poetic assessment of the dancer's art:

> You eat with your hands, dance on your legs.
> Eating can be right-handed or left-handed.
> Is dancing left-legged or right-legged?
> Any place is the centre.[1]

Dancing in Wales lends itself to Sontag's enigmatic conceit. First, in the practitioners' often experimental search for modes of physical expression, there is very often no real centre of meaning beyond the immediacy of the dancer's body; an often exhilarating ephemerality that, as in Antonin Artaud's desire to create a physicalized theatre, can create an understanding that goes 'beyond words'.

On a less recondite level, contemporary dance appears to have developed in a more open and confident way than many other Welsh artistic and literary practices in the last decade. It does not seem to see itself as having to be nationally representative, nor is it hampered by a received tradition. Both esoteric and accessible, declaredly experimental yet eager to consolidate its place in popular culture, dance here does not appear to elevate any one particular version of itself. All activity is the centre: be it the physical challenge and interculturalism of its Cardiff proponents, Sioned Huws's reticence, amateur folk and flamenco dance, Bharatha Natyam performed in south Wales's Indian communities, or the Friday-night drinker providing entertainment with a well-practised Tom Jones routine at karaoke night.[2]

Notes

[1] Susan Sontag, *Dancers on a Plane,* Catalogue of Jasper John/Merce Cunningham Exhibition at Anthony d'Offay Gallery (London, 1989).
[2] This essay has been adapted from 'Wales: Land of dance', in *Planet* 106 (August 1994), pp. 62–8.

12 • Genesis and Revelations: Theatr Clwyd

Bob Roberts

Theatr Clwyd Mold, or to be more precise, the Theatr Clwyd Arts Centre could, with some justification, be called the Eighth Wonder of Wales, notwithstanding the miscellaneous nature of the original Seven. In spite of protracted and clamorous opposition from the planning stage in 1972, the then Flintshire County Council under the dynamic leadership of the late T. M. Haydn Rees, the county's chief executive, pressed on regardless with the first phase of the development and it was opened officially by Her Majesty the Queen in 1976. A proposal to complete the project by constructing a concert hall/opera house was deferred indefinitely. The subversive Welsh Phantom of the Opera was active at that time too!

Mold is a small market town with a population of about 10,000. In the early 1970s, when the proposal to build a county civic centre complete with a sizeable theatre and an educational technology centre was made, the whole concept seemed to many people to be far too ambitious and elaborate given the size of the town. There was no apparent popular demand for a theatre, although the community did not possess one. It was considered that the school halls that were available to the community were adequate as performing venues. Particularly strong reservations were also voiced by many councillors and members of the general public regarding the problems of adequately funding such a monumental project and the awesome legacy of maintaining it once it was built. However, much of the hostility was parochial and insular in essence. Many people argued with sincerity and conviction that Mold and the adjacent rural localities simply could not sustain a development on such a grandiose scale. They could not, or probably would not, accept the fact that the instigators of the project had a wider and more relevant view of the demographic context. It is calculated that over 200,000 people live within fifteen kilometres of Theatr Clwyd, 575,000 within thirty kilometres and 2.5 million within fifty kilometres. It is estimated that fifteen million people live within two hours' travelling time. Of these, 412,000 live in the former County of Clwyd. Within the Clwyd area, the percentages of population by age are: under sixteen 20, sixteen–twenty-nine 21, thirty–forty-four 20, forty-five–sixty-four 21, over sixty-five 18.

When the cultural context is considered, one finds that the results of research into attitudes to the arts and attendance at arts events in Wales provide an important perspective on the place of Theatr Clwyd within the community it serves. The findings of the Beaufort In-Depth Attitudinal Research (November 1993) commissioned by the Arts Council of Wales include:

- A much larger proportion of the population of Wales than most people think, 56 per cent, attend a wide range of arts events, 51 per cent at least once a year or more often. (The definition of 'arts events' covers the full range of activities offered by Theatr Clwyd, including cinema and exhibitions.)
- Mid Glamorgan and Clwyd lead Wales with the highest proportion of arts attenders.
- Attendance appears to be affected by access and availability in different parts of Wales.

The presence of Theatr Clwyd within the region appears to be an important factor in the statistical evidence of the Beaufort research that 65 per cent of the population of Clwyd attend arts events. Thus, far from being a minority interest, the activities offered by Theatr Clwyd attract, or fall within the existing interests of, almost two-thirds of the population of the region. This evidence confounds the proposition that Theatr Clwyd's activities represent the interests of an élite minority.

Theatr Clwyd is located in a bilingual area of Wales. The Beaufort Research demonstrates that attendance at arts events, in English as well as in Welsh, is higher among Welsh-speakers. Although the role of the Theatr Clwyd Company has traditionally been to present plays in English, the arts complex as a whole has a clear responsibility to define a role within a bilingual culture.

Since 1976 Theatr Clwyd has developed broadly along the lines established at the outset, as a major English-language professional theatre company with a brief to tour within Wales, whose work is complemented by a programme of visiting performance activity (drama, dance, music, opera), film and exhibitions. The full potential of the educational technology centre was never realized and the television facilities were leased to HTV until they reverted to Theatr Clwyd in 1992. However, a range of Outreach education and community activities has been developed serving schools and communities throughout Clwyd.

The theatre's first arts administrator Roger Tomlinson, and its first resident artistic director George Roman, with the support of the Board of Governors, initiated a policy of presenting a varied international repertoire with an ongoing commitment to stimulate and support the work of Welsh-born dramatists, whether they work in English, Welsh or both languages. Furthermore, the policy also involved an obligation to arrange regular tours of the principal Welsh venues (Theatr Gwynedd Bangor, Theatr Y Werin Aberystwyth and the Sherman Theatre Cardiff) with suitable productions.

The Theatr Clwyd Company opened the theatre's activities in March 1976 with a production of *Macbeth* directed by George Roman, thereby defying the traditional theatrical superstition that this play is often the source of bad luck and even catastrophe! Since then, the company has presented nearly 220 productions, averaging eleven productions a year, which, by any standards, is a remarkably prolific output. There has also been, over the twenty years, a formidable input of professional and amateur drama in Welsh and English, ranging from the leading English-language touring companies, the professional companies working in Welsh, to amateur one-act play festivals and school productions.

A study of Theatr Clwyd's repertoire over the last twenty years will confirm that the policy laid down when the theatre opened in 1976 has been broadly adhered to. It certainly represents a strong international dimension, with regular productions of Shakespeare (about twenty in all). There is also an extensive choice of the definitive European classics (approximately seventy) and a formidable variety of modern plays, including serious drama, comedies (black and otherwise), farces and musicals. As to the clause in the policy which mentions work by Welsh-born dramatists writing in English, I could only count about thirteen plays in a period of two decades. This seems to me to be little more than a token representation, allowing for the fact that there is only a handful of dramatists of Welsh origin writing in English, and quite a number of those confine themselves to television. It is my contention that Theatr Clwyd could have made a more significant contribution in this area, had the directors commissioned more work by a wider selection of Welsh-born writers.

Theatr Clwyd's repertoire also reflected the main thrust of the European theatre since the beginning of the century. There were examples of 'naturalism' and the 'well-made play' pioneered by Zola and Ibsen, and examples from the 1940s and 1950s when playwrights started to modify the traditional rules and to introduce an extension of the subject-matter of drama in general. There were also plays representing new developments where the nature and function of theatre are questioned and dismantled. All in all, it was a comprehensive repertoire within an arbitrary historical framework. Inevitably, it had to combine popular tastes with the artistic priorities of the directors.

A rough analysis of the repertoire indicates that the selection of plays falls into the following categories: European classics, including Shakespeare (43 per cent), modern 'straight' drama (24), modern comedies, e.g. by Ayckbourn (22), plays by Welsh-born writers (6) and farces/musicals (5). I hasten to add that this is not a scientific analysis, but merely an indication that any regional theatre has to provide as wide a choice as is compatible with popular taste and its own artistic integrity. I should point out also that the above observations apply specifically to the Theatr Clwyd Company. When one considers the totality of the theatre's work, including the substantial input by visiting companies, then the balance could vary to some degree. The overall quality of the productions has been highly satisfactory, with a number of exceptional productions providing memorable theatrical experiences that extend the boundaries of drama as an interpretative art.

Over the two decades since 1976 the theatre has had three artistic directors and one associate artistic director. The first director (1976–85) was George Roman. He was of Hungarian origin, and a one-time lecturer at the University of Wales Swansea. His main characteristics were his natural ebullience, his depth of knowledge of European theatre in particular, and the continental musicality of his diction. In my opinion, George Roman was the most intellectual of the three directors. His productions generally resulted from sustained analysis of the texts and the application of ideas, which not only governed the treatment of the texts, but also the mode of their presentation. Occasionally, this resulted in an organic artistic unity which raised the productions above the ordinary. One example of this was his striking production of Dürrenmatt's *The Physicists* in November 1980. There were also occasions when this fusion of concept and content was absent, and these productions were not as successful.

After a period of nine years, during which he developed the company and put the theatre on the map, George Roman was succeeded by the distinguished stage and television director Toby Robertson. He was artistic director from 1985 to 1992. Ned Sherrin in his book *Theatrical Anecdotes* refers to Mr Robertson as 'an inspired provincial and touring director'. Toby Robertson brought his immense experience and know-how to Theatr Clwyd. He is a man of formidable presence and powerful intellect in the Tyrone Guthrie mould. His forte was his ability to get into the very core of a text and present it on stage in vivid theatrical terms.

He was particularly successful with dialectical plays – one memorable example was his production of Ibsen's *An Enemy of the People* in 1991. His extensive contacts in the higher echelons of the business enabled him to acquire the services of some of the most celebrated actors and actresses in the country, such as Eileen Atkins, Vanessa Redgrave and many more. This certainly raised the theatre's profile not only in Wales, but throughout the British theatrical scene.

Toby Robertson's associate artistic director was the irrepressible Annie Castledine (1985–7). Her productions stand out for their freshness, originality and sheer brio. Her particular contribution to Theatr Clwyd's repertoire was her ability to incorporate a feminist viewpoint in powerful theatrical terms. Not that all her productions were overtly feminist. Annie's vision was more universal and she was much more than a mere propagandist. She had a marvellous gift for using space creatively and for assembling stage pictures that evolved naturally from the texts. She could also put together intimate and intensely personal scenes with cinematic precision. There was always a basic clarity and vivacity in her productions that audiences found most appealing. Theatr Clwyd's third artistic director was the remarkable Helena Kaut-Howson (1992–5). She was a vastly experienced stage director, having worked in Poland and Israel and many other parts of the world. She had a particular gift for creating epic theatre. Her productions penetrated parts of her audiences' collective psyche that were never reached by run-of-the-mill productions. She had a theatrical vision which combined universality with a striking individuality, as exemplified by her productions of *The*

Devils (1992), *The Rose Tattoo* (1995) and *Full Moon* (1994). Unfortunately, her tenure was curtailed for internal political reasons and the extreme financial pressures that resulted from government policy. The termination of her contract caused a furore on which I do not intend to comment. However, I am convinced that if Helena Kaut-Howson had been given the time and the opportunity, she could have made Theatr Clwyd into a venue of international significance.

Theatr Clwyd can justly claim to have made a very considerable contribution to the cultural life of north Wales over the last twenty years. It has enabled local communities, as well as visitors from over the border in England, to enjoy high-quality professional theatre, music, dance and visual arts. It has given the theatre in Wales a prestige and an identity that it did not previously possess. It has enhanced the quality of life in these parts by becoming a focus for cultural endeavour for all those who are interested in the creative process, whether they are amateurs or professionals.

However, it must be said that the theatre had its downside as well. There have been personality clashes and disputes that have had an adverse effect on the theatre's work as well as its image. The constant battle against financial constraints has also inhibited progress. The Theatr Clwyd Company, in spite of the distinguished performers and directors that have been associated with it, has not yet established a distinctive house style. Furthermore, the Welsh dimension of its work is still not nearly as significant as it should be: this is a theatre in Wales and not in the Home Counties.

In spite of recent traumas and tribulations that resulted in the theatre having to suffer a great deal of negative publicity, it is hoped that, with the appointment of a new artistic director imminent (and likely to be the very experienced Terry Hands), the theatre can look forward to a period of renewed creativity and co-ordinated endeavour. It has tremendous potential both as a national centre of excellence and as a focus for local aspirations. Many of the theatre's detractors were of the opinion that Theatr Clwyd had been skating on thin ice for a long time, and they wanted to be there when it cracked. However, it did not crack and I, for one, hope that it never will!

13 • The Graveyard of Ambition?

Greg Cullen

From the deprivation of housing estates in London's Hackney, and its vibrant arts centre, Chats Palace, where I worked variously as an actor, playwright and director, I arrived to be told that sheep outnumbered people in Powys. In September 1983 I attended my first company meeting at Theatr Powys and found that I could barely squeeze into the room. Over forty people were perched on broken chairs, window sills, radiators and were liberally strewn across the dubious-looking carpet. The debate was angry, informed, hilarious and stressful. We all knew times were getting harder. The room was full of smoke. When the Manpower Services Commission stopped its support for arts workers in 1984 the job losses at Theatr Powys were reported on national network news.

I had been appointed writer in residence, the second person to hold such a post at Theatr Powys thanks to Welsh Arts Council funding. The contract was for six months during which time I would write a version of the Snow Queen for the annual Christmas tour of Wales and a small-scale show to tour Young Farmers' Clubs in Powys, in spring 1984. The WAC was very disappointed that the job had not gone to a Welsh writer. The fact was that at that time there were few Welsh playwrights around.

With the job came a huge dose of confusion. Working in the East End I was used to people's suspicions of 'artists'. In Powys you are simply labelled 'hippy'. This expression seemed quaint to me, it does not any more. I despise its connotations as much as I despised the attitudes of the National Front. I consider myself to be Anglo-Irish, the son of a Catholic family from Dublin and a Protestant, Orange Order, family from Londonderry; my childhood was full of conflict, stories and significant places. After twelve years Mid Wales has become a significant place to me for reasons other than my career but including my imagination.

In Llandrindod Wells the theatre and dance companies were a social group within the town. They knew few if any local people.

They drank together, partied together and slept together. Here was the largest community arts organization I had ever worked for and yet they had few links with the community. Few company members had a real feel for the area and most saw their stay as a stopping-off place on their careers.

Theatr Powys was touring Theatre in Education (TIE) projects to the primary and secondary schools, touring theatre venues with large-scale tours such as *Julius Caesar* and *Accidental Death of an Anarchist*, small-scale touring to targeted audiences such as youth clubs or the WIs. Then there was the annual Christmas show which attracted about 7,000 people.

Bob Thomson the director of the company when I arrived was a dynamic and skilful manager as well as an accomplished director. Alongside John Greatorex, the company's founder, now county drama adviser and nominal artistic director of Theatr Powys, this dynamic community organization had flourished and increased its audience by 500 per cent. The constant stream of work was akin to being on a roll-on-roll-off ferry and unsurprisingly the theory behind the work was woefully thin at times. When things went wrong the company blamed Bob, whilst he in turn could blame the company democracy. The tussle, both ideological and practical, between manager and collective continued throughout my time with Theatr Powys until in 1990 the company all but imploded. The desire to get to grips with the theory behind what we were doing played a part in that.

After the MSC withdrawal the surviving artists included five core actors (known as actor/teachers in the trade). They were paid for by Powys County Council and were on contracts which were the envy of theatre workers in Wales. Accordingly some had chosen to remain there for over ten years. New, young personnel brought with them the revolutionary imperatives of the decaying inner cities and radical, urban, sexual politics to the apparent permanence of rural Mid Wales.

Whilst Theatr Powys workers were viewed as 'hippies', the shows I saw before joining were politically oblique or downright reactionary. They were all superbly produced, however. It was as if the company feared their audience. I was told, for example, not to include any audience participation in the Snow Queen because the 'Welsh Character' was very shy. I had nightmares in which row upon row of blushing farmers refused to warn the goodies of impending disaster.

I abandoned everything I knew about people and popular forms of theatre and instead tried to write according to this thing everyone talked about but nobody could define, 'the house style'. The response to the opening scene on the first night of the Snow Queen was a spontaneous outbreak of communal foot stamping. From that moment on I determined to take everything with a dose of salt and trust myself a little more.

Subsequent Christmas shows sought to use the conventions of pantomime in new and imaginative ways, whilst presenting a visual and aural feast which borrowed aspects of everything from performance art to modern dance. Aware that for many people this was their first or annual experience of live theatre, I treated it as a showcase for what theatre could do.

With *The Snow Queen* I went back to the original story in which trolls create a distorting mirror called 'the Mirror of Reason'. A tiny fragment of this becomes lodged in the heart of a boy, Kay. This makes him susceptible to the dispassionate Snow Queen who seduces him into becoming her successor. For many there was a parallel with Thatcher and her distortion of greed and selfishness to the rank of social virtues. To others perhaps it was an adventure story about a girl who showed a stubborn belief in Kay's (humanity's) better nature and saved him.

The Christmas shows were political stories as much as they were entertainments. They had applied to them the same considerations as we used for other shows at the time: What is happening in the world? What can we say we know about it, think about it and feel about it? What is the prevailing ideology telling us about it? Whilst these considerations may sound at odds with the mythic qualities of fairy stories, they produced plays which worked on different levels, to be interpreted by each individual depending upon their level of perception and understanding. I did not want to lose the ability of these stories to reach unconscious human feelings and desires by making them politically bald.

Over the subsequent three years we raised our audience to over 10,000 people for this one annual production. The audience came to trust our qualities of a strong story, vivid theatricality, comedy, meaning and high production values. These shows put me in front of a whole cross-section of the community. As their trust grew, they came to see everything else that we did and we could estimate 2,000 extra audience if a play was written by me. It took years, but it was worth it if only to prove that a writer can make a relationship with an audience in Wales.

The audience expectation of our Christmas shows sometimes weighed heavily about my neck and meant that both I and the company felt we could not change what I was doing. I did eventually move in another direction with a production of *A Christmas Carol* which I wrote and directed. However that was in 1990, seven years after joining the company. It was a very successful production, with a design by Janis Hart which remains the best work I have seen by her and superb lighting by Paul Howey. Excellence, a strong story imaginatively realized with magic, mime, movement and music, carried the audience with us quite effortlessly. Ironically, the actors who had derided the panto-style of earlier shows complained that this had no audience participation in it. By this time I was only too aware that writing Christmas shows was an attempt to please everyone from the wardrobe mistress who wanted a chance to make something extravagant to a four-year-old who might be terrified by the results. Everything I was writing was becoming a political football within the company and it was time to leave.

Theatr Powys's attempts to find an alternative popular show with other writers failed and the slot was abandoned within two years of my resignation. This was what some company members had wanted: to lose the Christmas show would free the schedules, it was thought, and allow the company to develop more serious (or in the lingo, 'challenging') pieces for children. In 1995 Theatr Powys toured an excellent, devised, play directed by Louise Osborn called *My Old Jumper*, set in a cellar in Sarajevo. This exemplifies the change of direction, but it was a long time before they reached that goal, with many salutary lessons in between, not least the loss of their largest audience of the year.

There is a dilemma for companies who have social objectives for their work and see themselves as part of a tradition of theatre which seeks to educate. The entire notion of popular theatre is still confused with populism, which is depressing but probably partly due to a tradition of formal dramatic conventions. The old left-wing equation that form follows content never did impress me, although I could see why it should have been correct. With popular theatre such as the Christmas shows many company members felt that form was the determining factor and found that unjustifiable and opposed to 'process'.

My attitude was simple and some thought it crass. It was that people clearly wanted these traditional shows, they wanted the rituals of participation. I do not feel that it is my job to 'educate' people out of their culture (or for that matter, mine). I was deeply concerned by the superior sense of good taste that some members felt they held over their audience.

The pantomime form was there to be reinvented, and given content, it is gloriously self-referential and closer to the diverse dynamics of Shakespearean theatre than to the limited conventions of social realism. I looked at these shows as an opportunity to enlarge the stage to include the whole auditorium: for example, we had sea battles raging in *Swashbucklars!*, and in *Robin Hood* scenery made by schoolchildren in Theatr Powys workshops was meant to turn the whole space into part of the set. Music has always been a crucial part of my play-writing and excellent musical directors such as Tam Neal, James Machie and Steve Byrne contributed to our ability to produce moments of genuine beauty and meaning.

If I had lived in the Soviet Union I would have been condemned long ago as a formalist, but for me a house is not a home until a family make it theirs. We struggled to make shows which harnessed conventions to the story rather than the other way around. The writing process on *The Snow Queen* in 1983 was determined by Bob Thomson and the needs of the production departments. I had, for the first time, to write detailed scenarios saying what happened, how and why in every scene so that the designers and builders could begin work. It was gruelling and produced after six weeks a first draft which was slow and stale.

I was reminded of my technical drawing teacher who used to say 'You can't measure a line that hasn't been drawn, boy'. Bob had written for *Z Cars* and was a cerebral deviser. I am tactile, for me theatre is sculpture in action, characters are knowable only when they tell the writer what they would do in a situation. Writing scenarios and proposals is a completely different art form, but one I was forced to master. I felt as though the writing process was a question of colouring in a line drawing. It lacked thrill and danger, passion and perversity. Though I learnt a great deal from Bob and his methodology, I still only really find the play once I have written it. Once I have taken on the personalities of the characters and let my unconscious mind, intuition and emotions, skate with them through the story. Then I look at what I have got.

On *The Snow Queen* I had assurances that I would be able to work with the actors to improvise and redraft the entire play in rehearsal. The plan was to get the actors into character as deeply as possible and then let them improvise the play with me, restructuring, reinventing and assimilating their inputs into a finished script. As the finished script begins to arrive so it can be rehearsed, say, in the morning, whilst the afternoon is left for improvising the next sequences. This staggered process allows me to write in the evenings and weekends. This was an approach I had taken on three previous scripts and knew it well. However, on day one the associate director began blocking the actors. I was only able to rewrite because the play was too long. This was a classic lesson for a writer to learn. Directors say 'Yes' just to get you to shut up. They think theirs is the most important job because they are in the greater panic. When the actors also start to panic then the momentum is overwhelming. The writer shuts up. In subsequent years, however, we adopted this process to great effect. It is a process which believes in actors and is particularly useful with an ensemble who devise at other times of the year. I resolved to control the process of my own writing. With odd exceptions I failed because in the context of a company there are too many diverse pressures and competing wants. Now when I have complete control over my own methodology I sometimes feel lost.

Following *The Snow Queen* I was given the go-ahead to write for a tour of the YFCs who would 'host' the show, taking a cut of the box office to motivate them to rally an audience. This had worked successfully with WIs the previous year. The YFC committee had asked for a comedy. Some members of the company were rather prudish about YFC stickers saying that they 'did it in wellies' and decided that the show should deal with sexism (surely wellies are the most asexual footwear ever invented?). I was once again faced with the dilemma of some company members feeling that their purpose was to correct their audience. In fact, I was increasingly aware that the company, whilst producers of shows with excellent standards were as much grafted onto their audience as the concept of Powys had been grafted onto Montgomery, Brecknock and Radnorshire. Something had to change.

I had proposed a play based upon research I was doing into the bombing of the Welsh Guards aboard the *Sir Galahad* in the Falklands War. The company was very nervous about the material and largely abstained on the vote. Although the proposal was

narrowly carried, the following day Bob Thomson and I agreed that
to tackle a controversial subject like this I would need the support of
the actors. Later that morning I began writing a comedy about sexual
attitudes.

I constructed a myth about a 'Gothic' Baron who wanted to create
the perfect woman. Enlisting the help of a vengeful surgeon, the
Baron has the brain of a man placed inside a woman's body. It all goes
absurdly wrong of course. *The Bride of Baron Duprave* remains one
of the funniest shows I have ever seen, yet beneath its bawdy and
referential surface lie some deeper comments about power, sex,
misogyny and permanence. Though I was pleased that I had made a
farce work and technically I had learnt a lot, this was not what I
wanted to write. I was doing a job, it was not what I had imagined.

The tour opened to tiny houses because I suspect the YFC had not
really taken to the prospect of working with a bunch of
interventionist 'hippies'. When the regional YFC organizer came out
of obligation the tour took off. She remarked after the show that we
really should have told her that it was going to be this good. Curious:
but thanks to her we played to packed houses thereafter and had to
retour, such was the demand for the show.

That was the end of my contract and I expected to return to
Hackney and to writing about somewhere that I knew and
understood, but it was not to be. The company asked me to return to
direct and write a TIE piece for six–seven-year-olds. A fateful
combination of love and employment kept me in Wales. I had two
objectives, first to research and write about this area so that both I
and the company could actually learn something about it. Secondly to
inject some much-needed theory into the TIE.

I was fascinated by the work of Dorothy Heathcote, having been
reintroduced to her work via the Standing Conference of Young
People's Theatre (SCYPT). This organization holds two annual
conferences on the theory and practice of TIE. Its significance to the
life of companies like Theatr Powys has been very strong and
therefore I will spend some time dealing with it.

SCYPT was at that time brimming with member companies from
throughout the UK. A small but extremely articulate group within it
were either in or closely associated with the Workers Revolutionary
Party. The WRP were more akin to a cult than a political
organization. They could answer any question, were the true
inheritors of all that had ever gone right for Revolutionary Socialism,

the bibles were anything by Trotsky or the paranoid leadership of the party. Leadership was their obsession. Each new recruit convinced them further of their own beliefs, they became necessary for this reason.

Arguments were won in an atmosphere whipped to a frenzy by assertions that capitalism was going to collapse any day now, or that Thatcher's 'Bonapartist dictatorship' would subside into open fascism, or that SCYPT could build 'community councils' (soviets) with training facilities for the young unemployed and thus lead the revolution. Thus with visions of a Fascist Hell and the promise of a Trotskyist Heaven (brought about by angels whose real powers were greatly exaggerated), the WRP condemned their sceptics for possessing 'a lack of faith' in the working class. Laughable revolutionaries? Yes, but exhausting, obsessive and occasionally brilliant, SCYPT conferences had the ability to affect one's thinking for a whole year. They provided a showcase for some exquisite TIE.

At times however the WRP contingent drew a narrow and self-fulfilling agenda. Debates about gay or lesbian issues and perspectives were deemed 'diversionary', and discussions about relating to the exciting growth of Welsh-language TIE companies were dismissed because the revolution did not appease pre-existing bourgeois cultures. Theatre, like reality, would become knowable if we all applied their 'scientific' analysis to it. My spirit rebelled first, my brain followed. Whatever my attitude at the time, there is no denying that as a writer working in Mid Wales these people were the one main source of analysis, outside of the company, that I was exposed to. They influenced my work even when I was distancing myself from SCYPT by 1985.

Of course not everybody needed to feel ridiculously important and large numbers did not fall for the idealistic nonsense and belief in their own propaganda as did the WRP. Much has changed since the party destroyed itself rather than capitalism. SCYPT continues to be the major theoretical school for TIE development and long may it continue. Probably the most damaging effect of the WRP was to keep SCYPT purely as a theoretical hothouse and to deny it a role as the major lobbying forum for TIE in Britain. Explaining our work, which takes place in schools away from the public eye, was confused with the publicity-driven policies of Thatcherism and the Saatchi and Saatchi school of image creation and styling. By the time it started to campaign publicly in the 1990s it was too late, the companies were closing across England and SCYPT's membership was decimated.

When considering the artistic programme for a community company one can draw circles of influence, one around the company, the next around the immediate locale, a third around your touring area, a fourth around the country. In the case of Theatr Powys a further circle has to be drawn around SCYPT. A company can gauge how it is regarded and the effectiveness of its work by analysing each circle of relationships it should have with every project.

The first circle equates to the internal artistic ambitions of the company members as individuals and as a collective. Sometimes companies make mistakes when they place too much emphasis upon what they want to do without considering the needs of the communities within the outer circles. When a company is disengaged, as I believe Theatr Powys was in 1983, from its community the artists can only look at their needs. Of course the alternative extreme, of not considering the motivation of the artists, is to make them civil servants and they will not stay for long.

Any company is based somewhere and so has a relationship with its immediate neighbours. Theatr Powys has always been viewed with more suspicion in Llandrindod Wells than anywhere else. Making a positive relationship locally is vital, especially if one lives there. The third circle, one's touring area, allows you to judge the company's impact across the diversity of communities found within one geographical area. The national circle relates to building an audience for theatre in Wales, creating a theatre at the centre of our national life and projecting Wales beyond our borders. The danger of the circles around the company and SCYPT are that these can and did at times become the only two anyone really related to. Sometimes, perhaps cynically, I thought Theatr Powys's community was SCYPT.

As the writer, a lone worker, it was easy to become submerged beneath the imperatives of the acting company. A lone voice demanding consideration can easily sound like a selfish voice. Couple this with the so-called scientific assertions of the WRP within SCYPT and I began to feel not only as if my reasons for writing were not being valued but that the role of the unconscious in creating art was incorrect practice. It was becoming hard to see myself in the work I was producing.

It was the case, I believe, that few if any company members understood the particular needs of a writer. As Theatr Powys devised 50 per cent of its work it was difficult for the actors to switch to, perhaps, serving the needs of the writer. This led to my serving the company rather than developing my individual voice, the reason I had started to write in the first place. This situation was fraught with contradictions, not least the desire to be seen as a theatre worker who shared the objectives of the collective, whilst also realizing that writing was ultimately an individual activity.

The TIE project *Past Caring* in 1984, which I had been asked to direct, did inject Dorothy Heathcote's theory and practice into the work, and a new form arose which mixed theatre, participatory drama and role-play, analytical discussion and visual devices to deepen meaning. That form survives and has been developed by Theatr Powys up to the present day. Under the directorship of Louise Osborn, one of the original devisers of that project, Theatr Powys has created some of the most brilliant TIE to be seen anywhere in the world.

The project successfully answered the needs of the company in understanding its area. Furthermore it involved children in that understanding. When shown to SCYPT Wales, valid criticism was made and the work was clarified before two more tours took place. It was selected as Wales's contribution to the ASSITEJ (Association Internationale du Théâtre pour l'Enfance et la Jeunesse) international register of excellent theatre for children and requested from as far afield as Malaysia. This was an exciting time when we felt breakthroughs were being made and that Theatr Powys was beginning to play a major role in the development of TIE theory and practice. Unfortunately this period coincided with the abandonment of SCYPT by leading Welsh TIE companies such as Gwent Theatre and the wholesale rejection of it by Welsh-language companies. An alternative Welsh-language conference was set up and the two organizations have remained separate ever since, to the great cost of both, and to the development of TIE in Wales.

Following that project Theatr Powys secured funding for another six months and I was to write the next Christmas show, based on Aladdin, and a new play which would tour the whole of Wales as well as the usual Powys venues. My pressure to be able to write what I really wanted to write was finally acknowledged and the company supported me in writing *Taken Out*, the play dealing with the so-called 'Bluff Cove' disaster during the Falklands War. Here was a play which reached out across all the circles of influence to which the company should relate.

Bob Thomson resigned to become artistic director of the Queens Theatre in Hornchurch and was replaced by the experienced actress, but inexperienced director, Sue Glanville. *Aladdin* became about a young man who comes to possess great power but turns his back on his community in pursuit of his selfish desire, the Princess. We toured during the miners' strike of 1984/5. The company shared the conviction that this monumental strike had to be won. *Aladdin* was a story about the importance of community above individual solutions. The traditional hero, Aladdin, became someone who made mistakes.

Significantly, Sue was willing to try working with the actors to produce the finished script in rehearsals. It was a frantic scrabble towards the end. I was still rewriting after the third performance. Our new relationships not only included the director, but the designer, costume mistress, musical director, two actors and production manager. Perhaps the company would have been justified in saying to me, 'Listen, we've got enough to deal with, just go away and write the bloody thing!' We produced a brilliant second act, but I never did set the story up well enough in the opening scenes. I knew I needed a greater understanding of my craft. One of the problems I have constantly encountered in companies is who I can go to with no vested interest in the shape of the play. In London I could go round to a mate's house and read it to them. In Wales the nearest other writer I knew was Charlie Way in Abergavenny and I did not know him well enough to foist my unruly child upon him.

Theatr Powys staff were instrumental in establishing a miners' support group in Brecon and Radnor and in supporting the re-emergence of a Trades Council. Slowly but surely the company members began to have a relationship with the community which went beyond our fleeting visits in a van. More was needed and with the arrival of Guy Roderick in late 1984 we had a majority within the company able to envisage new forms of theatre in the community.

First, however, came the Falklands play *Taken Out*, which dealt with the aftermath of over fifty Welsh Guards dying during a bombing raid when they had been left sitting aboard the *Sir Galahad* in broad daylight. The *Sir Galahad* was carrying a cargo of weapons. It was said that these were unloaded in preference to the men. The company had to be persuaded over a period of a year to risk letting me write what I wanted and on such a controversial subject. My contacts for the story were outstanding. I had been in touch with soldiers, wives and parents of men who had died, and the officers involved. The nerves of the company jangled until the first draft was delivered, which convinced the actors that the risk of letting me write something that I had a personal conviction about was right. However, John Greatorex had to fend off the fury of the head of the Theatr Powys management panel, Colonel Stephens, whose son was serving in the Welsh Guards at the time. Cold feet were treading all about me.

The BBC in Cardiff had just appointed a new radio producer, Adrian Mourby, who wanted to discover new writers and new plays. He had funding for a season on Radio Wales and my play, *Taken Out*, was commissioned alongside the Theatr Powys stage version. I now made the BBC nervous as well. Besides touring nationally Theatr Powys was venturing into radio production as a way of reaching into the national circle of influence for the first time. The success of this initiative was to be repeated the following year with a new play about the miners' strike called *Spoiled Papers*.

These opportunities were also what I needed as being in parts of urban Wales is isolating enough and even more acute in the rural hinterland. I am still relatively unknown in Cardiff despite writing over thirty scripts in Wales, all of which have been produced. On my first weekend at Theatr Powys a trainee director referred to Mid Wales as 'the graveyard of ambition'. Twelve years later and still stone broke I sometimes find myself agreeing with her.

Via the radio *Taken Out* eventually reached an estimated audience of four million. However, Theatr Powys tried to tour the stage version in the summer when the universities had closed and sunny evenings competed for an audience's attention. The publicity was botched and the marketing non-existent. I suspected that a low profile had been adopted for the piece just in case it was too dangerous. Paranoid? Isolation can make a person so. The few reviews and audience feedback for *Taken Out* were tremendous, but Theatr Powys found themselves with the best play the company had ever commissioned, playing to one of the smallest audiences in recent years. It took eighteen months to write and one month of touring to realize that the play itself was not enough.

When Sue Glanville left Theatr Powys she immediately restaged the play in London. Her support had been crucial to me during the writing process when, through fear, I could have attempted to provide what I thought other people would accept. She encouraged me to write from my heart and from my anger, whilst Adrian Mourby helped me with the play's complex structure: a good combination. I wrote eight drafts of that play, plus numerous revisions. When the play went on in London I was flooded with reviews and suddenly I was recognized as a writer working from within Wales who was of serious interest. That momentum was to be lost until I jumped ship and wrote for the English company Red Shift in 1989.

The Welsh press is ignorant of the theatre and its uniquely immediate ability to contribute to our understanding of where and how we live now. The English press ignores Wales, with the very occasional exception of the *Guardian*. A writer in Wales is 'invisible', to coin an Ed Thomas phrase. Stylistically, I was sick to death of watching neo-Brechtian community shows liberally splattered with songs to make the hairs on the back of one's neck rise. They invariably had a character who was either a natural Marxist or who became a Marxist at some point during the show – if not a Marxist, it was someone who said the right things.

Taken Out was an experiment in editing and weaving story lines, relationships, different times and locations into a web. I no longer felt that as a writer I was addressing an audience whose experiences and attitudes could be assumed. The so-called post-war consensus was smashed. Socialism had become about getting a bigger slice of the cake, its desire to progress human civilization had been forgotten in Labour's stabs for power. The 'web' allowed me to write diversely: to draw diverse people into the centre of a web of implications which defined them as part of a society and made them responsible for its development.

I abandoned the prescriptive 'scientific' designation of characters into roles and instead freely wrote characters whom I 'felt' were needed. There were no rallying songs, no characters who summed it all up. Suddenly my characters were all lost, confused, clutching at straws, trying to make sense of the world. It was poetic. I enjoyed writing, I felt real, honest and vulnerable. There was no doubt that *Taken Out* was a reaction to the orthodoxies of SCYPT, it was a personal liberation from applying myself to that circle of influence. Instead I felt a responsibility to those who had suffered so much because of what happened that day in the South Atlantic. I owed them their dignity. They did not deserve to be turned into political viewpoints.

When *Taken Out* was performed at SCYPT conference that year Sue Glanville was assaulted as WRP evangelicals denounced it as reactionary and said that the play should have supported (the murderous, drunken, fascist) Galtieri: their reasoning being that for the world revolution it was more important in the short term that a colonial power such as Britain be defeated. Given that Thatcher's regime was fully instituted as a result of winning that way, one is only left to wonder what excesses Galtieri might have enacted against his population given victory. With *Taken Out* I had begun a long search through my political 'beliefs', finding many things I had accepted without question. It was changing my writing.

I had clarified my purpose at Theatr Powys. I wanted to write for the area and about the area in which I worked but those two things are not necessarily combined. Perhaps it is more accurate to say that I wanted to write because of this area. Secondly, I wanted to create in-roads into the community in more permanent ways than touring in a van provided. Lastly, whilst I wanted to work with an excellent acting company, I knew that I had to have the opportunities to write with a personal passion.

My position became permanent in 1985, despite objections from some Powys county councillors. In 1986 Sue Glanville left Theatr Powys and we abandoned completely the role of company director. We had become fully self-managing. Sue helped that process. I and the company began developing a series of new initiatives with the community which involved them in creating for themselves. The theoretical side of our work had blossomed with everyone contributing. The company was being regarded as a model of efficient collective practice with the support of the Arts Council. We began working with freelance directors on the community touring side of the work, whilst we directed the TIE and participatory community projects in-house. The advances in both fields of work made us feel that no one person was capable of leading the company's three directions.

I had argued along with others for this new structure, not realizing that it would have unsatisfactory consequences for my writing. I had looked forward to learning from a host of directors, but found that freelancers were not really concerned with developing new plays and a new writer so much as getting something on which worked slickly, did not damage their reputation and made them popular with the actors. My writing, despite the success of *Taken Out*, was again being manufactured for the company and now the guest directors. Whilst I had a great say in shaping the artistic policy of the company I had very little say in shaping my plays.

The company was facing cut-backs and needed to increase its box-office income. I adapted Dickens's *Hard Times* for a national tour in 1986 and wrote two more Christmas shows. In the mean time BBC Radio was beginning to offer me other opportunities for dramas based upon research into aspects of modern Wales such as *Spoiled Papers* about the miners' strike, and the comedy *New World in the Mourning* about a Labour candidate trying to maintain his respectability against the odds during a general election.

I began to develop a split identity. At Theatr Powys I was the community writer, whilst at the BBC I was being re-created as the writer who researched contemporary Wales. I was even deemed by one overenthusiastic producer a Welsh David Hare. However, like most writers I am at my best when I am writing about myself, in that I must know what it is like to be in that or a similar situation. In this respect good writers are like good actors.

By 1987 I had had enough and asked for a year in which I would develop new work with the community. This led to me writing plays with schoolchildren and to the creation of the Mid Powys Youth Theatre. Guy Roderick was given the chance to direct MPYT's first production, which I would write. We devised it thematically in workshops with young people, then I went away and trusted to the research and improvisations I had stored away in my mind. The play *Mary Morgan* was scripted in about six weeks and remains one of the most exciting and disturbing plays I have written.

Mary Morgan was a fifteen-year-old local girl who worked as a kitchen maid in 1804. She became pregnant, birthed the child alone in her room and cut its throat. The father of the child, the young man of the house, sat on the jury which convicted her. His cousin was the judge. I laced the story with the struggle between the gentry and the King for power, the multi-nationalism of the East India Company against the old land-based wealth of the aristocracy. This was a play about how the world changes and how children are its first victims. The play mirrored the rise of the so-called New Right, and their agenda for the welfare state, justice and enterprise.

In November 1987 we opened the play at the Wyeside Arts Centre to the amazement of the local community, Theatr Powys and ourselves. The young people who took part had a natural quality of conviction one rarely sees in professional actors. The first night remains one of the proudest of my career and the final performance was up until that date the best performance of a piece of my writing that I had seen.

Working with community groups and in particular with the MPYT (Mid Powys Youth Theatre) finally gave me the means to get inside the locality's skin. Besides all the altruistic reasons for starting a youth theatre, my selfish want was to write on a large scale. The major theatres were bemoaning the fact that no one was writing large plays anymore and I was sick of twisting my plays so that the actors could double up, change costume and get everything that was needed into a van.

We took over the Market Theatre at the Wyeside and performed *Mary Morgan* in promenade with a cast of twenty-three and an orchestra of eleven. Currently MPYT's membership stands at eighty-strong. We attract 1,000 people to every five performances of our plays. The annual autumn show has become a local institution. In the past four years the company has toured and made videos. MPYT have performed at the National on two occasions, won numerous awards including a BBC Arts Award. We are capable in this country of producing excellence given access and opportunity.

Without doubt the work of Theatr Powys in the late 1980s was spectacularly good, inventive and diverse. Devised TIE projects such as *Grandmother's Footsteps* and *Careless Talk* took the formalistic developments of *Past Caring* into new territory and are TIE classics. The acting company was excellent. Under Roger Wooster the company developed Welsh-language TIE, an initiative which has seen Theatr Powys become a bilingual company. With Guy Roderick we took over entire schools and put all their furniture into our decrepit removal truck. With the children as designers we turned every inch of the school into environments within which the children would perform a play they had written with me.

The democracy within the company was working because the level of understanding about what we were trying to achieve was shared. Each artist was considered in relation to the needs of the community, a community we were increasingly researching and becoming personally and professionally involved with. Democracy however is a frail thing. As personnel moved on, the new recruits were bringing, as I had done, new agendas. Unfortunately these were sometimes personal and career-orientated. The company democracy fell apart as we became increasingly hedged within the first circle of influence, the wants of the company members. Our work ceased to be drawn from real lives and the locality. Once again we saw the battles of the old SCYPT, abstract and unlikely, pushed forward, not, I ever felt, from conviction, but from the desire to oppose, to win, to lead and so progress one's own career. A working democracy was so easily hijacked that I seriously doubt whether I would leave the work of a company so exposed again.

Whilst we tried to maintain the thrust of our work with developments such as a community play at Llanidloes written by Peter Cox and a multi-arts package touring alongside my play *Tarzanne*, the willingness of the company to perform this work had been effectively undermined. The TIE work began to serve the frustrated desires of actors to be directors and playwrights and the development of our work was shattered.

By 1990 I had actors on stage performing my work who simply never learnt their lines. People who had developed Theatr Powys from being an organization grafted onto the community into a company whose work was part of and in demand from the community were having nervous breakdowns or leaving. I left whilst maintaining my role as director of the MPYT which I defended furiously from the machinations of Theatr Powys. Strangely, with the company abandoned by its most innovative members, those who had sought the artistic leadership of the company fled. Fortunately, Louise Osborn returned to lead the TIE work and reshape the company democracy. Chris Ricketts became the administrator and returned the functioning of the company to highly acceptable and principled standards.

As my departure became necessary so I began to look further afield. I wanted to write about two Mexican painters, Frida Kahlo and Diego Rivera. These were two artists who had helped to create a sense of national identity and culture from the ravages of the Mexican revolution and civil war. I proposed the play to Theatr Powys in the first instance, coupled with a proposal to link it with a celebration of visual arts in Powys and the commissioning of public works of art depicting our modern world and our history.

The play was thought irrelevant to Wales. This decision was part of the process of undermining personnel within the company, but the play was also turned down by another Welsh company because it was not set in Wales. I think this attitude has changed somewhat and that we are big enough now to have Made in Wales commission Dic Edwards in 1995 to write a play about the US murderer Gary Gilmore without such parochialism. At the time, I began to despair until Red Shift commissioned the play and won a Fringe First at Edinburgh for their troubles. *Frida and Diego: A Love Story* was their most successful tour up until that point and the play has subsequently been produced in Europe, North and South America.

My favourite production of the play remains the 1993 version by the Mid Powys Youth Theatre. When performed at the National Theatre the belief was electrifying. Here was a play which ignited young Welsh people to the point that Richard Eyre got up on stage and said, 'It was everything theatre should be.' This was a play for Wales, albeit set in Mexico, which captivates people of all nationalities. Despite its success, when I won the Fringe First award my first thought was: 'If they think this is good they should see the work we do in Wales.'

It felt for a brief time that I was reaching out from Mid Wales to the world, that finally recognition was coming our way. In 1990 both *Taken out* and *Frida and Diego* were playing to full houses in London. What happened? I do not know for certain: a divorce, an agent who wanted me to write for television, poverty inclining me towards accepting work I should not have bothered with, a return to Welsh rural isolation, a market fearful of empty houses. My subsequent plays have been better than *Frida and Diego* but they were only seen here in the 'graveyard of ambition'. A fully functioning Welsh media which operated with a sense of belief in itself could have done a lot to alleviate this situation. It is hard not to feel sorry for new Welsh playwrights who appear only to disappear because no one acknowledges their importance and because no Welsh theatre will give them a main stage with a decent promotional budget.

Subsequently I have continued to develop new plays for BBC Radio with Jane Dauncey and Alison Hindell and unsuccessfully for television. Television has been ripped apart and reassembled in the image of its financial masters to such a degree that people who experiment with form, in the way I naturally do with theatre and radio, are viewed sceptically. Debates which are crucial to our lives are dubbed controversial and 'politics' have become a setting for fictional thrillers rather than analysis of who we are now. Thrillers are 'sexy', truth is unfashionable. Naturally it does not help when the television world knows you live in Wales, a backwater, and the Welsh know that you are 'English'.

Being an authentic, mongrel, nationless immigrant has its disadvantages, but I share this condition with many millions across the globe. Few here are ready to accept our place whilst authentic white, Welsh voices remain so shamefully underdeveloped. With the invention of Ed Thomas daylight has appeared. Ed fits the bill exactly, bilingual, butcher's son, Valleys boy, rumoured to have worked in the steel industry, articulate and more than any of these attributes he wants to write about Wales and the Welsh at the end of the twentieth century. Phew! Now perhaps other Welsh writers can write about whatever they want rather than be constantly brought to the altar of 'what it means to be Welsh?', every time someone wants to commission them. Besides, Ed does it so well. The fact that Dic Edwards wrote a play about an American anti-hero speaks volumes to me about Wales today. My own play, *The Informer's Duty*, which dealt with the relationships surrounding Shostakovich when he conceived the Fifth Symphony, also strikes me as particularly Welsh, with its concerns for cultural continuity versus cultural revolution.

This large-cast play was commissioned by the inspiring Paul Clements, at the Welsh College of Music and Drama. It formed part of a year's work as their first writer in residence. The production was the first collaboration between the music and drama departments in twenty years. An eighty-piece orchestra performed as part of the play. We gave ten performances and not a single national newspaper reviewed what was surely one of the most extraordinary theatre events to be seen in Britain that year. Despite the best efforts of many people to persuade me otherwise I still wonder, if a truly great Welsh play was written, would anyone know?

Made in Wales, the ghetto for new writing in the English language, favoured whipping boy of all those writers who cannot see beyond this trough to the larger problems of writing in Wales, finally commissioned me and have given me incredible freedom to write. I have chosen to write about a town near to where I live. Of all the things I have wanted to write about over the years my decision to write about this place at first surprised everyone. This place has entered my blood. My anger now resides here as much as it has done anywhere else. Certainly the people I love most are here.

Whilst I still feel rootless and alien in many respects in Wales, this is how I would feel anywhere and I recognize that the people of this town might feel similarly even though they have lived there for generations. I can write about what I know and it can be about this place. This is very different from how I felt when I first wrote for Theatr Powys. Undoubtedly, the Mid Powys Youth Theatre has been my greatest source of attachment, insight and understanding: I do not think I could have written so genuinely without them. In the isolation of Mid Wales, they have taught me about writing as much as I have taught them. It was also my solution to the problem of creating work and getting it on.

With my departure from Theatr Powys in 1990 went the post of writer in residence, after a brief period of replacement by Dic Edwards. It was the only such post in Wales. To some extent the old anxiety of actors who devise their own work returned and they felt uneasy about an individual writer having a hallmark influence over a company. Theatr Powys continues to commission new plays but the dramaturgical process is something of which they have no experience. Some of the work has been poorly written, other work ill-suited to the broader circles of influence the company has to accept as its community.

One can say anything, create a play about anything, for the communities in Powys. It is how you say and show it that counts. A writer attached to the company has a chance to understand how to write specifically for that audience. Hiring writers who profess to have no interest in the community, but wish instead to write about ideas, misses the point. I see no value in touring plays which alienate one's audience; who then are they for? In cities the populations are large enough for theatre to cater for every taste. To tour a community with theatre which does not make sense to it is a fatuous exercise which only those who are removed from the community they serve can attempt to justify.

Not everyone is made for writing for community companies. It can be a big mistake to suffocate one's own voice, obsessions and concerns. Certainly one learns the craft, gets one's work on and is never short of personal criticism; in this respect a writer can serve an apprenticeship. Some writers who think that they are the creators of theatre and everyone else facilitates their art could benefit from the experience. The company has a responsibility to make sure that it understands the implications of hiring a writer, that its job is to nurture that voice, not use them to lessen the burden of constantly devising new work. Having done that, every company in Wales should have at least one writer attached to it. In fact Charles Way has made the equation that there should be one writer for every administrator.

We currently have a situation in Wales where its most experienced writers are not recognized within our own borders, where media criticism of the work is rare and largely of pathetic quality, where the main stages are foreign fields, where writers drink themselves to death or, worse, give up and write soaps for television, where Welsh-produced work cannot be seen beyond our borders with funding from the Arts Council of Wales. Young writers do not have a career to follow. We are barely off square one. Yet there is a body of work which exists, is excellent, but has been seen only by small audiences in specific parts of Wales.

The Welsh Playwrights Company, an organization of leading Welsh playwrights, is seeking to address these issues. The publishing of new plays in Wales will hopefully reach other practitioners in Wales who remain startlingly ignorant of the work of other companies, let alone Welsh writers. It is the work of writers which has been most undervalued in Welsh theatre and this must change if we are to create something which has life beyond short-term objectives and which can reflect and comment upon contemporary Wales in all its diversity. If we mean what we say when we want a theatre in Wales which is at the centre of our national life, then it will not come without huge investment in writing. The correct space for writers, given their personality and obsessions, must be granted. The main stages must be open to them. A theatre in Cardiff dedicated to new writing must be established with touring facilities for its most successful productions.

I have stayed with the MPYT for ten years because it is simply an exciting context. Real relationships are formed which fuel the work. Experimentation is uncritically encouraged and the lust for art is palpable. The MPYT is like my play *Taken Out*; it is a web of relationships devoid of correctness. I may have squandered some of the best years of my life as some people have told me, but here, with them, I have created theatre which affects the lives of our community, which transforms people, which is amongst the most vital, in every sense, that I have seen in the past ten years. The ordinary becomes extraordinary. Surely that is my job.

14 • The Space Between – Work in Mixed Media: Moving Being 1968–1993

Geoff Moore

The space I am thinking about has several meanings:

- the space before starting, the empty slate, the unmarked canvas, the blank sheet of paper, the cleared room;
- the space of time, twenty-five years, unbelievably a quarter of a century, half a working lifetime;
- the space between things, at the edges of objects, the space that defines one thing from another, one form of expression from another;
- the symbiosis of form and content, the dialectic of art and life;
- the space of possibility.

One of the first pieces I made in the 1960s was called 'Space': white background, white floor, a group of figures in primary colours moving in silence. This early work with Moving Being reflected naturally enough the priorities of the period and my own formative background. At the time both inner and outer space were seemingly innocent unpolluted frontiers. It was as if we had the privilege of starting on a new journey. For me, an art school education in painting and sculpture fed a dominant interest in the visual and the physical – as opposed to a drama school or university background, which is the more usual apprenticeship for directing theatre in Britain, where the text is the primary focus and *raison d'être*.

Most people I knew were more into movies than anything else. The montage and flow of 'the art form of the twentieth century' left the rest standing. Films were the visuals, and rock'n'roll was the soundtrack. The 1960s saw many explorations and mergings of forms investigating notions of a non-text-based theatre. It seemed to me then that a polarity was being set up between defenders of the old faith and those who saw 'the well-made play' as the enemy in their quest for a more real visceral expression. As the history of the last quarter-century has shown, we were presented with a false dichotomy. Why lose language, why lose the eye, why lose the body? Both ancient and non-Western forms of theatre were powered by an eclectic and dynamic alliance of music, dance and visual signing through objects and costume as equal parts in the dramatic telling. American musicals and directors in Europe worked naturally with such hybrids. It was only in Britain, perhaps because of the critical establishment and the Arts Council, that we were hung up on categories.

I remember a conversation with Tim Albery at the ICA. He was putting together a programme of new work which involved texts, but did not want to give out the wrong signal. He asked me what I would call it. I suggested 'Theatre not plays', a title which he used. At this distance such semantic wrestling seems precious, but it represented something very real – the need to define a theatre for the twentieth century, a protean theatre growing in tandem with a changing society and rapidly evolving cultural forms. It was a theatre in touch with its audience. The audience was as engaged as the practitioners in the excitement of innovation. The unspoken agreement was that we were finding things out together. If you did not come out of a performance challenged, potentially changed, with a feeling that you had been taken further, you had been cheated.

We are now faced with exactly the opposite. Our present cultural climate is one that is completely opposed to innovation and risk. The space of possibility has become a void. Theatre in Britain appears to be facing a crisis of decline, crippled as much by lack of vision as of funds. It is a theatre run by accountants. If a project does not fit a subscription season, if it is not attractive to sponsors, if it is not a set text with a guaranteed audience, or something cobbled together to celebrate local interest, or this or that centenary offering requisite marketing advantages, if it is not safe and familiar, it is not on. Artists no longer have any power. The initial purpose of the Arts Council, enshrined in the phrase 'to respond to initiatives from artists', has been completely usurped by its own new bureaucrats who are now writing artistic policy themselves in the language of business-speak.

This process of disempowerment is of course part of a much wider picture, a sea change in public life so profound, that to bang on about the role of the artist may seem inappropriate if not ridiculous. Perhaps we get the art and the theatre we deserve. We have failed to shift a government who have been in power long enough to breed a generation and a half who know no better. There has been a centralization of power for so long that for most people alienation from the political process is now almost complete. A sense of powerlessness and a deadly lack of confidence are the result.

When we began Moving Being there was an established sense that artists had a role and a purpose, that they operated in a necessary space between art and society, that they may even have some influence on social and political life. In the age of postmodernism, artists of all kinds have been obliged to recognize their efforts as merely one more commodity in the all-powerful market-place. In the light of such circumstances theatre has to think very clearly. Instead of capitulating and selling itself short, it should make itself more and more difficult to sell.

Then, paradoxically, people will want to buy it again. If theatre has lost its power and its audience, it is because it has given in. Theatre is not meant to be easy, it is not meant to be reassuring, it is not meant to be complacent and conforming. From its earliest days, in the cradle of Greek drama, it has been a social irritant, it has been a terror, it has been a scourge. That is its purpose. If our theatre has lost its way in the hands of chief executives, managers and marketing consultants, it has also lost its challenge and its dignity.

In the early 1970s, probably coinciding with the unprecedented growth of subsidy, new companies, and new venues for the arts in Britain (which in hindsight takes on the look of a golden age), there was also a fashion for explaining things. Companies developed what were called lecture-demonstration programmes, which were designed to spread the rather patronizing word to the populace at large. So there was 'Ballet for All', 'Opera for All', etc. It was suggested to Moving Being that we might put together a 'Mixed Media for All', which was so bizarre a proposition it was almost interesting. It obliged me to look carefully at what sources and influences lay behind the work. The history of mixed-discipline performance is probably the unwritten, unofficial story of the development of theatre in the twentieth century. From Richard Wagner to Robert Wilson, from Vsevolod Meyerhold to the Wooster Group, from Diaghilev to Robert Lepage. The influence of the other arts, of painting, of poetry, of music, dance, film, even television on the theatre is clear from mainstream stages and the opera house to small studio theatres that take on the look of art gallery installations.

For the purpose of our demo piece, called 'The Idea, the Image and the Space Between', I drew up a list of sources which neatly enough

happened to form an ABC of background references and heroes –
Artaud, Brecht, Cage. An outrageously ambitious synthesis, probably
unachievable, but which many strive for: Antonin Artaud, physical
poet of the irrational, the dark soul, the transformed body, the
inarticulate cry, the signals through flames; Bertolt Brecht, a theatre
of clarity, of instruction and analysis, of social and political
usefulness for an audience who 'did not hang up its mind with its coat
in the entrance'; John Cage, a Zen view of wit, humour, and cool
beauty – courtesy of Merce Cunningham and Robert Rauschenberg,
the complexity of elements left to their own, random, intrinsic value,
which cannot be defined in terms of single meanings but leave
connections for the onlooker to make for themselves. They become
active contributors to the meaning.

In Britain, such a manifesto is automatically pretentious and
embarrassing. Interestingly enough, the only missing ingredient is
psychological realism, which has been the backbone of British theatre
for over a hundred years. Actually, I like that too, but I think there
should be room for alternatives. What we are talking about is making
a space for complexity. As Howard Barker says,

> Art is a problem. The man or woman who exposes himself to art
> exposes himself to another problem. It is an error typical of the
> accountant to think there is no audience for the problem. Some people
> want to grow in their souls. The only resistance to a culture of banality
> is quality.

I love a good movie. I love bad movies. I love crashing out in front of
the television like anyone else. Theatre offers something different.
Another kind of attention. You have to go out. You are required to be
part of a social transaction. Your humanity is called upon. You have
to 'be' there with others. This higher demand often leads to higher
frustration. It is a price well worth paying. For theatre cannot
function unless the space that is made for the audience is filled. I am
not of course just referring to the proverbial bums on the seats.

The space theatre offers is a human space, a societal space, a
political space. Theatre's job is to keep that space relevant, and to
keep it always open to question. This is why filling it up with pap is
such a crime. Good theatre is never just about itself. There is always
another agenda. Unlike the other arts, theatre does not deal in
completed objects. Theatre is a process, a measure of where we might

be at a given moment, a dialogue, a dialectic, a debate with history, society, morality, time present. What theatre is worth pursuing now? Which writers are best to be looked at now? As I write, I feel a sense of pride and solidarity with a friend, Susan Sontag, who is directing *Waiting for Godot* by candlelight in Sarajevo.

Those of us who care about it make extravagant claims for the theatre, fully aware that we are speaking of and to a tiny minority within a minority that is, like everything else, adrift in the vast sea of mass culture and the corporate entertainment industries. The more this is so, the more theatre matters. It really is a case of 'where two or three are gathered together'. It may be that to retain its seriousness, theatre will have to go underground again for a time. So be it. It has happened before in history. The important thing is that we are still finding ways to talk to each other, still trying to tell the truth. Moving Being made its reputation in the 1960s as the pioneers of a new kind of non-narrative theatre. Howard Barker, one of the most important voices in contemporary theatre and a master of language with whom the company worked in 1990, says 'The narrative form is dying in our hands'. Whilst knowing exactly what he means, I would put it another way. We must find new kinds of narrative. It is over seventy years since T. S. Eliot in *The Waste Land* signalled the dislocation of this century: 'I can connect/Nothing with nothing'. Those artists who have worked across the borderlands and edges, between the spaces of forms, have reflected this fragmentation as a condition of truth, that 'meaning' has to take account of the randomness, discontinuity and plurality of contemporary experience. Moving Being used texts from the earliest dance-based days, bits from newspapers, poems, quotations of all kinds. Later, assemblages were from a particular writer, at first from literature rather than drama. More recently I have found the bringing together of great plays from the past, counterpointed with those from the present, provided a rich space in which to find new meaning. Little did we know way back then that we were headed down the road of deconstruction to the place called postmodernism.

If one of the meanings of that overworked catch-all phrase is that it has all already happened, that somehow with the triumph of free-market capitalism we have reached the end of ideology, even the end of history, we are in trouble indeed. The idea that there can be no new moment, no fresh expression, that we are condemned to recycle past styles in an endless pastiche, is a kind of hell. Sitting in our separate cocoons with our VCRs rerunning the history of the world in a pick'n'mix fashion, fast forwarding the difficult bits, and smoothing out the chaos and contradictions of contemporary reality with our individually selected personal stereo soundtracks (*mea culpa*).

Everybody knows this slippery feeling of distance from modern experience – literally not being able to get hold of it because it is all surface. Equally, everybody knows it is not on; we know there is trouble up ahead from all those things 'we can do nothing about'. This is why our forms of communication are so important. We need a way of reminding ourselves that we are not invincible, that we are flawed and only partially in control. Theatre is still sweaty and vulnerable, it is unedited and anything can happen. As Artaud reminds us, 'We are not free, and the sky can still fall on our heads. And the theatre has been created to teach us that first of all.'

There is a paradox at the heart of all this, one that I have long wrestled with: that theatre, by its very nature is/should be resistant to technology, that essential theatricality equals low-tech: the 'poor-theatre' aesthetic which means less equals more. There is certainly a truth in this, theatre does proceed through an economy of means. But if it is to remain connected to our present realities theatre must incorporate technology, however critically, and show the human being and the human scale in relation to the extensions of ourselves in and through electronic media.

Theatre has certainly travelled a considerable distance in the twenty-five years we have witnessed. From the gilt and red plush to the austere black box to the disused industrial site where we stand around in the cold watching the last rites of something, or is it the birth pangs of something else? The system has a great capacity to absorb, process and remarket the various radical challenges it throws up. Artists are there to remain one step ahead. It is hard to see where theatre might be headed, when the form itself seems to be up against the challenge of history. We are faced with real questions that are not only financial.

It was in 1968 that Peter Brook published his seminal theatre lectures *The Empty Space*, redefining Western theatre's purpose for a whole generation, and placing that word 'space' at the heart of the matter. I am sure it was in some memory of this that I called the old building that Moving Being was converting to new purposes ten years ago, St Stephen's Theatre Space.

For a decade St Stephen's was by common agreement the most exciting theatre in Cardiff, if not in Wales. It was a theatre of seriousness and joy. It was a theatre of visionary poets – William Blake, John Webster, William Shakespeare, August Strindberg, Henrik Ibsen, William Morris, Bertolt Brecht, Karl Kraus, Vaclav Havel, Harold Pinter, Peter Handke, Heiner Muller, Joseph Beuys, Alan Osborne, Edward Thomas. It was the preferred home of dancers, musicians and visual artists who knew the value of its unique atmosphere. It was a theatre that created actors, directors and companies. It was a theatre valued and loved by its audiences, but it was not a theatre of patronizing crowd-pleasing pap, so it was closed by the accountants, the only arbiters of value in today's climate. The accountants worked for the Arts Council, now a cocktail of bureaucrats, politicians, and in Wales, rank amateurs, all of whom think they know more about the theatre than the artist.

St Stephen's was lost because it refused to fit the new mould. It was artist-created, and artist-led, and that leaves no room for the legions of consultants and marketing experts who know all about what people want. So, after two decades of building theatre in Wales, the first at Chapter, the second at St Stephen's, we are relegated by the Welsh Arts Council to the position of a 'project', a category that has been reneged upon even in its first manifestation.

In the end, the only power an artist has is the strength of an idea. Peter Mumford, a founder member of Moving Being, recently reminded me of a conversation in the early days when I apparently said, 'We'll give it a couple of years and see what happens.' Well much has happened. The potential space has been filled and cleared, filled and cleared again according to changing times. It will be so again. New and complex narratives wait to be formed.

Contextual note

The above was written on the occasion of Moving Being's twenty-fifth anniversary production, *The Darwin Project*, in 1993. The company had recently lost its revenue status and as a result its base, St Stephen's Theatre Space. Subsequently Moving Being has produced single site-specific projects; for example *The Changing Light* at the National Museum of Wales in 1994.

15 • Talking Theatre:

A Conversation between Playwrights

Lucy Gough and Dic Edwards

Dic: Have you finished the play you were working on yet?

Lucy: I've started again . . . Scrapped the lot.

Dic: I know how you feel! There's a good chance this play I'm working on at the moment will be workshopped at the RSC. So I cut half a scene this morning. It's been with me for three years and now I wonder if it was the right thing to do. Suddenly the mind is concentrated, and anything that hints at self-indulgence has to go.

Lucy: Yes, the reason I had to go back to the drawing board with my play *Head*[1] was that I couldn't let go of ideas and images which had actually done their job and ought now to go. You hold onto these things, fight tooth and nail to keep them and then finally when you let go the play takes off again. I keep doing it each time, I don't learn!

Dic: I think in both our cases it's actually a part of the process built into the way we work. Our writing tends to be an investigation of all the themes thrown up by what we want to write about. As in a criminal investigation it would be unjust to prejudge the final account.

Lucy: That's true. I just wish there was a short cut sometimes. Once the play is finished I can see why I had to go through a particular process, and this is why I find 'treatments' can be problematic, I really don't know exactly what I'm writing until it's finished.

Dic: Which is precisely what's wrong with television. These days television playwrights are treated like film scriptors, you have to pitch an idea in some detail, then if they're interested in that you have to offer a detailed treatment. It's all a bit like putting the cart before the horse for stage playwrights. How do we know how a story is going to reveal itself when we haven't had the opportunity to discover the integrity of the characters. What happens to the characters is what the story is about after all.

Lucy: It's this search which is the reason why part of the process of writing is always such a wrestling match, always challenging oneself about the inner integrity and internal logic of the play. My feeling is that this is why the philosophy behind television drama initiatives like 'Wales Playhouse' are wrong, seemingly based on a 'treatment' competition rather than a good starting-point with the experience and integrity to achieve results. It is worrying that this 'sell us an idea' stand is creeping into theatre.

Dic: Yes, you've identified two things there that are antagonistic to one another. The first is the challenge inherent in all of the best art, and second is the desire to put bums on seats, whether in the living room or in the auditorium. In the latter instance the mere production of the piece becomes the justification for its existence rather than the subject-matter. For me there is a moral implication in this. If our art is determined by requirements other than the 'wrestling with ideas' as you put it and the moral responsibility that goes with it then it ceases in most senses to be art. All we are left with is one form of propaganda or another.

Lucy: I really believe that we are doing something useful when we write a play, but we need to retain freedom to explore our subjects as deeply as we wish. If we get to a point where in order to survive we become like story factories, then theatre dies because we cannot justify the existence of theatre or its writers within society.

Dic: I've been reading Arthur Miller's autobiography and his account of the McCarthy years has frightening resonances today. I believe we are living with what I call a McCarthyism of the soul. I've been writing a speech for a character in my new play *The Idiots*. The character is a night-club singer, she sings political songs that nobody is interested in. Any audience only goes to look at her body. Her feeling is that society is in the process of throwing certain words out of our language, that we seem to be hell-bent on rendering existence in all its richness negligible. It's this collusion with denying our language and consequently our freedom. That's the McCarthyism of the soul!

Lucy: In effect we could be seen as defenders of freedom because we dig around in the subtext of life. It always fascinates me the way some writers often write about events that then occur. It is part of our role within society, not that we foretell the future but that we are in touch with our time.

Dic: I think this is to do with the responsibility an artist has for understanding his or her society, in the sense that humanity is understandable. There really isn't much point for me in an art which merely paints a representational picture of the way things are. This hinges on the old philosophical dichotomy of 'appearance' and 'reality' which plays such a major part in Shakespeare's thinking for instance. If we write plays that describe the mistakes we know we've already made we've produced something only as satisfying as an autopsy. If we write a play that anticipates the mistakes we might make in the future then we may be able to change a few things.

Lucy: Given all this, how do you feel about this new initiative to establish a National Theatre for Wales?

Dic: This is nothing new, last time it was Theatre Wales based at the Sherman, commonly called 'Theatre 125' because most of the big people involved with it lived in London and they used to travel up on the Intercity 125 train!

Lucy: Do you think having tried at least once and failed, this project has any chance of success this time?

Dic: I think it's a question of identifying exactly what people mean when they talk about a National Theatre. Either they are talking about a national theatre culture, or a building. If it's the former there are many practitioners in Wales who would resent the implication that in effect they've been doing nothing for the past fifteen years since Theatre Wales. If the latter, so what!

Lucy: Except that a building would soak up all the money and disenfranchise the rest of the theatre community in Wales. I fear that the effect of this would be to diminish theatrical output in the rest of Wales.

Dic: It's a paradox, to set up a National Theatre would actually undermine the culture.

Lucy: That could be the danger. I can see the need to have a focus for Welsh theatre culture, to raise the profile, but we need to avoid overcentralization.

Dic: There are things more important than buildings: for example, publication. Publication establishes the existence of work in all its diversities. It is a worry that a building is going to reflect only one voice; that of the Artistic Director. This would be all right if there were lots of buildings, but this centralizing is likely to work against a democratic Welsh theatre art.

Note

[1]   Broadcast on BBC Radio 4, November 1996.

16 • Physical Theatre and its Discontents

Paul Davies

Volcano is a national and international touring theatre company. The artistic directors are graduates of the University of Wales Swansea and the designer and technical director was born and educated in Neath. Their work has not focused on the 'problem of Welshness' – identity, division, unity, past, present or future. One consequence of this is that it might be said that Volcano has made little impact within the Principality.[1] Nevertheless the work has been widely seen outside of Wales, in Hong Kong, Greece, Spain, Macedonia, Germany, Montenegro, France, Italy, Russia, Holland . . . At the same time, Cardiff, in particular, and to a lesser extent Swansea, Aberystwyth and Builth Wells, have remained vital platforms for the development and promotion of the work of Volcano. Indeed Volcano was probably one of the first Welsh companies to play at the newly opened Taliesin Arts Centre in Swansea in 1983.

Adapting the work of Steven Berkoff and Jonathan Moore provided the basis for the early touring success. The 1980s were a difficult decade. Conservative politics had not yet targeted the cultural infrastructure within Wales and Great Britain as whole. Thatcherism had older scores to settle. As a young Anglo-Welsh theatre company rooted in a dissident, sometimes Marxist, sometimes oppositional, sometimes just bloody-minded tradition, it appeared to us that Welsh theatre was curiously unprepared for the challenge that Thatcher's modernizing rhetoric posed. Culture and the place of theatre within that awkward claim does not just go on; it gets redefined, left behind, obliterated, the subject of doctorates and so on.

Just what happened to the culture of theatre in Britain in the 1980s is perhaps a story that remains to be told. Certainly the success of New Right ideology and the collapse of the Communist utopia signalled the end of one way of looking at, and living in, the world. Radical rethinking of a Marxist and non-Marxist hue declared that we were now living in 'new times'. The old definitions would not do and various attempts were made to reinvigorate our political, social, sexual and cultural vocabularies. Whilst it is too early to say how successful any of this rethinking has been, it cannot be doubted that postmodern theory casts a long shadow over all modern strategies for change. Furthermore it would be a mistake to see these developments as purely narrow, academic concerns. The collapse of political, and to a lesser extent experimental, theatre can be viewed within the context of the triumph of the market and postmodern excess.

Of course the situation is more fluid than this account suggests. Rearguard battles were fought, but whatever the outcome of particular struggles, it was clear that the 1980s were a critical decade for culture and capitalism in Wales. There was, for example, within funding bodies (and this to some extent remains true) a crisis of definition. Were they funding new work on the basis of old criteria or old work on the basis of insufficiently articulated new criteria?

It was from within this particular historical conjunction that Volcano developed as one of Britain's foremost proponents of physical theatre. The term physical theatre is imprecise. Volcano has not sought to articulate, or represent, an essentialized account of this new school of performance. We are historical animals and whatever the seductive charms of naturalism, theatre has always been, in some senses, physical. Nevertheless there was within Volcano the feeling that theatre had, unfortunately, turned its back on what was an increasingly complex political situation. And here the emphasis was on an expanded definition of the political. Sexual politics were now at the very centre of both our theatre practice and our imaginary speculations as to how we might live. There was in addition the problem of the text, the author and the audience. We needed to use movement and words to break through what we considered to be irrelevant patterns of performance and inherited patterns of response. In a very obvious way this was theatre that was young, angry and urgent. However, beyond this immediate response Volcano had chosen its material carefully. The concern was to unlock the modern/ postmodern debate in ways that revealed new and unexpected theatrical possibilities.

Combining movement and text, dynamic and exhilarating versions of Tony Harrison's *V, Medea: Sex War,* Shakespeare's sonnets *(L.O.V.E.)* and the Communist *Manifesto* were produced. The focus of these productions was in some senses the same. Volcano sought to disturb and sometimes destroy the classics (ancient and modern), to suggest that the tradition - be it political, cultural or sexual – is not so smooth, not so seamless. More recently we have examined the legacy of Ibsen in *How to Live,* the influence of Nietzsche and Baudrillard in *After the Orgy* and Chekhov's *Three Sisters* in our post-Tarrantino, post-feminist thriller, *Vagina Dentata.* The belief has been both that a truly contemporary theatre must draw on a variety of sources and that the market system of production, exchange and ideology is differentiated but universal. The Anglo-Welsh experience can be seen within the logic of late-twentieth-century capitalism.

The vexed problems of nations, states and identities have not been addressed. Rather, Volcano has sought to reinvigorate theatre, reminding us of theatre's popular, even Dionysian, potential. The enemy here is, on the one hand, the complacency that surrounds much of our theatre practice; and on the other developing systems of technology that may render the culture of theatre an increasingly formal thing of the past.

This scenario is not doom-laden, although we have our problems in Wales. Foremost among these are: a coagulation of theatre, its practitioners and funders around Cardiff (although I would say that, as Volcano is based in Swansea!), a slender base for the production and touring of work within Wales and lastly a culture that when in retreat prefers the past to the present and the known to the unknown.

But these things change. Certainly our experience over the last ten years in Wales has seen the development of a more flexible approach to the problems, a willingness to discuss them – and sometimes even to do something about them! Diversity in theatre seems to us to be more of a healthy sign than some kind of national style or characteristic and as the end of the century approaches we seem to have more of the former than the latter. Whether the current situation reflects the policy of arts councils and the practice of artists is another matter. The profound challenge that the 'happy consciousness' of postmodernity offers to artists and funders alike seems, as yet, to have provoked little in the way of practical or theoretical response.

Our own intentions remain the same: to move between Wales and Europe, to find ourselves somewhere in the middle, on the edge – perhaps off the map. In this vein we have planned a production of Dylan Thomas's *Under Milk Wood* with Welsh, Albanian and English actors and a Croatian director. But, wait a moment, we can't get the rights, they (who are they?) are performing it at the National. Oh well that's different isn't it, see . . .[2]

Note

[1] Although the recent success of Frantic Theatre company, who have worked with Volcano, and are recipients of ACW project funding does not bear out this claim.

[2] Volcano did eventually tour *Under Milk Wood*. Unfortunately it had to be withdrawn from production due to problems with Thomas's estate.

17 • Speaking to the Nation

Gilly Adams

Confronted with the need to explain why a performance of three plays in Cardiff's docklands aspires to be a major cultural event, I find myself tracing the history of my own involvement with theatre writing and the development of the Made in Wales Stage Company. The two things seem somehow inextricably bound together. It is a good time to examine the past. We are in the middle of 'blitzing' our offices, engulfed in costumes, papers and props after the recent production of Charles Way's *Search for Odysseus*. The hour has come to be ruthless and brave in penetrating the depths of the damp storage cupboard we share with the Welsh Academy. Strange objects appear from the darkness – a plastic helmet and shield, mocked up British Rail uniforms. Shorn of the particular theatrical context to which they belonged, these props appear incongruous and worthless. Given our lack of storage space, why did we hang on to these particular things? Anything that cannot be recycled now finds its way into a bin bag preparatory to being taken to the dump.

Part of the tidy-up involves a long-planned reorganization of the photographs and posters which line the walls. Glass clipframes give the posters a new lease of life, which emphasizes the blatant technological changes of the last decade. The poster for the original tour of *Bull, Rock and Nut* to Bethesda Arts Centre in Merthyr Tydfil in 1983 now looks as though it hails from another, more primitive age compared with the high precision of more recent advertising.

Two events precipitated the foundation of the Made in Wales Stage Company. One was a Play for Wales competition organized by the Welsh Academy in 1981, the other a late-night performance of Dic Edward's play *Late City Echo* in the same year. The Play for Wales competition, thanks to comparatively large prizes and the promise of (some kind of) performance for the winning play, occasioned a mass turning out of drawers and an influx of dusty plays. They divided roughly into the following categories: historical plays where the history substituted for any dramatic impulse; reworkings of *Under Milk Wood;* arson plays written by people who did not know the difference between Cymdeithas yr Iaith, Plaid Cymru and Adfer; 'returning home' plays in which a Son of Wales comes back to the old country, usually to attend a parental funeral, and confronts left-over family issues in the process. (Theatr Clwyd was later to do the 1980s version of this play in Keith Barter's *Barnaby and the Old Boys* – the returning son was gay and accompanied by his black lover!); and mining plays in which the solidarity of the working class and its ability to sing hymns at the drop of a disaster were paramount. Among a lacklustre selection, Alan Osborne's fragment of *Bull, Rock and Nut* shone like a mysterious beacon.

In 1984 Made in Wales embarked on a development programme which has continued ever since. The focus of the workshops has been to stress the theatricality of theatre, i.e. that play-making is different from novel-writing since the page-to-the-stage process is a collaborative one involving the talents of actors, designers, directors, technicians, composers, as well as writers.

Many workshops and readings later, there is a network of writers in Wales who have worked with the company and, strangely, some of the most vivid memories attach to written fragments which blossomed in the workshops but never reached a public stage. Some of the best jokes have emerged from that area of risk and experiment too. This is the underbelly of Made in Wales's work, an area where the challenge has been to focus writing towards the goal of the professional stage, rather than leaving it as personal therapy or further education, although both these activities have their place. It is an area where ideas may germinate to appear as full-blown plays several years later; where the emphasis is on process rather than product – something that is especially important in the nurturing of young writers or those whose voice is underconfident. Whilst much writing remained privately in the workshop room, other fruit of the development programme demanded a vehicle for public expression. Touring does not allow for short or experimental work – traditionally the theatre circuit demands the full-length play – and so the company invented the Write On! Festival, which began at the Sherman in 1985. The first festival was a seat-of-the-pants affair with ten actors rehearsing and learning six plays and involving themselves in six rehearsed readings as well. The logistics of the rehearsal schedule were staggeringly convoluted because of the cross-casting which meant that nothing could be rehearsed in 'one go': actors had to grapple with several different plays in one day. I have a vivid memory of Roger Stennett's play *Out of the Sun*, set on an air base in the Second World War, in which several scenes finished with the signal to 'scramble'. It was always touch-and-go whether the actors would return to the right scene or even to the right play! Over the years, the core acting company for Write On! has got smaller, the mechanics of its organization have become smoother, but the ambitions for the festival have continued to expand, with ever more plays in the same period of time. Early festivals had a dangerous edge which has never been lost. For example, Edward Thomas's early play *When the River Runs Dry* featured in Write On! '86, changed radically between its first and second performance at the insistence of the playwright. The first Write On! finished with an emotional reading of Alan Osborne's *In Sunshine and in Shadow,* which played to a packed house. Write On! '93, the most ambitious festival to date, also finished with *In Sunshine*, but for a different reason. That festival, which was the culmination of the previous eighteen months' development work, involved eighty actors, writers, directors, etc. in the presentation of a total of twenty-five plays in ten days and a significant feature of the festival was a retrospective of Osborne's work.

Looking back through a random selection of production photographs from the years that Made in Wales has been in existence there are plays which were landmarks in the writer's development rather than for the audience, plays which were loved by some and hated by others and plays of real significance and merit — many of which never reached the wider audiences that they deserved. If Wales had a theatre tradition that compared with Ireland's perhaps the audience would not be so elusive – a chicken or egg situation?

Made in Wales has not had a monopoly of new work. Ed Thomas, Tim Rhys and Ian Rowlands set up their own companies; Greg Cullen worked extensively with Theatr Powys and now with the Mid Powys Youth Theatre; Frank Vickery has found a professional home for his work at the Sherman Theatre. Considering all this writing, it *is* possible to see some common threads in the plays of the last decade. Some serious academic analysis would be worthwhile but my feeling is that any study ought to identify the proliferation of male writers from urban south Wales whose work is rooted in the economic and cultural deprivations of the communities from which they come. Laurence Allan, Alan Osborne, Dic Edwards, Edward Thomas, Ian Rowlands, and Tim Rhys all fit into this mould, although each has a distinct voice, characterized by a vivid, racy and poetic use of language. Regrettably, there has been a lack of major work by female playwrights.

A writer of a different kind is Charles Way, whose wonderful adaptation of Bruce Chatwin's *On the Black Hill* (in the pantheon of Made in Wales's greatest hits) took the essence of the novel and transmuted it into another medium. He is also known for his plays for younger audiences, which often take myth as a starting-point, as in the recent *Search for Odysseus*. Tony Conran is another writer who has used myth to powerful effect. He took the story of 'Branwen' from *The Mabinogion* and developed it dramatically and poetically to emphasize its contemporary resonance. BBC Radio 4's arts programme *Kaleidoscope* described this play as 'speaking to the nation through the walls of the theatre', something which we surely aim to do all the time, even if it is a rarely achieved ambition.

Beyond any comparisons between playwrights, what strikes me most is the power and character of so many individual plays. Often the question of identity is implicit in their subject-matter, an issue which is far more complex for the Welsh writer writing in English than for the Welsh-language writer – although it is only Edward Thomas who has run full tilt at 'the matter of Wales' by addressing the need to reinvent ourselves, our country and our language at the end of the twentieth century. This may explain the strong appeal of his work, which seems to feed a particular hunger.

And that is reassuring, given the increasing difficulties of producing new plays in an economic climate where the talk is of 'performance indices' and 'quality assurance' rather than ideals and ideas. It is depressing that the perennial arguments for a 'national theatre' in Wales are always made in terms of the bricks and mortar rather than the artists. It is the latter who would make such a building vital and viable. When we speak of the Abbey Theatre in Dublin, it is the writers and artists associated with it who matter. That is a situation we must imitate in Wales. Beware of theatre led by committees of the great and the good!

In many ways, it is astonishing to me that Made in Wales has survived for so long, given the fragile nature of the plays performed and the difficulties of finding audiences for them. There is no consensus between those who run the performance venues in Wales and those who produce theatre, about the value of indigenous work: the gulf between the two now seems unbridgeable. Whilst ignoring this major problem, the Arts Council of Wales has kept faith and continued to invest in new work, although the cycle of favour and disfavour is often characterized by the need to chastise the company at regular intervals for failing to find the great Welsh play, the 'hit' which everyone dreams of, and upon the merits of which we will all be able to agree, of course.

What is it worth, this struggle to push the large stone of Welsh writing for the theatre up the hill again to have it, as in Sisyphus' struggle, roll back down again on all our heads? In the age of video and film, the theatre remains one of the few places that offers a *live* experience, a place where people can come to participate in an event and receive emotional, mental and spiritual nourishment; a place where excitement can be palpable, where risks are taken, and where dangerous things may happen; a place where ideas can be discussed and shadows dispersed. I am not suggesting that all these things happen all, or indeed even some of, the time. But the possibilities and the potential are there and, since that is the case, it is essential that the voice of the living artist, the contemporary playwright, should be heard talking to us about our lives now. People are hungry for this experience and there is not enough of it about.

In 1992 Made in Wales organized a conference called 'No place to go?' It looked at the theatrical record of the last decade or so in Wales through extracts from the best plays in both languages. There was a tangible sense of excitement and pride at what had been achieved. The conference also discussed ways of solving the problems of finance, touring and apathy, in order to create recognition and demand for what theatre in Wales has to offer. One of the problems identified was the lack of a proper critical forum for the performing arts in Wales, outside the *Guardian*'s reviews (which have now almost disappeared). This situation is compounded by the difficulties of getting plays published. (Seren has more recently published a book each of plays by Edward Thomas and Charles Way but has incomprehensibly turned down Alan Osborne's *Merthyr Trilogy*.) These things conspire to make Welsh theatre invisible. It happens and then disappears without trace, only leaving a memory in the minds of those that saw it and a few relics such as photographs and programmes. Somewhere in all of this we are also dealing with the 'prophet in his own country' syndrome, which means that a play has to be celebrated in London or Edinburgh before it can be taken seriously in Wales.

Encouraged by the conference, Made in Wales's answer to these problems has been to find a venue in Cardiff which can act as a focus for the new theatre-writing community as a whole – a place where seasons of work can be staged so that new plays are not seen, and judged, in isolation but contextualized and allowed time to breathe. In this way, plays can develop and have some chance of reaching their proper potential. Originally this idea seemed impossible. The financial climate is against the opening of a new venue and Made in Wales itself does not have either the people or financial resources to run a venue. However, it has been brought to fruition by the imaginative decision of an established graphic design company, The Design Stage, to buy St Stephen's Theatre Space in Cardiff's docklands area and offer it as a model for a partnership between business and the arts. The building has been renovated with the help of a grant from Cardiff Bay Development Corporation, and renamed The Point. It will be the venue for a season of four new plays from Made in Wales – the first extended season of work since the company's inaugural season at the Sherman in 1982.

The success of the season will obviously depend on the quality of the plays themselves. Recent discussions with the Arts Council of Wales restated the council's desire to see plays which explore Welsh cultural and political issues – the 'matter of Wales' again. However, Welsh writers seem to resist that pressure, feeling that their identity is implicit in the people and communities about which they write and in the way that they use language. What is clear is that they want to work on the edge, offering work that is dangerous, shocking and powerful.

Certainly this is true of the work which will be on offer at The Point. Gary Gilmore, the American murderer, is the central character of Dic Edwards's surreal play *Utah Blue;* Lucinda Coxon's period play *Waiting at the Water's Edge*, begins in Harlech in the 1920s and follows its central character, Vi, to the New World in the guise of a man; Peter Lloyd, whose brilliant play *The Scam* took Made in Wales to the Traverse Theatre for the 1989 Edinburgh Festival, continues his investigation into alienated youth in *I've been Eddie Mostyn*. In addition, Made in Wales will play host to the recently formed Thin Language company's adaptation of Caradoc Evans's novel *Nothing to Pay*, which deals with the hypocrisy endemic in Welsh life. Difficult and uncomfortable plays all – but plays that will excite, challenge, entertain and provoke.

We may not yet be speaking to the nation, but we will be.[1]

Note

1 This article has been adapted from *New Welsh Review*, 27 (Winter 1994–5), pp. 62–6; reproduced with kind permission of the editor.

Appendix I

Chronology of Theatre in Wales

The Existing Structure

1949:   Arts Council of Great Britain set up out of wartime ENSA, with a Welsh Committee for the Arts.

1949:   The Castle College founded (later Welsh College of Music, with drama provision from 1952).

1962:   Welsh Theatre Company established, later Cwmni Theatr Cymru emerge as Welsh-language national theatre.

1967:   Welsh Arts Council, establishment of Arts Associations across Wales, which were subsequently dissolved when Arts Council of Wales was established as separate body funded by Welsh Office in 1994.

1971:   Chapter Arts Centre founded in Canton, Cardiff, upon localized arts initiative.

1972:   Aberystwyth Arts Centre built, and heralds an extensive period of civic and college investment in arts and theatre spaces throughout Wales.

1973:   Sherman Theatre built.
Theatr Powys founded (out of Breconshire Theatre Company), the first of several, very successful Theatre in Education companies throughout Wales.

1974:   Department of Drama, University of Wales Aberystwyth, founded.
Expansion of drama education, with university departments set up in Bangor, Swansea and at postgraduate level in Cardiff.
Centralization of provision on Aberystwyth in 1984/5 results in running down of Swansea and Bangor departments, and taught Masters degrees at Cardiff cease.
Later initiatives in drama teaching at degree level are then outside the University of Wales, at Trinity College,

          Carmarthen, Bangor Normal College, the Welsh College, and at the University of Glamorgan.

1975:   Theatr Gwynedd built in Bangor.

1976:   Theatr Clwyd opened in Mold, with production of *Macbeth*.

1977:   Torch Theatre opened in Milford Haven.

          Foundation of Theatr Bara Caws, and distinctive, devised mode of working.

After the Referendum

1979:   Bara Caws, *Bargen*, at Royal National Eisteddfod.

1980:   Odin Teatret tours Wales.

From early Campaign for Welsh branch of Equity, eventually
1980s: set up with subsequent consequences for development of S4C.

1981:   Brith Gof founded in Cardiff by members of Cardiff Laboratory Theatre, subsequently moves to Aberystwyth.

          First major production, *Branwen*, at Harlech Castle.

          Moving Being, *Y Mabinogi*, in Cardiff Castle.

          Made in Wales Stage Company set up by Hugh Thomas and Gareth Armstong.

          Death of Gwyn Thomas.

          Welsh Arts Council Dance Committee set up.

1982:   Opening of S4C.

          Dic Edwards, *At the End of the Bay*, for Made in Wales.

1983:   Financial crisis in Cwmni Theatr Cymru (Welsh-language national theatre).

          Brith Gof with Cwmni Theatre Cymru, *Gernika!*

          Brith Gof, *Ymfudwyr (Emigrants)*.

1984:   *The Glory of the Garden*, Arts Council of Great Britain policy document advocating devolution to (English) regions.

          WAC report, *Priorities into Practice*, advocates setting up of mainstream theatre company in south Wales.

          Prohibition of Howard Brenton's *The Romans in Britain* in Swansea.

1985:   Sherman Company begins performances in Cardiff.

          Arad Goch theatre company founded in Ceredigion (out of Cwmni Cyfri Tri and Theatr Crwban).

          Death of Saunders Lewis.

1986:   *Theatre is for All* (Cork Report): recommends widening access to theatre, particularly through encouraging young and new audiences.
          First Magdalena Festival in Cardiff.
1987:   Brith Gof, *Disasters of War* (until 1989).
          Meic Povey, *Perthyn* (*Related*) at Porthmadog Eisteddfod.
          Alan Osborne, *The Redemption Song*, for Made in Wales.
1988:   Duncan Bush, *Sailing to America*, also for Made in Wales.
          Siôn Eirian, *Wastad ar y Tu Fas* (*Always on the Outside*).
1989:   Tony Conran, *Branwen*.
          Brith Gof, *Gododdin* (part of large-scale series of 'site-specific' works (*Disasters of War*), which was staged throughout Britain and internationally).
          Dalier Sylw founded.
          Sherman Theatre becomes a young people's theatre.
          Edward Thomas, *House of America*, for Y Cwmni.
1990:   Gareth Miles, *Hunllef yng Nghymru Fydd* (*Nightmare in Future Wales*) for Dalier Sylw.
1990/1991: Brith Gof, *Pax*, as antidote to *Disasters of War*.
1992:   Pam Palmer, *Yn Ein Dwylo* (*In Our Hands*): last play awarded Drama Medal Prize at Eisteddfod.
1993:   Gareth Miles, *Dyrnod Branwen* (*Branwen's Blow*).
          Greg Cullen, *Frida and Diego*, performed Mid Powys Youth Theatre in Mid Wales and at National Theatre.
1994:   Devolution of Arts Councils (Welsh Arts Council funded directly from Welsh Office).
          National Lottery set up.
          Theatr Gwynedd, *Cwm Glo* (*Coal Valley*): first professional (and bilingual) production of Kitchener Davies's play since 1935.
          Siôn Eirian, *Epa yn y Parlwr Cefn* (*Ape in the Back Room*).
          Lucy Gough, *Crossing the Bar*.
          Withdrawal of funding to Welsh writing development company Hwyl a Fflag.
          The Ark: Garw Valley Community Play, near Bridgend, one of many memorable large-scale, localized amateur plays staged throughout this period.
          Sherman Theatre, *A Generation Arises*, youth theatre production.

Opening of The Point, Cardiff Docklands: involving both young and established playwrights.

1995:   Edward Thomas, *Song From a Forgotten City*, for Y Cwmni, first Welsh play to go to London's Royal Court Theatre since Gwyn Thomas's *The Keep* in 1960.

Launching of National Theatre Campaign by Michael Bogdanov and Phil Clark.

Director Helena Kaut-Howson (appointed after Toby Robertson) leaves Theatr Clwyd. Theatr Clwyd's production of Pinter's *Old Times* with Julie Christie in West End, following successful transfer of Shaw's *Saint Joan* the previous season.

1996:   Lottery bid for opera house in Cardiff rejected, after long media battles over design.

Reorganization to unitary authorities, an immediate consequence of which is uncertainty over Theatr Clwyd's long-term future.

Volcano, *Under Milk Wood*.

1997:   Financial crisis in several theatre companies, not least Cardiff's Sherman Theatre, because of changes in local government funding. Lottery funding increases in size and in importance to companies and venues.

Theatr Brycheiniog opens in Brecon.

September Referendum.

Appendix II
Welsh Arts Council Schedules to the Accounts

Schedule 1 to the Accounts
FOR THE YEAR ENDED 31 MARCH 1993

DRAMA
Mainstream Producing Companies

Sherman Theatre	312,890
Theatr Clwyd	444,810
Theatr Gwynedd	163,804
Torch Theatre	151,540
	1,073,044

Welsh Language Producing Companies

Cwmni Hwyl a Fflag	103,883
Cwmni Theatr Cymru	11,040
Dalier Sylw	85,692
Theatr Bara Caws	117,363
	317,978

Theatre in Education and Community Touring

Arad Goch	112,886
Cwmni'r Frân Wen	52,641
Cwmni Theatr Outreach	50,470
Gwent Theatre	47,281
Hijinx Theatre	94,637
Spectacle Theatre	51,856
Theatre West Glamorgan	82,912
Theatr Iolo Morgannwg	48,341
Theatr Powys	88,185
	629,209

Development Production Companies and Projects

Brith Gof	116,970
Centre for Performance Research	64,030
Made in Wales Stage Company	125,155

Magdalena Project	34,530
Volcano Theatre Company	38,226
	378,911

Projects

Green Ginger	5,015
Moving Being	40,030
No Fit State Circus	7,020
Sherman Theatre	10,020
St Stephens Theatre Space	6,020
Theatre West Glamorgan	9,020
Theatre Hâd	11,020
Wales Actors Company	20,030
Whare Teg	37,030
WOT Theatre	10,020
Y Cwmni	50,030
Y Gymraes	5,015
	210,270

Touring Fund Enhancement (GB Fund)

Gwent Theatre	5,525
Marine Theatre Contractors	2,517
Moving Being	3,517
Sherman Theatre	14,020
Theatr Clwyd	14,020
Whare Teg	14,020
Y Gymraes	2,015
	55,634

Development Schemes Training

Arad Goch	1,515
Cwrs Drama Ieunctid Cymru	2,515
Dalier Sylw	1,195
Drama Association of Wales	80
Fallen Angels	260
Gwent Theatre	205
Is-Bwyllgor Gymraeg Assitej	1,010
Magdalena Project	460
National Youth Theatre of Wales	6,520
Sherman Theatre	455
South Wales Intercultural Community Arts	155
Theatr Clwyd	2,230
Theatr Powys	230

University College of Wales, Aberystwyth,
   Drama Department   3,025
Volcano Theatre Company   510
Wales Association for the Performing Arts   1,315
Welsh Language TIE Conference
   (Y Cynhadledd)   760
Awards to individuals   2,756
                                 25,186

Theatre Writing
Arad Goch   760
Dalier Sylw   1,010
Eisteddfod Genedlaethol Frenhinol
   Cymru: Aberystwyth   2,025
Hijinx   1,010
Hwyl a Fflag   1,010
Sherman Theatre   2,015
Spectacle Theatre   1,515
Theatr Bara Caws   1,515
Theatre West Glamorgan   1,515
Theatr Gwynedd   310
Theatr Iolo   1,515
Torch Theatre   810
University College of Wales, Aberystwyth,
   Drama Departement   510
Valley and Vale Community Arts   1,515
Wales Actors Company   1,010
Welsh College of Music and Drama   3,015
Y Cwmni   1,515
Awards to individuals   1,515
                                 24,090

Total as Note 6   2,714,322

SCHEDULES TO THE ACCOUNTS 31 MARCH 1981

DRAMA
Receiving Theatres and Arts Centres
Aberystwyth Arts Centre   79,000
Bangor: Theatr Gwynedd   92,500
Cardiff: Chapter Arts Centre   176,000
Cardiff: Sherman Theatre   92,700
                            440,200

Theatre Based Companies

Theatr Clwyd, Mold	144,800
Torch Theatre, Milford Haven	114,000
	258,800

Touring Companies

Cwmni Theatr Cymru	253,000

Experimental Theatre Companies

Cardiff Laboratory Theatre Trust	60,800
Paupers Carnival	14,000
	74,800

Young People's and Community Theatre Companies

Action Pie	21,500
Caricature Theatre	78,000
Clwyd Outreach	20,000
Cwmni Theatr Crwban	12,000
Gwent Theatre in Education	18,500
Open Cast Theatre	27,000
Spectacle Theatre	20,500
Theatr Bara Caws	20,000
Theatr Powys	25,000
	242,500

Theatre Projects

Action Pie	5,525
Bag and Baggage	10,500
Clwyd Youth Theatre	1,000
Cwmni Cyfri Tri	6,500
Cymru '81	2,500
Diamond Age	2,500
Drama Association of Wales	200
Gwent Theatre in Education	1,250
Llandovery Theatre	5,500
Masquerade	2,000
Merthyr Circus School	500
Open Cast Theatre	500
Small Change Theatre Company	10,750
Spectacle Theatre	2,390
Theatr Bara Caws	300
Theatre Camel	8,000
Theatr Powys	465

Theatre Wales	25,000
Torch Theatre	250
Welsh National Youth Theatre	2,500
Wyeside Youth Theatre	1,000
	89,130

Amateur Theatre
Drama Association of Wales   10,000

Miscellaneous Projects

West Wales Arts Association	172
Swansea Little Theatre	150
	322

Bursaries and travel grants	23,347
Playwrighting Commission Scheme	23,405

Total as Note 2   1,415,504

Accounts reproduced by permission of the Arts Council of Wales.

Appendix III
Chronology of Brith Gof Performances

1981

Branwen with students of UCW Aberystwyth (Harlech Castle, Aberystwyth)

Rhiannon with students of UCW Aberystwyth (Eisteddfod Maldwyn; Welsh tour)

Rhosyn Cochion (Red Roses) with students of UCW Aberystwyth (Ceredigion villages)

Gaeafdaith (A Cold Coming) with Paupers Carnival Theatre (residency in Llangeitho)

1982

Manawydan with Cwmni Cyfri Tri (Welsh tour; Denmark)

Gwaed Neu Fara (Blood or Bread) with students of UCW Aberystwyth (Eisteddfod Abertawe; Aberystwyth)

Bwyty Bananas (Ceredigion Schools)

Blodeuwedd (Welsh tours, 1982–3)

1983

Dros Ben Llestri (Over The Top) (Welsh schools)

Gernika! with Cwmni Theatr Cymru (Eisteddfod Môn; Cardiff)

Ann Griffiths (Welsh chapels 1983–5; Patagonia 1985)

Ymfudwyr (Emigrants) (touring 1983–5: Wales, Spain, Poland, Italy, Argentina, Eire)

1984

Pedole Arian (Silver Horseshoes) (touring 1984–5: Wales, Italy, Spain)

Rhydcymerau (Eisteddfod Llanbedr-Pont-Steffan; Welsh tour)

Lleuad, Lleuad! (Moon, Moon!) with Farfa (Wales, Poland, Italy)

1985

8961–Caneuon Galar a Gobaith (Songs of Grief and Hope)

(Eisteddfod Rhyl; touring 1985–7: Argentina, France, Italy, Germany, Eire, Poland, Norway)

Iddo Fe (*For Him*) (Poland)

Gŵyl Y Beibl (*Bible Festival*) with Teatr Osmego Dnia (Llanrhaeadr-ym-Mochnant)

Boris (Welsh Folk Museum)

1987

Pandaemonium: The True Cost of Coal with Theatr Taliesin (Tabernacl Chapel, Morriston)

Disasters of War: Part One (Wales, Denmark, Eire, Norway, Venezuela)

Disasters of War: Part Two/Hiroshima (Eisteddfod Porthmadog; Eire)

Disasters of War: Part Three/Besatt! with Grenland Friteater (touring 1987–8: Norway and Wales)

Disasters of War: Part Four with Rubicon Community Dance Project (Cardiff)

1988

Disasters of War: Part Five with students of Dartington College of Arts

Disasters of War: Part Six with students of UCW Aberystwyth

Disasters of War: Part Seven/Displaced Persons with Dance Wales (Cardiff)

Can Heledd (i Clifford Posum) London

Disasters of War: Part Nine/Arminius with Theaterlabor, Bielefeld (Germany)

Gododdin (Disasters of War: Part Ten) with Test Dept. (Rover Car Factory, Cardiff)

1989

Disasters of War: Part Eleven/EXX–1 (Cardiff)

Gododdin with Test Dept. (Italy, Germany, Netherlands, Scotland)

Pax Concerts (Westminster Abbey; Cardiff; Edinburgh)

Gododdin Installation (Cardiff)

Disasters of War: Part Twelve with Sand and Bricks (Hong Kong)

1990

A Oes Heddwch? (broadcast video, S4C)

Gododdin (broadcast documentary, HTV)

Llythyron O'r Nefoedd (*Letters From Heaven*) with Dance Wales and Cyrff Ystwyth (Llanbadarn Church)

Los Angeles I (Rhymni)
Pax Concerts (Westminster Abbey; Bangor Cathedral)
Pax (St Davids Hall, Cardiff)

1991
Gwynt, Glaw, Glo a Defaid (Wind, Rain, Coal and Sheep) (Cardiff)
Los Angeles II (Scotland)
From Memory (Welsh Folk Museum; Warwick 1992; Belgium 1993)
Pax Concert (Cardiff)
Pax, Glasgow with Jigsaw (Harland and Wolff Shipyard, Glasgow)
Pax, Aberystwyth with Cyrff Ystwyth (Railway Station, Aberystwyth)

1992
Patagonia (Swansea, Cardiff, Glasgow, Warwick, London)
In Black and White with disabled performer David Levitt (Cardiff, Glasgow, Llandrindod, Rhondda, Warwick, London; Belgium 1993, Spain 1993)
Los Angeles III (France, Switzerland, Argentina, Swansea 1993, Aberystwyth 1993, Belgium 1993)
Ar y Traeth (On the Beach) (Eisteddfod Aberystwyth)
Der Gefesselte (The Bound Man) with Peter Brotzmann (Germany; Cardiff)
Haearn Concert (National Garden Festival, Ebbw Vale)
Haearn (Old Iron Foundry, Tredegar)

1993
Haearn (broadcast documentary, S4C and BBC 2)
DOA (Cardiff; 1994 Warwick, Bangor, Aberystwyth, St Donat's, Wolverhampton)
Camlann (Cardiff; Recklinghausen 1994)

1994
Angelus with Peter Brotzmann (Hamburg)
Cusanu Esgyrn (Eisteddfod Glyn Nedd)
Arturius Rex (Cardiff)

1995
Y Pen Bas Y Pen Dwfn (television production in collaboration with Bangaw, S4C and HTV Wales)

Tri Bywyd (Lampeter)

1996
Prydain (Cardiff, Glasgow)
Once Upon a Time in the West (St Fagans; Cardiff, Aberystwyth)
Sawl Bywyd (Eisteddfod Llandeilo)

1997
Hafod (Ely Hospital, Cardiff)
Dead Men's Shoes (Cardiff, Swansea Museum)

Appendix IV

Investing in a New World

Phil Clark

In the late 1960s Saunders Lewis said at a National Eisteddfod, and in a radio interview, 'There is no hope for Wales until a generation arises that knows its own past.' It was this quote that became the inspiration and starting-point for the Sherman Theatre production of *A Generation Arises* in 1994. The Sherman Theatre is the major producing theatre in south Wales. The theatre has a specific brief to be a young people's theatre and to identify young audiences. *A Generation Arises* was a partnership between the Sherman Theatre Company (professional actors and artists), the Sherman Summer School (young people working in the theatre as artists) and established new and young writers.

The work started in 1992 with the writers and after various discussions and workshops eight writers gave their commitment to the project. The role of dramaturge/script editor was also established. The writers (four established, four new) made the decision with the production team to edit the quote to *A Generation Arises* believing that it allowed a broader canvas for invention and comment. Some writers used the complete quote, others used the abbreviated version. What was exciting was that the writers themselves were a generation arising whilst at the same time addressing the quote. It was clear that there should be few rules to the game, but an opportunity should be made for broad thought and partnerships. Some writers worked on their own, others worked together. Some experienced writers worked with inexperienced writers and the dramaturge/script editor liaised between the writers and the directors. There was always the danger that this was a recipe for disaster, but it was in fact this danger that ensured an edge of excitement that was prominent throughout the process, right up until the last performance. It became clear that it was the job of the script editor and directors to piece the disparate writings together to form a structure with dramatic integrity.

The process of the Sherman Summer Schools is about partnerships, sharing and equality of power. Professional actors, designers, writers, musicians, directors, electricians, stage managers, production staff and managers all worked alongside their non-professional equivalents with ease, comfort and equality.

Alongside the making of the show, BBC Wales commissioned the independent film company Teliesyn to make a documentary that recorded both the process and the product, but featuring the young participants with particular reference to the writers. The completed documentary was shown on BBC Wales (who had indeed sponsored the complete project) as part of the arts programme *The Slate*. The documentary was nominated for a Celtic Film Festival award.

After two exhausting years of germination and a four-week rehearsal period, *A Generation Arises* burst onto the stage in September 1994. We had successfully combined the energies of the professional theatre community with the talents and energies of Wales's young people. What had 'arisen' was an important statement on the culture of young people in the 1990s.

As a company we believe in 'giving voice' to the youth of Wales. *A Generation Arises* placed the voice of young people centre-stage, and raised questions for the future of Wales and its young people by making connections with youth culture throughout Europe.

What we saw, what we heard, what we felt and what we experienced in this production was often dangerous, experimental, opinionated, frightening, informed and exciting.

If we as artists cannot experiment with the 'new' then the generations of tomorrow will inherit a very 'old' world.

Appendix V
Main Theatre Companies Working Professionally in Wales

THEATRE IN EDUCATION/COMMUNITY THEATRE

ARAD GOCH
Aberystwyth, Ceredigion
Founded 1987 (out of combination between Theatr Crwban and Cwmni Cyfri Tri)

Range of work: Schools' and young people's work, community shows. Running workshops and training sessions. Mainly Welsh-medium productions, but performances also in English and some productions available through both languages. Devised and commissioned work from invited and resident dramatists.

Size: Resident director, actors, administrative and technical support. Prefers to work with stable group of actors over a period.

Particular features: As Arad Goch resulted from a fusion of companies (one with a distinct educational remit, the other more experimental and influenced by physically and visually confident Third Theatre), the style of the company is very distinctive. First and foremost, the group aims towards giving children (and adults) a theatrical experience, rather than an overtly pedagogical one. Futhermore, the company has aimed to use traditional Welsh modes of rhetorical and theatrical expression joined with wider European influences such as *commedia dell'arte* and physical theatre work. Evidence of the company's commitment to international links was the 1996 Agor Drwsau/Open Doors international children's theatre conference which it hosted.

GWENT THEATRE
Abergavenny, Monmouthshire
Founded 1976

Range of work: Produces issue-based dramas as well as work linked to National Curriculum texts. Teachers' packs are regularly provided to support schools' work. Not driven by National Curriculum, but Shakespeare projects have been prominent and successful features of the group's output. Most of the work is devised but company has commissioned work from writers. Gwent Theatre is a touring company that works across a range of ages. Most of the work is in English but company co-operates with Theatr Iolo on annual Welsh-language productions for top infants/lower primary.

Size: Seven (three actor/teachers, stage manager, part-time secretary, administrator, director). Musicians and additional actors have been brought in, but present funding is only for core company.

Particular features: Very strongly community-based, responds to local concerns. However, the company is not parochial, and sees its brief as fostering an interest in contemporary and historical issues. The company's work is designed to provoke discussion of current issues and to introduce children to the arts. All work strives to be imaginative and original, even when directed by the needs of the National Curriculum. The company serves a very diverse area, from rural prosperity to former mining villages with high rates of deprivation, and now works across five unitary authorities.

THEATR CLWYD YOUNG PERSONS' THEATRE
Mold, Flintshire
Founded mid-1970s (as Clwyd TIE)

Range of work: Young people's theatre, which is a mixture of TIE work toured to schools, and arranging visiting companies to present work for children and young people. Audiences can be brought in to see work, much of which is related to National Curriculum needs. However, company tours across north Wales and occasionally into England, and caters for the full range of schools and ages, including special schools. Workshops are provided as are teachers' packs.

Approximately 20 per cent of work is in Welsh, and the company works closely with youth theatre wing of Theatr Clwyd.

Size: There are no retained actors in the company, only an administrator, associate director and stage manager. Three to five actors are hired for individual shows.

CWMNI'R FRÂN WEN
Menai Bridge, Anglesey
Founded 1984 (at Coleg Harlech)

Range of work: TIE work, workshops for teachers and children. Tours to schools from infants to upper secondary. All work is in Welsh, and detailed workpacks are produced with every project. Most productions are devised under the guidance of the artistic director.

Size: Four full-time members: director, administrator, schools liaison officer and production manager. Up to four actors employed for each project.

Particular features: Long-standing and highly developed relationships with schools in old Gwynedd area, successful way of working that complements schools' education in the region.

HIJINX
Grangetown, Cardiff
Founded 1981

Range of work: Two strands of work: large tours throughout Wales and into England, and work for adults with learning disabilities. Aims to integrate audiences in many venues. All work was originally devised, but company has used writers in recent years, forging good links with Laurence Allan and Charles Way in particular.

Size: 3.5

Particular features: High-quality, accessible theatre taken into venues that normally have little association with theatre. All new work.

Much use of music, particularly in shows for people with learning disabilities. High emphasis on design and the visual aspect of theatre, as communication is not necessarily through the spoken word. Co-operative management with involvement of actors throughout process of production.

THEATR BARA CAWS
Caernarfon
Founded 1976

Range of work: Community theatre work. Primarily concerned with touring work to old county of Gwynedd (58 per cent of venues), but also travels to small, rural venues throughout Wales. Lends out equipment and costumes, offers practical advice to local organizations. Stages an average of three productions a year, which attract high audience figures. Work is devised, born of original ideas and discussions within the company, and then scripted.

Size: Co-operative company with six permanent members: administrator, two technical staff, one actor and two authors.

Particular features: Bara Caws has established a distinct, collectively based, devised style of production with a very popular base. Encourages audiences to look at local and national issues from the perspective of their environment and to recognize influences on their own lives.

THEATR POWYS
Llandrindod Wells, Powys
Founded 1972

Range of work: Theatre in Education, community touring to adults. Tours shows 'back to back' in Welsh and English. Mostly devised shows, with writers used regularly. Aspects of National Curriculum integrated into work. Offers workshops, teacher training, exhibitions at larger venues such as Royal Welsh Show.

Size: Director, three permanent actors, three production staff (design, stage management, wardrobe), three administrative staff.

Particular features: Highly developed and sophisticated TIE. Devised and new writing, commitment to tackling difficult subjects, such as war in Bosnia, racial hatred, child abuse. Issue-based work, updatings of classical subjects. Theatr Powys runs as a collective, and decisions are made as a team.

THEATR IOLO MORGANNWG
Cardiff
Founded 1987

Range of work: Primarily TIE, with some youth theatre. Projects taken into schools, with emphasis on participatory work. Some shows such as *Macbeth* designed for family audience. Majority of work in English, with annual Welsh-language production. Most of work devised, some scripted pieces. Commissions some writing (from authors such as Charles Way, Mike Kenny and Lucy Gough) and music. Three to five projects a year, with over 200 performances. At present runs County Youth Theatre.

Size: Director and administrator, would hope to increase. Cast for each project.

Particular features: Story-telling aspect very strong in productions, tries to reflect multi-racialism of south Wales. Uses multi-racial casts, and looks at 'Welsh culture' in widest sense. Based generally in schools in Cardiff and the Vale of Glamorgan, but has built up links with theatre companies in Austria and Norway.

SPECTACLE THEATRE
Porth, Rhondda/Cynon Taff
Founded 1979

Range of work: Caters for ages four to sixteen, in English and Welsh. Productions go directly into schools, or are toured to theatres. Has created projects in museums such as St Fagan's. Tours youth centres, community halls and FE establishments throughout Wales. Offers workshops and resource packs for teachers. Devises and commissions plays. At present playwright Dic Edwards is working on a long-term literacy project with the company. Works mainly within old Mid Glamorgan area but attends theatre festivals abroad.

Size: Four permanent staff (of whom three are part-time). Large pools of actors and design/technical staff to draw on. Policy of encouraging new actors and technicians.

Particular features: Tries to produce innovative work. Does not work to a particular formula or promote theatrical style as such. Works bilingually, image and action strong, with emphasis on clear narrative. Aims to create work that is relevant to Mid-Glamorgan and the Valleys, conscious that, in a socially and economically deprived area, Spectacle's shows may be the only contact with any kind of theatre. Trying to re-establish youth theatre work for ages fourteen to twenty-six within the company.

THEATRE WEST GLAMORGAN/THEATR GORLLEWIN MORGANNWG
Neath
Founded 1981

Range of work: Group works bilingually, at both local and national level, producing shows for adults and young people. Tours its adult shows, which often have a strong musical and popular element, throughout Wales. Work was always devised until recently when the company began to commission playrights and use existing plays. Does not tour schools, instead work is shown at Neath headquarters. Runs intensive play-writing course (in Welsh) to encourage new writing.

Size: Director, administrator, technical and acting staff.

Particular features: The company has developed a lively and popular style of presentation that frequently uses music and song. It has managed to tackle 'difficult' issues such as educational disadvantage and housing shortages in this popular form. Fully committed to bilingual working, the company has responded to very local issues in its work as well as representing broader Welsh-language concerns.

WRITERS' COMPANIES

DALIER SYLW
Cardiff
Founded 1989

Range of work: Production of established Welsh-language writers' work; particularly that of Gareth Miles, Siôn Eirian, Meic Povey and Geraint Lewis. Performs mainly in Welsh but is working increasingly in English. Developmental work on scripting and staging for younger writers.

Size: Artistic director, administrator. Actors and guest directors brought in for particular productions.

Particular features: A writer-centred company that invests considerable time in the writing process. Works across a diverse range of dramatic styles, from the intimate realism of Povey to the politicized, anti-naturalism of Miles.

MADE IN WALES
Chapter Arts, Cardiff
Founded 1981

Range of work: Production of new writing in English, using a mixture of established authors and new writers; for example 1996 season of new plays by women featured two established authors (Sian Evans and Christine Watkins) and new writer Afshan Malik. Encouragement of new writing that through its quality, variety and distinctiveness, makes a vital contribution to nation's culture.

Size: Director and administrator, trainee assistant director on Arts Council Scheme.

Particular features: Commitment to social and political issues. Successful developmental work in local area, which has resulted in a muli-cultural writers' workshop and showcases of work. Workshops held for young writers and individual support given to young writers. Links with Welsh College of Music and Drama.

Y CWMNI
Chapter Arts, Cardiff
Founded 1987

Range of work: Director's company – mainly dedicated to producing Edward Thomas's work, who is dramatist/director. Some radio, television and film work.

Size: Administrator, director, regular/company of actors and design staff who are committed to particular form of theatre.

Particular features: Through the close association of Thomas as writer/director within the company, Y Cwmni has developed a highly distinctive, witty and physically energetic mode of performance.

RESEARCH AND EXPERIMENTAL COMPANIES

BRITH GOF
Chapter Arts, Cardiff (earlier Aberystwyth)
Founded 1981

Range of work: Large-scale, 'site-specific' work, and more intimate personal performances. Workshops, research work, as with Department of Archaeology at Lampeter. Bilingual practice.

Size: 2.5: Sceneographer, director, part-time administrator. Committed group of actors, musicians, dancers and technicians who have regularly worked with the company to develop a physically charged experimental theatre.

Particular features: Extensive experiment into the nature of performance, with a constant search for new principles and practices. Wide variety of spaces used from Cardiff Bay warehouse to Tuscan quarry. Demanding and difficult work on occasion, for both performers and spectators.

CENTRE FOR PERFORMANCE RESEARCH
Cardiff and Aberystwyth (1996)
Founded late 1970s

Range of work: Research into nature of theatrical performance in the widest sense. Offers archival material, library, newsletters and now produces journal on performance. Arranges international conferences.

Size: Deliberately small: director, administrative and research staff.

Particular features: Commitment to non-Western theatres, and to 'Third Theatre' practices, above all to Barba's work. Sophisticated and influential organization that has done much to excavate and promote the work of lesser-known theatrical figures, as well as to the reassessment of 'past masters' such as Meyerhold and Artaud.

EARTHFALL
Chapter Arts, Cardiff
Founded 1987

Range of work: Although officially a dance company, Earthfall has done much to develop a physically energetic theatrical style, that incorporates spoken narrative, song and dialogue. Uses performers' own memories and stories alongside and within dance movement.

Size: Around five choreographer/dancers.

Particular features: Informed by knowledge of other cultures' dance and performance styles. Aligned to work developed by companies such as Moving Being and Brith Gof. Use of other media, for example sculpture and music.

ELAN WALES
Chapter Arts, Cardiff
Founded 1992

Range of work: Productions devised by the group toured in repertoire. Training is main thrust of organization, based on the principles of 'Performance Montage' developed by directors. Intensive training offered over ten to twelve days, resulting in performances mounted in front of audience. Also produces work for children and young people.

Size: Two full-time directors.

Particular features: Physically based training that draws on *commedia dell'arte* and other elements. Own method of training and performance. Devises from existing texts. International organization with bases in Italy and Germany.

THE MAGDALENA PROJECT
Chapter Arts, Cardiff
Founded 1986

Range of work: Committed to exploring and researching into women's performance. Creates possibilities of new work, with over forty projects set up in the last ten years. Runs conferences, has an archive, newsletter and annual journal. Cross-cultural exchanges and collaborative projects.

Size: Three part-time administrators, access to great number of women performers and researchers.

Particular features: Large network of women performers throughout world. Extensive conferences, advice offered to new and young theatre artists. Multi-cultural and interdisciplinary approach.

MOVING BEING
Cardiff
Founded 1968 (London), moved to Cardiff (1972): 1972–82 (Chapter Arts), 1982–92 (St Stephens, Cardiff Bay)

Range of work: Combination of dance, drama and movement. Mixed-discipline work. Visual and experimental performances; sometimes non-text-based collages, on occasion more 'conventional' work on classical and contemporary texts. Visual exploration of 'literary' theatre. In Wales, tried to establish theatre aesthetic that would not rely on English model. Epic 'site-specific' stagings that brought dance, film and animated texts together.

Size: Director. Company no longer in receipt of revenue funding. When in production, uses ensemble of twelve to fifteen.

Particular features: Used video and technology very early on, integrated other media and forms such as film, dance and sculpture into theatrical event. Memorable large-scale stagings such as *Mabinogi* at Cardiff Castle and *Darwin Project* at St David's Hall. Highly influential style and practice.

VOLCANO
Swansea
Founded 1983

Range of work: Radical reworking of classical texts, dramatic adaptations of contemporary literature. New writing. Workshops and training offered. Extensive links internationally, particularly with Eastern Europe.

Size: Two directors, designer/technical director, administrator, core actors.

Particular features: Radical, physically exciting style of performance. Challenging consideration and deconstruction of literary and theatrical heritage. Exploration of gender issues.

REPERTORY COMPANIES

CWMNI THEATR GWYNEDD
Bangor, Gwynedd
Founded 1985

Range of work: New writing which tends to be mainstream and popular, some classic Welsh plays, translations of European classics.

Three productions each year that are toured throughout Wales for eight to ten weeks.

Size: Director, administrator, technical staff on site. Casts vary, up to ten depending on production.

Particular features: Commitment to popular, accessible theatre. Some collaborations with other companies and outside directors. European dimension, with productions of French and Spanish dramatists. Artistic committee advises company; company offers *ad hoc* training in absence of theatre school in north Wales; training of Welsh-language technicians carried out by Theatr Gwynedd, for example.

SHERMAN THEATRE
Cardiff
Founded 1973 (built as part of university), 1985 established as repertory theatre.

Range of work: Full-scale productions with emphasis on classics and new writing, children's and young people's theatre. Several youth theatres run from the building. Lunch-time plays, shows brought in from Wales and abroad.

Size: Thirty-five to forty, including front of house.

Particular features: Commitment to developing audiences and making theatre accessible. Particular strength is Sherman's work for and with young people. Extensive events for a young audience. Youthful, contemporary atmosphere created in theatre areas. Encouragement of new writing.

THEATR CLWYD
Mold, Flintshire
Founded 1976

Range of work: High standards of production. Repertoire geared towards European classics and modern drama. Studio theatre. Tours productions throughout Wales, and has transferred work to West

End. Range of activities provided by theatre: exhibitions, films, youth theatre. English-language repertory theatre.

Size: Large-scale repertory company, with fifty to sixty staff.

Particular features: High levels of theatrical activity, several plays in repertoire at any one time. Ambitious and critically successful productions which have drawn in large audiences from across north Wales and north-west England. Emphasis on world drama, in a repertory theatre in Welsh rural setting.

TORCH THEATRE
Milford Haven, Pembrokeshire
Founded 1977

Range of work: Around three productions undertaken each year: new plays, modern and older classics, and adaptations of novels. Theatre also hosts other events, touring companies, films, children's theatre, etc.

Size: Director, administrator, casts for individual productions.

Particular features: Some productions tour throughout Wales, accessible classics. Repertory theatre in community that does not have wide access to theatre-going.

EMERGENT COMPANIES

Here it is less easy to list the companies as some are relatively newly established. At present the most innovative companies working in Wales are Alma Theatre in Cardiff, an all-women company that has developed a witty and visual style in its devised work; Theatr y Byd in Mid Glamorgan which has produced work by author Ian Rowlands, often integrating other media; Cardiff's Mappa Mundi with a fresh, highly popular approach to the classics; Frantic Theatre in Swansea and U-Man Zoo in Aberystwyth with an energetic physical style; and Y Gymraes, again an all-female group, this time working in Welsh.

There are also a good number of companies throughout Wales whose work can be described as 'semi-professional', in that professionals work alongside amateurs to produce very high standards of work. Such companies include Mid Powys Youth Theatre, Castaway Theatre Company in Aberystwyth, and of course productions in colleges and universities throughout Wales. On occasion this work can be more ambitious in its scope than professional performances constrained by budgets and small casts.

Bibliography of Contemporary Drama in Wales

Introduction: General Works on Welsh Theatre

Adams, David, *Stage Welsh* (Llandysul, Gomer, 1996).

Baker, Mike, 'Transporting a sense of place', in David Cole (ed.), *The New Wales* (Cardiff, University of Wales Press, 1990), pp. 111–22.

Jones, Dedwydd, *Black Book on the Welsh Theatre* (Lausanne, Iolo, 1980).

Price, Cecil J., *The English Theatre in Wales in the Eighteenth and Early Nineteenth Centuries* (Cardiff, University of Wales Press, 1948).

Price, Cecil J., *The Professional Theatre in Wales* (Swansea, University of Swansea, 1984).

Rabey, David Ian, and Savill, Charmian C., 'Welsh theatre: inventing new myths', *Euromaske* (Fall 1990), 73–5.

Stephens, Elan Closs, 'Drama', in Meic Stephens (ed.), *The Arts in Wales* (Cardiff, Welsh Arts Council, 1979), pp. 239–96.

Stephens, Meic (ed.), *The Oxford Companion to the Literature of Wales* (Oxford, OUP, 1986), pp. 152–3.

Tighe, Carl, 'Theatre (or not) in Wales', in T. Curtis (ed.), *Wales: The Imagined Nation* (Bridgend, Poetry Wales Press, 1986), pp. 239–60.

1. Welsh Drama in English in the 1960s and 1970s

Abse, Danny, *The View from Row G: Three Plays*, ed. James A. Davies (Bridgend, Seren, 1990).

Curtis, Tony, *Danny Abse* (Cardiff, University of Wales Press, 1985).

Davies, Hazel, *Saunders Lewis a Theatr Garthewin* (Llandysul, Gomer, 1995).

Jones, Alun R., and Thomas, Gwyn (eds.), *Presenting Saunders Lewis* (Cardiff, University of Wales Press, 1973).

Mathias, Roland, *Anglo-Welsh Literature: An Illustrated History* (Bridgend, Poetry Wales Press, 1987).

Richards, Alun, *Plays for Players* (Llandysul, Gomer, 1985).

Thomas, Gwyn, *Three Plays*, ed. Michael Parnell (Bridgend, Seren, 1990).

Thomas, M. Wynn, *Internal Difference* (Cardiff, University of Wales Press, 1992).

Williams, Raymond, 'New English Drama', in John Russell Brown (ed.), *Modern British Dramatists* (Englewood Cliffs, New Jersey, Prentice-Hall, 1968), pp. 26–37.

2. Welsh-Language Drama since 1979

There is very little published work on the drama of this period. Accounts of productions can be found in *Barn* and *Golwg*. Some plays have been published including Gwenlyn Parry, *Y Tŵr* (Llandysul, Gomer, 1979); Meic Povey, *Perthyn*; Bara Caws, *Bargen;* Dewi Wyn Williams, *Leni* (all Llanrwrst, Carreg Gwalch, 1995); and Siôn Eirian, *Epa yn y Parlwr Cefn;* Geraint Lewis, *Y Cinio;* Gareth Miles, *Hunllef yng Nghymru Fydd* (all Cardiff, Dalier Sylw, 1995).

3. Patterns of Theatre-Making

Cork, Kenneth, *Theatre is for All: Report of the Enquiry into Professional Theatre in England* (London, Arts Council of Britain, 1986).

Davies, Andrew, *Other Theatres* (London, Macmillan, 1987).

Jackson, Anthony 'The repertory theatre movement in England', in Klaus Peter Muller (ed.), *Englisches Theater der Gegenwart: Geschichte(n) und Strukturen* (Tübingen, Gunter Narr, 1993), pp. 99–116.

Kershaw, Baz, *The Politics of Performance* (London, Routledge, 1993).

Morgan, Kenneth O., *Rebirth of a Nation: Wales 1880–1980* (Oxford, OUP, 1981).

Pick, John, *The Theatre Industry* (London, Comedia, 1985).

Rees-Mogg, William, *The Glory of the Garden: A Strategy for a Decade* (London, Arts Council, 1984).

Rowell, George, and Jackson, Anthony, *The Repertory Movement: A History of Regional Theatre in Britain* (Cambridge, CUP, 1984).

Taylor, Anna-Marie, 'A national theatre?', *Planet*, 110 (April/May 1995), 61–8.

Williams, Gwyn Alf, *When Was Wales?* (Harmondsworth, Penguin, 1985).

Yarrow, Ralph (ed.), *European Theatre 1960–1990* (London, Routledge, 1992).

4. Theatre in Education

Boal, Augusto, *Theatre of the Oppressed* (London, Pluto, 1979).

Heathcote, Dorothy, *Selected Writings*, ed. L. Johnson and C. O'Neill (London, Hutchinson, 1984).

HMI Wales, *A Survey of Theatre in Eduction in Wales* (Cardiff, HMI, 1989).

Itzin, Catherine, *Stages in the Revolution* (London, Methuen, 1980).

Jackson, Anthony, *Learning Through Theatre: New Perspectives on Theatre in Education*, 2nd edn. (London, Routledge, 1993).

O'Toole, John, *Theatre-in-Education: New Objectives for Theatre* (London, Hodder and Stoughton, 1976).

Reddington, Chris, *Can Theatre Teach? An Historical and Evaluative Analysis of TIE*, (Oxford, Pergamon, 1983).

Robinson, K. (ed.), *Exploring Theatre and Education* (London, Heinemann, 1980).

Savill, Charmian C., 'Theatre in Education in Wales', *Planet*, 67 (February/March 1988).

Schweitzer, Pam (ed.), *Theatre in Education* (London, Methuen, 1980).

5. Actor's Training

Clements, Paul, *The Improvised Play: The Work of Mike Leigh* (London, Methuen, 1983).

Mitter, Shomit, *Systems of Rehearsal* (London, Routledge, 1992).

Stanislavsky, Konstantin, *On the Art of the Stage,* tr. David Magarshack (London, Faber and Faber, 1950).

— *An Actor Prepares*, tr. E. Hapgood (London, Methuen, 1980).

Zarrilli, Phillip (ed.), *Acting (Re)Considered* (London, Routledge, 1995).

6. Theatr Fach, Llangefni

Jones, Llewelyn, *Francis George Fisher: Bardd a Dramodwr* (Caernarfon, Argraffwyr Gwynedd, 1983).

Morgan, Enid R., 'Theatr Fach Llangefni yn dyfod i oed', *Y Llwyfan* (Summer 1969), 8–9.

Shaw, Dilys W., *Theatr Fach Llangefni 1955–1983*.

7. Community Drama

Jellicoe, Ann, *Community Plays: How to Put Them On* (London, Methuen, 1987).

McGrath, John, *A Good Night Out: Popular Theatre, Audience, Class and Form* (London, Methuen, 1981).

8. Experimental Theatre
Artaud, A., *The Theatre and its Double* (London: Calder and Boyars, 1970).
Bachelard, G., *The Poetics of Space* (Boston: Beacon, 1994).
Barba, E., *The Floating Islands* (Holstebro, Bogtrykkeri, 1979).
— *Beyond The Floating Islands* (New York, PAJ Publications, 1986).
— 'Theatre anthropology', *The Drama Review*, 26/2 (1982), 5–32.
— and Savarese, N., *The Secret Art of the Performer* (London, Routledge, 1991).
Beck, J., *The Life of the Theatre* (San Francisco, City Lights, 1972).
— Rostagno, A., and Malina, J., *We, The Living Theatre* (New York, Ballantine, 1970).
Eliade, M., *Shamanism* (Princeton, NJ, Princeton University Press, 1972).
Goffman, E., *The Presentation of Self in Everyday Life* (Harmondsworth, Penguin, 1971).
Grotowski, Jerzy, *Towards a Poor Theatre* (London, Methuen, 1968).
Levi-Strauss, C., *The Savage Mind* (Chicago, University of Chicago, 1966).
Schechner, R., *Public Domain* (New York, Avon, 1969).
— *Between Theatre and Anthropology* (Philadelphia, University of Pennsylvania Press, 1985).
— and Schuman, M., *Ritual, Play, and Performance* (New York, Seabury Press, 1976).
Southern, R., *The Seven Ages of the Theatre* (London, Faber and Faber, 1962).

9. Brith Gof
Brith Gof, *Brith Gof: A Welsh Theatre Company, i. 1981–1985* (Pontypool, Mid Wales Litho, 1985).
— *Brith Gof: A Welsh Theatre Company ii. 1985–1988* (Pontypool, Mid Wales Litho, 1985).
Foster, Hal (ed.), *The Anti-Aesthetic: Essays on Postmodern Culture* (Washington, Bay Press, 1983).
Schechner, Richard, *Environmental Theatre* (New York, Hawthorn, 1973).
Shank, Theodore, *American Alternative Theatre* (London, Macmillan, 1982).

10. Theatre and the World

Anderson, Benedict, *Imagined Communities* (London, Verso, 1985).

Aston, Elaine, and Savona, George, *Theatre as Sign System* (London, Routledge, 1991).

Bhabha, Homi K. (ed.), *Nation and Narration* (London and New York, Routledge, 1990).

Brith Gof, *Y Llyfr Glas* (Cardiff, Brith Gof, 1995).

Clark, Phil (ed.), *Act One Wales* (Bridgend, Seren, 1997).

Davies, Hazel W., a series of interviews with Welsh playwrights in *New Welsh Review* (1994–7).

Elam, Keir, *The Semiotics of Theatre and Drama* (London, Methuen, 1980).

Read, Alan, *Theatre and Everyday Life: An Ethics of Performance* (London, Routledge, 1993).

Taylor, Anna-Marie, 'Women and words (not writing): the Magdalena Project in Wales', *Books in Wales* (Summer 1993), 7–9.

Turner, Victor, *From Ritual to Theatre: The Human Seriousness of Play* (New York, Performing Arts Journals, 1982).

— *The Anthropology of Performance* (New York, Performing Arts Journals, 1986).

11. Dance Theatre Wales

Adshead-Lansdale, Janet, and Layson, June (ed.), *Dance History* (London, Routledge, revised 1994).

McFee, Graham, *Understanding Dance* (London, Routledge, 1992).

Index